Radical Intimacy in
Contemporary Art

Also available from Bloomsbury:

Intimacy, by Christopher Lauer
Philosophical Skepticism as the Subject of Art, by David Carrier
Queer and Deleuzian Temporalities, by Rachel Loewen Walker
The Changing Boundaries and Nature of the Modern Art World, by Richard Kalina

Radical Intimacy in Contemporary Art

Abjection, Revolt, and Objecthood

Keren Moscovitch

BLOOMSBURY ACADEMIC
LONDON • NEW YORK • OXFORD • NEW DELHI • SYDNEY

BLOOMSBURY ACADEMIC
Bloomsbury Publishing Plc
50 Bedford Square, London, WC1B 3DP, UK
1385 Broadway, New York, NY 10018, USA
29 Earlsfort Terrace, Dublin 2, Ireland

BLOOMSBURY, BLOOMSBURY ACADEMIC and the Diana logo are trademarks of Bloomsbury Publishing Plc

First published in Great Britain 2023

Copyright © Keren Moscovitch, 2023

Keren Moscovitch has asserted her right under the Copyright, Designs and Patents Act, 1988, to be identified as Author of this work.

For legal purposes the Acknowledgments on p. ix constitute an extension of this copyright page.

Cover design: Ben Anslow
Cover image: Leigh Ledare
Me and Mom in Photobooth (2008)
Courtesy of the artist

All rights reserved. No part of this publication may be reproduced or transmitted in any form or by any means, electronic or mechanical, including photocopying, recording, or any information storage or retrieval system, without prior permission in writing from the publishers.

Bloomsbury Publishing Plc does not have any control over, or responsibility for, any third-party websites referred to or in this book. All internet addresses given in this book were correct at the time of going to press. The author and publisher regret any inconvenience caused if addresses have changed or sites have ceased to exist, but can accept no responsibility for any such changes.

A catalogue record for this book is available from the British Library.

A catalog record for this book is available from the Library of Congress.

ISBN: HB: 978-1-3502-9818-7
ePDF: 978-1-3502-9819-4
eBook: 978-1-3502-9820-0

Typeset by Deanta Global Publishing Services, Chennai, India
Printed and bound in Great Britain

To find out more about our authors and books visit www.bloomsbury.com and sign up for our newsletters.

To my mother

Contents

List of Illustrations viii
Acknowledgments ix
Abbreviations x

Introduction: Intimacy Revolts 1

Part I Leigh Ledare: The Subject on Trial

1 Imagining Intimacy 25
2 A Poetics of Abjection 48

Part II Genesis P-Orridge: Radical Sensibility

3 Ritual and Revolt 81

Part III Ellen Jong: The Object in Revolt

4 Sex and the Symbolic 113
5 Object-Oriented Intimacy 132

Part IV The Politics of Subjects and Objects

6 Postcolonial Intimacy 157
7 Subjectivity Reclaimed, Reoriented 176

Coda: Being is Heard in the Intimate 201

Notes 207
Bibliography 232
Index 240

Illustrations

Color Plates

1. Genesis P-Orridge, *B-Right-On*
2. Ellen Jong, *Lily NYC*, 2010
3. Leigh Ledare, *Mom with Hand on Bed*
4. Leigh Ledare, *Mom's Profile in Seventeen Magazine*
5. Leigh Ledare, *Untitled (Entire Roll)*
6. Leigh Ledare, *Hot Licks*
7. Leigh Ledare, *Mom in New Home*
8. Breyer P-Orridge, *You Are My Other Half*
9. Leigh Ledare, *Mom with Neck Brace*
10. Ellen Jong, *Two Chairs Two Coffees NYC*, 2010
11. Ellen Jong, *Cum NYC*, 2010
12. Ellen Jong, *In the Window NYC*, 2010
13. Ellen Jong, *Red Door NYC*, 2010
14. Barbara DeGenevieve, *Gordon #6*

Figures

1	Leigh Ledare, *Mom Fucking in Mirror*	28
2	Leigh Ledare, *Me and Mom in Photobooth*	62
3	Laure A. Leber, *Jackie and Genesis, November 5, 2006*	105
4	Lorraine O'Grady, *The Clearing: or, Cortés and La Malinche, Thomas Jefferson and Sally Hemings, N. and Me*	180

Note: Please be aware that the images in this book contain sexually explicit material.

Acknowledgments

A book such as this could only have been accomplished in intimacy. I owe a debt of gratitude to many people in my life, both personal and professional, and those lines are characteristically blurred. First and foremost, a warm and lifelong thank you to my mentor Ewa Płonowska Ziarek for her kindness, professional wisdom, and generosity of spirit. George Smith has extended decades of teaching on life as an artist-philosopher and has created a unique community in which to develop these ancient skills, for which I am immensely grateful. Simonetta Moro has been a sharp and incisive advisor on my academic journey. Silvia Mazzini provided much needed encouragement toward the manifestation of the project in book form. I am so thankful to Christopher Lauer for his own research on intimacy and for our talks that continually invite me to rethink my assumptions. A heartfelt thank you to Tom Huhn for years of friendship and support for my many intellectual projects. Much gratitude for Ateret Sultan-Reisler's eagle eye. Thank you to Marcus Coelen for listening. To all the professors, teaching assistants, and students at the Institute for Doctoral Studies in the Visual Arts, I thank for forming the backbone of my growth as a philosopher, especially Angelalynn Dunlop, Gabriel Reed, Jennifer Rissler, and Jeff Siemers. Shannon Rose Riley, Christopher Yates, and Stacey Tyrell each provided valuable insight towards key aspects of my research. My colleagues and students at the School of Visual Arts and Parsons School of Design at The New School provided decades of camaraderie and conversation on contemporary art and helped construct my artistic psyche in its ever-evolving form. Perhaps most importantly, I could not have completed the work necessary to produce this volume if it were not for the support of my family, especially my mother Dorit Yaron, who is a lifelong inspiration and ally. And finally, to my love Tom Benton, without whom I would not even begin to know the full meaning of the intimate.

Abbreviations

ISA	*Ideological State Apparatus*
OOF	*Object-oriented feminism*
OOO	*Object-oriented ontology*
RSA	*Repressive State Apparatus*
TG	*Throbbing Gristle*
TOPY	*Thee Temple ov Psychick Youth*

Introduction
Intimacy Revolts

This is a book about intimacy. It was born out of the friction, rebellion, and compassion that accompany the deeply intimate. It grew out of the need to understand, the desire to be understood, and the knowledge that the intimate evades understanding. It celebrates the creativity and invention that result from this very evasion. This book is an investigation of intimate revolt in contemporary art practice, and the ways that artists participate in social and political upheaval by turning subjectivity inside-out. It began with a whisper, a notion, a suspicion. It ends with a declaration and with new questions. The psychoanalytic philosopher Julia Kristeva speaks of revolt as perpetual turning, permanent motion, and eternal questioning. She advocates a continual re-turn to the moments before the subject-object begins its process of cleavage, its *being* torn apart, sparking its initiation into patriarchal order and separation from the maternal body. Through the experience of ejection, desire is born in the eyes of the newly formed subject—the division that grants the subject the identity in which it will forever be confined. She calls for a return to the intimate as a process of revolt and the reconfiguration of the subject at its point of inception. Kristeva notes her gratitude to Freud's discovery of the unconscious and the impact of analytic speech on the revolutionary. Revolt, she states, "is the idea that being is within us and that the truth can be acquired by a retrospective return, by anamnesis, by memory. The return to oneself leads the individual to question his truth."[1] The act of questioning truth and concepts enables a shift in thinking, temporally interwoven with a shift in ontological positioning; as we think of being in new and radical ways, our very being is transformed. In intimate exchange with each other, with ourselves, and with speech, we redraw the borders of our subjectivity until they become porous and flexible, open to change, foreclosing the possibility of an object. As thinking and questioning beings, we are eternally morphing in our very ontology—thinking ourselves and our surroundings into new shapes. Kristeva tells us that "[t]he intimate is where we end up when we question apparent meanings and values."[2] Thought and intimacy go hand in hand, relying upon one another to transform consciousness and, more importantly and poetically, our unconscious fantasies and defenses. In intimate exchange, we may take new shapes than those previously visible to us—fueled by radical thought and guided by an ethos of intimacy.

I write this book as a researcher of theories and histories of ideas. I also write as an artist and as someone who has wrestled with the intimate through my own practice, searching for language to describe what my hands and body already know. I have searched for a home among these words and ways to understand radically intimate art beyond its shock value. How do works that push against many viewers' edges, their comfort zones and their sense of propriety, actually function? Why is it important, even essential, to continue looking? I have come to believe that artists who operate through radically intimate praxis—breaking accepted notions of the erotic to generate uncertain spaces with inconsistent boundaries—question the hegemony of subjectivity and, with it, of ideology. In doing so, these artists may find themselves outcasts. Through the slippage of inside and outside, subject and object, qualities escape conceptualization. In artistic practices sometimes deemed objectionable, dangerous, and disgusting, abjection operates ontologically, as a questioning and shaking of foundations of meaning, and a rejection of perceived truths. In revolt, artists plumb the depths of memory to awaken primordial drives and new approaches to being. Kristeva emphasizes the role of pleasure and, perhaps more importantly, unslakable jouissance in the psychic apparatus of subject-formation. Implicitly, she continually invites us into the realm of sexual intimacy, for it is there—in enjoyment and pain—that the greatest ambivalence emerges that spurs us to question the very foundations of our subjectivity. Kristeva notes that "the word [intimacy] comes from the Latin *intimus*, the superlative of *interior*, thus 'the most interior.' So, although it includes the unconscious, the intimate does not have to be reduced to it and may go well beyond it."[3] By shaking the bedrock of modern notions of "I," including the psychoanalytic split subject, radical sexual intimacy proposes alternatives to the hegemonic structures of twenty-first-century civilizations and hints—sometimes forcefully—at new ontologies ahead. By engaging radical intimacy, the artist-philosopher participates in a revolution of being.

How does intimacy operate as radical activism, and how can we understand the employment of radical intimacy in contemporary art practice? This book argues that intimacy has the capacity to operate as a radical disruption of ideological constructs and therefore possesses political agency. Furthermore, contemporary art that employs radical intimacy may be deployed as ideological-political activism. In this way, radical intimacy can be a powerful tool in practices of poetic resistance and aesthetic activism. Grounded in Kristeva's psychoanalytic-poststructuralist theories, particularly her research on intimacy, abjection, and revolt, the book positions intimacy as an ambivalence of subjectivity and borders, inside and outside. Radicality is understood as a disruption of subject-oriented ontologies and meanings, and a practice of continually generating new forms of thought. Kristeva clearly articulates the personal and philosophical stakes of intimacy, which she believes plays a uniquely singular role in the human psyche. According to Kristeva, "the intimate is what is most profound and most singular in the human experience . . . this interiority that the Greeks called 'soul' (*psukhê*), defined by its proximity with the organic body as well as by preverbal sensations."[4] Intimacy thus operates in the philosophical gray zone where mind, body, and memory collide to uncover being at its most elemental. By delving into the interior space beyond subjectivity—so interior that it manages to blur the boundaries of inside and outside, thus creating space for endless creation— the artist operates as cultural producer and shifter of consciousness within the deepest strata of the human psyche.

The theoretical arc of this book engages a diverse group of artists and theorists, each of whom offers a perspective and a set of tools for understanding radical intimacy as a pathway toward new ontological models. The project examines the practices of several contemporary visual artists and their collaborators, namely Leigh Ledare, Genesis P-Orridge, Ellen Jong, Barbara DeGenevieve, Joseph Maida, and Lorraine O'Grady, to suggest artistic vocabulary and frameworks for radical intimacy as a tool of resistance in the twenty-first century. Beginning with Freud's subject of the unconscious and the eroticism of psychoanalytic discourse, and continuing into Lacan's split subjectivity and desire, I then follow Kristeva's and Luce Irigaray's poetics into a discourse of ambivalence between subject and object. Judith Butler's theories of gender performativity inform the project throughout. Each of these artists and theorists, in their own ways, blur the boundaries between potentially compartmentalized aspects of human experience, cleaved by modernity and waiting to be reunited. Kristeva's theories, in particular, guide us through the workings of intimacy and its ideological implications. Referring to both the individual body and the sociopolitical realm, she argues: "Psychical life is this interior space, this place within, that allows one to take attacks from inside and outside. . . . The imaginary metabolizes them, transforms them, sublimates them, and works on them: it keeps us alive."[5] Intimacy, Kristeva argues, is essential for our survival. Engaging Althusser's theories on interpellation of subjectivity and ideology,

I situate radical intimacy in contemporary practice as a rejection of oppressive ideological constructs, including subjectivity itself. By dissolving the hegemony of subject-object relations as interpellated ideologically, radical intimacy gestures toward an ecological ethos of coexistence. The project concludes with an engagement with object-oriented feminism (OOF), a relatively new school of feminist praxis grounded in the contestation of the hegemony of subjectivity and a turn to objecthood. I engage the writings of OOF's founder, artist and theorist Katherine Behar, as well as philosophers Frenchy Lunning and Timothy Morton to explore new ontologies and forms that generate opportunity for ethical, sustainable coexistence and collaboration. This final step situates radical intimacy in contemporary art within the political arena of activist practices, demonstrating the ways that abjection, revolt, and the dissolution of categories catalyzed by intimate practice effect an ontological shift from subjectivity to objecthood. By doing so, radical intimacy disrupts the modern hegemony of subjectivity, suggesting a new language for the contemporary philosophical era ahead.

From Subject to Feminist Object

Despite not directly addressing the issue of intimacy, Freud muses on the break with the ego as a sense of self as experienced in love and sexual desire. He describes this subjective rupture as a "feeling of an indissoluble bond, of being one with the external world as a whole."[6] The autonomous subject defines Enlightenment-era philosophy and entrenches itself in art criticism through the Kantian canon; Freud's discovery of the unconscious, however, disrupts this secure and independent sense of self, revealing subjectivity as a stratified entity, in constant tension between inner and outer reality. Beyond our encounters with other subjects, Freud indicates, we are in eternal confrontation with the other inside ourselves. Our conscious selves, however, maintain the clear boundaries between inside and outside, self and other—with one important exception. Freud argues:

> There is only one state—admittedly an unusual state, but not one that can be stigmatized as pathological—in which it does not do this. At the height of being in love the boundary between ego and object threatens to melt away. Against all the evidence of his senses, a man who is in love declares that "I" and "you" are one, and is prepared to behave as if it were a fact.[7]

That Freud would characterize this moment of perceived dissolution as "threatening" shines light on a notion perhaps adjacent to love but not synonymous with it, which is that of *intimacy*. While "love" promises unity, embedded in this joyful union is a dangerous loss of boundaries and with these lost boundaries, a lost sense of an autonomous self.

My inquiry focuses on the period since the 1968 protests in France, which marks a dramatic shift in both the ontology and the politics of subjectivity in the West—a movement in which Kristeva was a key intellectual player. By considering Kristeva's frustration with the state of revolt in the arts post-1968, we have the opportunity to reformulate our thinking on intimacy in relation to the subject in permanent revolt—an essential paradigm shift for Kristeva in her use of psychoanalytic concepts to reorient the political manifestations of revolution. We witness the change in thinking that occurs when subjectivity itself begins to dissolve—not just theoretically but in practice. In parallel, an ambivalent, decentered being emerges in Lacan's theories leading up to the upheaval of 1968. Insisting that Freudian theory in the UK had abandoned key tendencies in Freud's work, and therefore wrongly worked toward the healing and buttressing of the ego, Lacan instead focuses on the subject as a fractured entity. Rather than making peace with a false sense of self, an illusory identity housed in the imaginary ego, Lacan suggests, the subject must make peace with its split and unconscious existence in language, which is itself an ever-shifting structure. This instability of subjectivity has been an ever-present specter in theory since the 1960s, circling questions of autonomy, freedom, and representation that I will address throughout my exposition. It is my intention, however, to pierce the tautology of these questions with the disruptive potentiality of radical intimacy and open up new ways of thinking outside subjectivity without re-entrenching ideology in the object.

Psychoanalysis provides useful frameworks for a discourse of intimate materialist art practice. Lacan's distinctions between the imaginary identification, symbolic sociality, and the real of the drive are important to understanding the role of language in the unconscious, as well as the role of the drive in our exploration of radical intimacy. If language is unstable, then so is the unconscious, which is structured like a language. Therefore, the key to integration into the symbolic order—the realm of culture and civilization—lies in language itself, and its tether to the intimate may be located in the drive. Lacan characterizes the function of the drive as a "constant force"[8] that sets out to penetrate the impossibility of the real. In describing Freud's use of the term *Trieb* (drive) over the more biological *Drang* (thrust), Lacan notes that "the *Reiz* [excitation] that is used when speaking of drive is different from any stimulation coming from the outside world, it is an internal *Reiz*."[9] Rather than aiming toward the satisfaction of needs such as hunger or thirst, which can be satisfied with food or water, the drive cannot be satisfied. Lacan goes so far as to say that "the function of the drive has for me no other purpose than to put in question what is meant by satisfaction."[10] Through an examination of the selected artists' work, we will see how Lacan's understanding of the Freudian drive plays a significant role in Kristeva's theories on abjection and revolt, supporting my own inquiry into radical intimacy as a questioning of boundaries, categories, and the notion of a unified subject. Particularly, the notion of challenging the very concept of satisfaction plays out for Lacan in the physical, material world of sexual intimacy, as well as in the experience of attempting to make meaning in language. As Lacan says: "In other words—for the moment, I am not fucking, I am talking to you. Well! I can have exactly the same satisfaction as if I were fucking. That's what it means. Indeed, it raises the question of whether in fact I am not fucking at this moment."[11] Lacan's provocative game questions the very notion of meaning, through the metaphor and materiality of sexual intimacy and its relationship to radical thought.

Kristeva further develops Freud and Lacan's thinking on language and drive by stressing the poetics of analytic speech, which she highlights in her theories on intimacy, abjection, and revolt. Kristeva, in the lineage of Lacan, brings the notion of subjectivity into the realm of poetry. As a literary theorist, semiotician, novelist, (reluctant) feminist, activist, and clinical psychoanalyst, Kristeva spans a wide range of philosophical positions and discourses. Her writings feel exciting, multifaceted, and open to infinite readings, but her grounding in the Freudian structure of psychoanalysis, itself an ideological field, continually presents a point of resistance to radical thought. A rereading of Kristeva's ideas through the shifted frame of object-oriented feminism, however, allows for a feminist materialism to emerge that challenges the patriarchal categories of psychoanalysis while remaining grounded in female and feminine materiality.

Of particular interest to my inquiry is Kristeva's explicit disappointment in the state of the art world after the May 1968 protests rocked the ideological foundations of the academic and intellectual spheres. Kristeva addresses what she deems as the failure of contemporary art institutions and creative practices to revolt and cites the lessons she believes can be learned from the psychoanalytic tradition. In free association, the analysand experiences a continual renewal of the possibility of meaning, which is neither cure nor resolution but an important mental exercise keeping the psyche nimble and creative. Psychoanalysis, she claims, leverages speech and memory, and the poetic variances of analytic discourse, to effect the subjective transformation needed for true revolution. This book situates Kristeva's thoughts on intimacy within this shift/rift in thinking and suggests that radical intimacy, as enacted via feminist artistic praxis, possesses political agency. Through the lens of radical intimacy—blurring the edges of subjectivity and destabilizing seemingly fixed categories of meaning entrenched deep within the psyche—we witness the workings of art practice as philosophical discourse and its participation in heralding new eras of thought.

Kristeva's relationship to feminism presents challenges to considering her ideas within this landscape. In an interview with Philippe Petit, *What's Left of 1968?*, Kristeva minces no words regarding her disdain for the feminist initiatives that arose around her in the post-1968 resistance movements, including accusing one group of outright totalitarianism. Though she states, "I don't consider myself a theorist of feminism," she notably stops short of recusing herself from feminist praxis. She aligns herself specifically with a wave of feminism which asks how the wielding of power may be "modulated in terms of the specifics of feminine experience, with all the complicity it implies—intimacy, sexuality and those matters closest of all—nature, the child?"[12] How might we understand Kristeva's feminism, and her relationship to radicality in context to contemporary philosophical positions on gender, particularly those that heavily critique the notion of binary sexual difference? Kristeva hews closely to the psychoanalytic models of gender difference tempered only by psychic bisexuality, the Oedipal, and the maternal/paternal functions, so how might we engage her theories in ways that are inclusive of queer identity and praxis?[13] This book presents an array of feminist perspectives that function as both counterpoints and redirects of Kristeva's theories, searching for new pathways through her theories in dialogue with the selected artists' works.

As we will see, the question of essentialism recurs frequently in the attempt to formulate a psychoanalytic discourse based in the materialism of the body. According to Butler, whose psychoanalytic theories on performativity inform my chapters on artist Leigh Ledare as well as the book's shift toward performative object-orientation, Kristeva's conceptions of the semiotic do not sufficiently subvert the patriarchal language of the Lacanian symbolic order, and her deference to the dominance of the paternal function renders her "self-defeating theory" a "failure of her political strategy [that] follows in part from her largely uncritical appropriation of drive theory."[14] Butler argues that "Kristeva reinstates the paternal law at the level of the semiotic itself . . . a strategy of subversion that can never become a sustained political practice."[15] I suggest, in opposition to Butler's critique, that the semiotic entrance into these very symbolic laws is precisely what radicalizes Kristeva's notions of the subject on trial, and in process, and her notion of poetic revolutionary practice. Kristeva's contribution to a feminist praxis grounded in positionality and female materiality detached from subjective wholeness and identity will prove significant in my exploration of object-oriented feminism and Behar's suggestion for a feminist art praxis that bounds itself to the barriers of language and the law in order to subvert it. For Kristeva, this is a necessary post-thetic moment, which she refers to variously as the signifying process, practice, and the subject on trial.

In addition to Butler's performativity, I will introduce a range of feminist theories that collectively lead up to my concluding exploration of OOF as an intersectional feminist praxis. Donna Haraway's theories on situated knowledge inform a practice of radical intimacy that deploys positionality as a tool and that suggests that intimacy is grounded in a positionality attached to signification rather than the subject. Alongside Kristeva's discourse on poetics and revolt, Irigaray's poetic challenge to Lacanian theory and her performative writing, destabilizing objecthood, decenters and de-unifies the psychoanalytic subject. Finally, O'Grady's subject-oriented discourse considers the intersection of race, class, sex, and gender in subject-formation, and questions the psychoanalytic model from a postcolonial perspective that nevertheless acknowledges the impact of psychoanalytic ideology on Black subjectivity. Paradoxically, O'Grady's call for the reclaiming of subjectivity invites an object-oriented approach that frames radical intimacy in terms of abjection and revolt. Throughout, Behar's object-oriented feminism presents an opportunity to read the artwork presented in this book through an altered lens—a lens that operates on the levels advocated by Kristeva in her discourse on intimacy, abjection, and revolt, but that also offers a more intersectional and performance-based approach to feminist praxis in the lineage of feminist new materialism. I acknowledge the critiques of Kristeva's approach to gender and sexuality, as well as her adherence to the Lacanian Symbolic. In seeking alternate, yet complementary, routes toward a feminist praxis of radical intimacy in the twenty-first century, I find solidarity between Kristeva's theories and new forms of thinking in contemporary art and philosophy. Particularly, O'Grady's contributions to a discourse of intimacy that situates race as a central component of ideology, and that critiques the structuralism of psychoanalysis, operate as an important counterbalance to Kristeva's theories which are heavily indebted to the Freudian-Lacanian and Kleinian traditions while still leaving room to see alignment between these thinkers. My hope is that the diversity of voices included in this book, written with Kristeva's own intertextuality as a guiding post, enacts a more diverse theory of intimacy.

In researching the topic of radical intimacy, I have been particularly interested in the contemporary experience and the expressions of my own contemporaries in the fields of art practice and theory. As a practicing analyst, Kristeva notes the differences between contemporary patients and those treated by Freud, producing a discourse reflective of twenty-first-century imagination. She states: "These new patients are suffering less from repression or inhibiting prohibitions than from the lack of reference points, such that their psychic apparatus hasn't really established itself: they're having difficulty representing their internal or external conflicts."[16] Here she takes the Lacanian position of privileging the role of the symbolic realm—the locus of language, authority, and the law—as one component in establishing the subject in process, along with the semiotic working through and attacking the limits of language. She likens the ability to inscribe aggression and the death drive to the function of photography, with the psyche acting as a visual intermediary between the real of the drive and the inscriptions of language:

> If ultimately the point of the psychic apparatus is to make a *camera obscura* inside which these internal and external aggressions are inscribed, verbalized and symbolized, so as to defend the subject from these attacks, well then, with the new patients, this defense is down. When psychic representation is in default, it takes the form of psychosomatic illnesses, drug abuse, or acting out—from botched actions to perverse violence, like paedophilia and social vandalism. What can't be represented is abreacted in a violent act or else goes deep down inside where eventually everything self-destructs—organs, self-awareness and life itself.[17]

For Kristeva, the contemporary condition is defined by the inability to visualize coherently, or to put into words the destructiveness of the death drive, by the psychical camera apparatus of the mind's eye. Although some of the pathologies she cites here have been historically used to label dissenters and activists as perverse, dangerous, and sick,[18] Kristeva makes a distinction between violence and acting out against others in antisocial, perhaps even unethical, ways, and the representation of the drive through radical manifestations in art and poetry. Kristeva claims that rules and regulations—the structures of society—in fact are necessary for revolt and that the working out of violent tendencies through acts of signification proposes radically new forms of meaning and being. She argues that "[t]here is no revolt without prohibition of some sort"[19]—prohibition which revolt puts into question; in a society of seeming permissiveness, revolt disappears. Though Kristeva's loyalty to certain cultural, clinical, and social structures threatens to subvert her own call for radicality, her grounding of revolt in the prohibitions of law and society has led me to search for ways that her theories on intimacy can puncture those very structures while working within and in radical exteriority to these very ideological mechanisms.

Intimacy

Though Kristeva's gender essentialism raises concerns about the potential contribution of her theories to a praxis of resistance in the twenty-first century, her persistent focus on the intimate sets her work apart from other, dominant threads of thought. "Intimacy" is a term that, even when found embedded in philosophical theory, is often taken for granted, conflated with love or divinity, or ascribed to spatial definitions relating to interiority, with few qualifying concerns for the simultaneous exteriority that lends the intimate its uniquely subversive timbre and otherness. Kristeva, by contrast, directly addresses the intimate in two books on the practice of psychoanalysis, as it relates to the practice of writing. In *The Sense and Non-Sense of Revolt* and *Intimate Revolt*, Kristeva lays out a theory—and praxis—of intimacy.

Kristeva's interest in the intimacy of psychoanalysis lies in her belief that it is a relationship based on mutual love and hate, in transference and countertransference. She suggests that initiation into the symbolic order is a precondition of intimacy, which will lead to the questioning of that order. In analysis, she states, "[t]he result is that you are initiated into law and otherness, insofar as they are the intra-psychic conditions for the constitution of an 'interiority,' i.e. a subjective intimacy that allows the patient to acquire a psychic autonomy and only through that, confidence, desires and a capacity for creation and challenging things."[20] Kristeva's argument hinges on the intimacy of analysis and the integrative nature of analytic speech by which the analysand transforms the repetition compulsion of the past, endlessly relived as present, at least partially into memories in the symbolic, via the construction of representations. For Kristeva, the analytic act is analogous not just to intimacy broadly but to art, as well as to the intimacy of sexual differentiation and desire. For Kristeva, intimacy not only operates as a deconstructive mechanism—decoding memories, speech, and identity—the origins of individual subjectivity; it also operates as a constructive mechanism, imbuing newly situated subjects with the capacity to create and think. This creative platform is also an opening for intimacy, one that generates an ambivalence between inner and outer space, a poetics of self, constituting perpetual revolt.

If we are to situate radical intimacy in the political arena, extended from the personal experience of transformation and metamorphosis made possible by radical thought, we must also understand how this openness may translate into political rebellion and the construction of a new ethos. Kristeva states that "going into analysis is an internal experience enabling a person to situate herself in openness."[21] Herein lies the personal poetics of intimacy, as enacted in analytic speech, but also its ethics as it pertains to the global stage. Kristeva defines revolt as

> a return to the sense of the drive and vice versa, in order to reveal memory and to restart the subject. In short, to begin, endlessly, the questioning of value systems, which is neither belief nor nihilism. It is being able to take a position in order to assume a judgment in a specific situation and being capable of questioning things from the place of another subject.[22]

For Kristeva, the ethos of intimacy at the heart of psychoanalysis, and the quality that perhaps lends it its political power, is the way it retrains the psyche to leave its own well-constructed subjectivity aside and operate from the perspective of an other.

We may find Kristeva's roots in Freud's discourse on subjectivity in heightened states of sexual love and arousal. Implied in Freud's observation of a "man in love" is the fleeting nature of such sensations of groundlessness, infinity. Freud states: "one of the forms in which love manifests itself—sexual love—has given us our most intense experience of an overwhelming sensation of pleasure and has thus furnished us with a pattern for our search for happiness." Such happiness, he claims, is also sought in the realm of beauty, as "'Beauty' and 'attraction' are originally attributes of the sexual object"; however, Freud cannot reconcile the apparent ugliness of the genitals, "the sight of which is always exciting, [but which] are nevertheless hardly ever judged to be beautiful."[23] Freud's curious ambivalence toward the genitals mirrors the simultaneous attraction and repulsion we find in public and critical response to artists working with radical sexual intimacy as material. In his separation of beauty and subjectivity from the boundlessness of the oceanic, Freud also introduces the enjoyment that operates in excess of pleasure and which shall later, in Lacanian theory, be termed "jouissance." Freud believed in channeling this excess energy left over from the impossibility of happiness via sexual gratification into the arts—sublimation. Lacan's and Kristeva's thinking on intimacy as a conflation of inner and outer space mirrors Freud's discovery of the schism between inner experience and consciousness. Kristeva's extension of these ideas into a rigorous investigation of the intimate helps transform the interiority discovered in psychoanalysis into an understanding of sexual intimacy as a radical ontological stance with the potential to dissolve borders between self and other, and also borders within the self.

In her writings on intimacy, Kristeva argues for a renewed urgency to revolt through the arts, claiming that humanity is in a state of crisis that requires the intervention of the intimate. Important to my inquiry is her desire to develop a culture of revolt that reconnects us to the interiority of the soul, through the sensibility of the body, taking us beyond what she considers to be "the invasion of the spectacle."[24] She states:

> There is an urgent need to develop the culture of revolt starting with our aesthetic heritage and to find new variants of it . . . faced with the religious and political impasses of our time, an experience of revolt may be the only thing that can save us from the automation of humanity that is threatening us. This revolt is under way, but it has not yet found its voice, any more than it has found the harmony likely to give it the dignity of Beauty. And it might not.[25]

In an interview with the artist Anish Kapoor on the occasion of his 2015 exhibition at Châteaux de Versailles, Kristeva remarks on the subversive function of his work in relation to the beautiful.[26] Kristeva says to Kapoor: "I am captivated, struck by this way you have of lacerating the splendid beauty of the site without insulting it. You force something frightening upon it. . . . This embrace does not reject Versailles, it invites us to grasp it from within."[27] Kristeva is captivated by Kapoor's installations as symbolic chasms, doorways to the divine, and agents of intimacy—that ambivalent space in which the seemingly rigid boundaries of inside and outside collapse. She asks: "Could the hideous, frightening and orgasmic appropriation of this space of calculated rapture represent a striving for the sacred? Its rehabilitation in disillusioned modern eyes?"[28] By introducing the question of beauty and the sublime into her discourse on revolt, Kristeva invites us to examine contemporary art practices in terms of their ability to move the human psyche into a beyond, in the lineage of religious sublimation of the death drive. Much of Kristeva's discourse on beauty and the sublime relates to religiosity outside of, or beyond, ideology. In my chapter on Genesis P-Orridge, I explore these ideas alongside Brian Massumi's writings on form and the occurrent arts to recalibrate our understanding of the function of the sacred in contemporary art practices beyond the religious and toward the intimacy of ritual.

The term "intimacy" itself does not appear frequently in Freud or Lacan's writings, leaving us the task of defining it for the purposes of this inquiry.[29] Kristeva argues for the intrinsic intimacy of psychoanalysis and is faithful to a concept in Lacanian theory that is particularly relevant to my inquiry and which takes as its basis the very ambivalence of inner and outer space that intimacy presents. According to Jacques-Alain Miller, Lacan's term "extimacy" designates "the unconscious as discourse of the Other, of this Other who, more intimate than my intimacy, stirs me. And this intimate which is radically Other." Also drawing from etymology, Miller describes how we may locate intimacy in Lacanian theory, wherein "the exterior is present in the interior. The most interior—this is how the dictionary defines 'intimate' (*l'intime*)—has, in the analytic experience, a quality of exteriority." This slippage of inside and outside takes place throughout the psychoanalytic structure, from the relationship of the unconscious to the ego, to the structure of the *objet a* and language itself. Beyond the foreign intrusion of the Other into the private realm of the unconscious, "extimacy is a term used by Lacan to designate in a problematic manner [the] real in the symbolic."[30] In other words, the real asserts itself in the innermost sanctum of the psyche—the unconscious—and makes our very insides strange and unknown to us, all the while emitting signs of itself in the form of elusive symptoms and ambiguous representations. According to Miller, "extimacy is not the contrary of intimacy. Extimacy says that the intimate is Other—like a foreign body, a parasite."[31] At the deepest levels, exteriority and otherness is baked into our psyches, and an intrinsic alienation of self from self defines human subjectivity as a struggle between the inner feeling of formlessness and the outer tension of the Ideal-I—the fate of the split subject. The notion of the presence of exteriority and otherness, as a translucent specter deep within individual being, informs the psychoanalytic structure employed by Kristeva in her formulation of the intimate as that which questions the meaning and value of subjectivity. Topologically and structurally, Lacan's formalization of extimacy is less a loss of borders than an invasion that inserts the Other into the core of subjectivity. By disrupting subjectivity, and questioning and destabilizing its autonomy, intimacy as radical exteriority disrupts the foundation of ideology.

Ideology

This book argues for the radical potentiality of intimacy, in its ability to disrupt and destabilize ideological constructs. Althusser tells us that "[i]deology represents individuals' imaginary relation to their real conditions of existence,"[32] an argument that I will revisit throughout the project to understand the workings of the imaginary, the symbolic, and the real in constructing subjectivity. We will see that for Althusser, ideology always involves the ideology of subjectivity. Therefore, rather than attempting to interrogate which specific ideologies intimacy ruptures, and how it ruptures them, I focus on the broader notion of *ideology in general* and its relationship to modern subjectivity. If we understand radical intimacy as the continual erasure and redrawing of ontological categories, and a challenge to the very concept of subjectivity, then we might see intimacy as inherently radical, in so far as it disrupts ideology in its constitutive form—subjectivity.

I suggest that ideology has an intimate dimension and that intimacy operates ideologically—in other words, intimacy operates within and through the borders of ideology while also undermining those very boundaries and edges that define the individual's relationship to reality and the notion of "self." Furthermore, the intimate dimension of ideology derives from interpellation as a process of mutual recognition of subjecthood, and from ideology's interiority and the ways it breaches the public/private division. Althusser contends: "what thus seems to happen *outside* ideology (to be very precise, in the street) really happens *in* ideology. What really happens in ideology thus seems to happen outside it."[33] Ideology deliberately confuses the borders between the autonomous subject as a free agent and the material, environmental workings of subjectivity as interpellated en masse, through the collective indoctrination of individuals into modes of thought. Rather than being mere reflection of reality, ideology reveals the subjected status of individuals at the same time as it perpetuates said status. Ideology makes individuals who have already been born into being subjects, act in ways that continue to reproduce the same relationship between thought and conditions of existence—that of subject to external reality. In sum, we see ourselves as independent, freely thinking agents, despite the fact that we are reenacting and reproducing our very conditions of subjection, and this is precisely how ideology keeps us ensnared. Intimacy both participates in this mutual recognition and leverages it toward an ethos of connectivity. This book's thesis does not posit that ideology itself is dangerous, oppressive, or reductive; rather, that the ability to constantly question the very foundations of thought is a human quality that must be preserved and that can be preserved in the intimate. If ideology is understood as having an intimate dimension and intimacy an ideological function, then we can better articulate the subversion of radical intimacy as a form of radical thought that leads us through the continual metamorphosis of human consciousness.

Althusser himself seems to credit subjectivity—the mutually constitutive element of ideology—with the capacity to revolt. He argues that "the ritual practices in which a 'primary' ideology is realized can 'produce' (in the form of by-products) a 'secondary' ideology—thank God, since, otherwise, neither revolt nor the acquisition of revolutionary consciousness nor revolution would be possible." This statement invites the question: Is resistant subjectivity the secondary ideology that makes revolution possible? Before I address the issue of radicality as regards to revolution, allow me to note the weight of responsibility that Althusser places on artists and educators. He reminds us that "the externality of the superstructure [of the Ideological State Apparatuses (ISA's)] with respect to the [economic] base . . . is an externality exercised, in large measure, in the form of *interiority*."[34] ISAs such as cultural and political institutions infiltrate our homes and our private interior lives while at the same time impacting, serving, and helping to perpetuate an economic infrastructure that relies on subjectivity to operate. Apparent in this schema is the intimacy of ideology, enacted by state actors who may not even realize the extent of their complicity in the ideological mechanisms of subjectification. How might artists leverage this intimate access to disrupt the automation of subjectivity in its ideological modes of production? What does it mean to be radical today, and interrupt and subvert the automotion of subjects marching in formation?

Radicality

The question of radicality is persistent in contemporary art and activism. In my own work as an artist, researcher, and educator, I come across the term being used both casually and with passionate conviction, and it is always asking to be unpacked and redefined in context. My argument for the revolutionary potentiality of sexual intimacy to disrupt ideology and its expressions in contemporary visual art requires a tether to the language of radicality. Baudrillard's discourse on radical thought has helped me to consider the ways that artists enact radical practice and disrupt hegemonic principles. I also situate Kristeva's work on revolt within the same theoretical field. Kristeva emphasizes that revolt and its impact on subjectivity are historically contingent, and, in alignment with Althusser, argues that modern subjectivity itself provides the tools necessary for intimate revolt. She argues that "the tension toward unity, being, or the authority of the law (although always at work in modern revolt) is accompanied by centrifugal forces of dissolution and dispersion."[35] These forces of contradiction, in conjunction with the simultaneous drawing and erasing of borders, privilege the intimate in my search for a theory of radical praxis in the twenty-first century.

Of particular interest to this project is the hegemonic principle of modern subjectivity and my contention that radical intimacy challenges and undermines categorical notions of self as subject. Far from being confined to the individual, radicality disrupts the entire system of knowledge and being that is entrenched in the modern relationship to reality and is the substrate of social and economic infrastructure. By engaging Baudrillard's notion of *radical thought*, I position radicality not as a direct ideological substitution—the exchange of one ideological regime for another—but as an overhaul of thought itself. Rather than attempting to see the real through the fog of illusion, radical thought "seeks to restore the illusion of this world, and aspires to being party to it."[36] Thus, an intervention into subjectivity is an intervention into the individual's, and by extension, the society's relation to the real. Baudrillard describes the laughable absurdity that "defines the insoluble relationship between thought and the real." He posits that while "a certain form of thought is bound up with the real. . . . The other thought, in contrast, is eccentric to the real, ex-centred from the real world."[37] In this book, I explore the alignment between intimacy and radical thought to support my exposition of radical intimacy in contemporary art practices. Just as intimacy can be understood as an ambivalence of inner and outer space, subject and object, Baudrillard argues, "radical thought lies in the violent intersection between meaning and non-meaning, between truth and untruth, between the continuity of the world and the continuity of nothingness."[38] Radical thought is intimate thought. It transgresses borders without setting new ones and continually re-forms itself to escape rigidity. As a philosophical stance, it grounds itself in the materiality of the imaginary realm of playing with illusion while exposing it, as well as facts, as illusory. In contrast to rationalist discourses that attempt to articulate meaning and the truth of the objective world, "radical thought gambles on the illusion of the world, aspires to being an illusion that restores the non-veracity of the facts, the non-signification of the world, advances the opposite hypothesis that there is nothing rather than something, and looks for the nothingness that flows beneath the apparent continuity of meaning."[39] Baudrillard's radical thought is playful, elusive, and constantly in motion, situating itself in the realm of illusion as our lived reality and opening the mind to the possibility of nothingness.

For the purposes of this book, I posit sexual intimacy, along with art practice, to be a materialist practice. My aim is to situate Baudrillard's radicality in its imaginary and fantastical dimension alongside the materiality of sexuality and its constructions to show how radical intimacy disrupts the borders between the symbolic, imaginary, and real. This material dimension of radical sexual intimacy is a necessary component of a discourse of ideology since, according to Althusser, "[i]deology has a material existence."[40] In opposition to the ideological imaginary relation to the real, the involvement of the physical body in sexual intimacy enacts materially the formation and dissolution of subjectivity and therefore disrupts the imaginary relation. According to Althusser, "the material existence of the ideology in an apparatus and its practices does not have the same modality as the material existence of a paving-stone or a rifle. But . . . I shall say that 'matter is discussed in many senses,' or rather that it exists in different modalities, all rooted in the last instance in 'physical' matter."[41] I thus understand the workings of radical sexual intimacy in contemporary art to be grounded in the material reality of the body and artistic production, embedded in the sensuality of the drive, even as radical thought brings it into the realm of conceptual play. According to Baudrillard, "[r]adicality is not a more sublime virtue of theory. It means isolating in things whatever allows for interpretation, whatever overburdens them with meaning."[42] If we are to understand interpretation as an attempt to assign stable meaning to signifiers, then we may posit that radicality intervenes directly on the stage of meaning, disrupting any attempt at codifying psychic representations or societal imperatives, including the ideology of modern subjectivity and the ideologies of sexuality that have been constructed in tandem.

Baudrillard offers an analysis of radicality via the language of metamorphosis and posits that rather than the disappearing subject or the annihilation of meaning, radical acts operate via the mechanism of "instant commutation"[43]—the continual replacement of the subject in an eternal process of becoming. The subject, according to Baudrillard, is constantly changing its own constitution and positionality, altering its reflections of itself, and even questioning its own existence. The playful movement of radical thought disallows subjectivity a stable place from which to perch and judge the external world. How might the rituals presented in the selected artists' works irreversibly alter the landscape of interpretation, if they are to be considered radical in scope? Baudrillard states:

> There is no longer any metaphor, rather metamorphosis. Metamorphosis abolishes metaphor, which is the mode of language, the possibility of communicating meaning. Metamorphosis is at the radical point of the system, the point where there is no longer any law or symbolic order. It is a process

without any subject, without death, beyond any desire, in which only the rules of the game of forms are involved.[44]

Rather than the replacement that metaphor provides, metamorphosis, like Kristeva's signifying process, changes subjectivity on an elemental level and defies the stability of meaning—even if fleeting—that metaphor inherently implies. Rather than shifting from one shape to another, one form referencing another, metamorphosis ensures that we are constantly morphing and that no singular representation may ever take hold. Instead of narcissistic attachment to the illusion, we play with the illusion. Despite Baudrillard's insistence that "what psychoanalysis has to say about mythology is an abuse of metaphorical language,"[45] in Kristeva's words, this type of play available in the analytic process may be understood as "a sub-version, a re-volt in the etymological sense of the word (a re-turn toward the invisible, a refusal and displacement)."[46] We will see this very same mechanism in object-oriented feminism, in which artists playfully appropriate and *work with* identifying attributes such as gender, race, and nationality in order to subvert their hegemony. Artistic practices that assume roles in order to subvert them engage Baudrillard's discourse on "the ancient principle of metamorphosis, going from one form to another without passing through a system of meaning . . . a form of extraordinary expansion."[47] Such metamorphosis proves to be a radical mechanism when deployed deliberately in an intentional set of artistic acts of intimate revolt, aimed at diffusing the control and limits of ideology.

How might a culture of revolt look? One way that Kristeva answers this question is by turning to a materialist feminist approach to radical intimacy. She asserts: "The universe of women moreover allows me to suggest an alternative to the robotizing and spectacular society that is damaging the culture of revolt: this alternative is, quite simply, sensory intimacy."[48] In the text that follows, I address Kristeva's call for intimate revolt, grounded in sensual experience and displacement of the past, via Baudrillard's radical thought as a destabilizing relation to the real. I present object-oriented feminism as a materialist praxis of radical intimacy and radical thought that, by challenging the hegemony of subjectivity, challenges ideology in general. OOF offers an exciting new approach to feminist praxis that challenges the very ideological construction of feminist thought, a position which aligns with both Kristeva's and Baudrillard's concerns about the rigidity of all ideology. This project emphasizes art practice as a tool for the emergent subject in revolt and asks: How do the artists in this project work within, along, and through the bounds of the law in order to renovate and reinvent it, and themselves?

The Arc of Chapters

In Part I, I introduce Leigh Ledare's examination of his own mother's sexual life in the project *Pretend You're Actually Alive* using psychoanalytic theory, as well as adjacent theories of performativity and situated knowledge. In Chapter 1, I suggest that Ledare both fully occupies his role as interpellated subject and questions and challenges this ideological position through radically intimate praxis. I point to intimacy as complicit in the process of ideological subject-formation, while it simultaneously operates as a destabilizing mechanism from within this very same structure. I demonstrate that Ledare enacts a ritualistic reproduction of his own ideological subjectification as a subject of patriarchy and the Oedipal cycle, and that this gesture of self-recognition, and perpetual self-questioning, can be understood as a radical act. I then read Ledare's practice through Kristeva's theories on the maternal and the corpse in Chapter 2, in order to locate the role of the abject in rupturing meaning and subjectivity. I extrapolate on the ways that Ledare and his mother, in intimate collaboration, employ radical intimacy to effect an ambivalence of inside and outside, which ultimately confuses subject-object relations and operates as an interruption of patriarchal, capitalistic, and individualistic ideologies. I discuss the ways that Ledare's work engages the drive, embodying Kristeva's notion of the artist as borderlander, working in a space between representation and the unrepresentable, deconstructing subjectivity, time, and language.

Part II explores the lifelong practice of Genesis P-Orridge, whose dedication to challenging subjectivity, gender, and oppressive ideology in general through intimate life-art practice explicitly employs Kristeva's notions of abjection and revolt in performance practices frequently deemed repulsive or threatening. I introduce three distinct moments in P-Orridge's life-practice—COUM Transmissions and their collaborations with Cosey Fanni Tutti, particularly the *Cease to Exist* performances (1967–81); Thee Temple ov Psychick Youth (TOPY) and orgasmic sigils (1982–91); and P-Orridge's partnership with Lady Jaye Breyer P-Orridge and their collaborative project Pandrogeny (1993–2020). I introduce Massumi's notion of occurrent art to situate P-Orridge's work as activist practice and demonstrate the analogy between intimacy as embodied ritual and Massumi's ideas about form and activism. I investigate how Kristeva's early ideas about abjection develop into her more recent etymological query on revolt and argue for the radical potential of intimate, abject aesthetic practice. I frame the physicality of P-Orridge's practice in terms of radical sensibility, which

I explore as continual metamorphosis and a rejection of divisions between body, mind, and the sacred.

Part III introduces the work of Ellen Jong, whose practices extend beyond the disruption of subject-object relations into an embrace of objecthood as projected onto her husband's sexual body in the monograph *Getting to Know My Husband's Cock*. Jong's practice suggests that an object-oriented approach to sexuality and the body may in fact operate as a more radical, contemporary intervention into oppressive ideologies than simply re-situating subjectivity itself. In Chapter 4, I query Jong's work in context to Lacan's famous maxim that *there is no sexual relation*, and Irigiray's feminist response that both critiques the phallogocentrism of the psychoanalytic model and introduces language for considering intimacy as radical, poetic speech. Chapter 5 goes into more detail on object-oriented feminism in the context of contemporary feminist art practice and situates Kristeva's abjection as a materialist component of object-oriented theory.

The final section of the book, Part IV, articulates the political stakes of subject-object-based thinking, as it relates to contemporary art production, dissemination, and discourse. I argue for the employment of intimacy as a conceptual ground for developing more nuanced, sensitive and responsible approaches to sexuality and difference in the aesthetic field. Intimacy's radicality reveals itself as a poetic intervention that operates on ideological, political, and institutional levels. In Chapter 6, I introduce Barbara DeGenevieve's *The Panhandler Project* and Joseph Maida's video *Hula Kahiko Kane* alongside his photographic project *New Natives*, to frame the issue of postcolonial intimacy and inquire as to how intimacy can and should operate within a hegemonic space and in relation to the object of desire. I discuss photography as an ideological medium, as well as one that enacts power structures, and argue that the artists produce an intimate space that acknowledges and works through the breakdown of subjectivity in intimate practice, while I continue to question their intentions and manifestations of their power. Finally, in Chapter 7, I introduce the practice and theory of Lorraine O'Grady, as regards to her work *The Clearing*, to reengage the political stakes of subjectivity and the role of art and intimacy in both reclaiming and destabilizing the ideology of subjectivity. O'Grady's discourse will work in concert with Sheldon George's writings on trauma and race, as well as object-oriented approaches, to challenge and reframe the traditions of psychoanalysis and ontology through feminist intersectional praxis.

Suggesting our own blindness toward change as it happens in our time, Kristeva invites us to imagine a better future and a radically intimate life. In a hopeful nod to the power of artistic production, she states: "Faced with the invasion of the spectacle, we can still contemplate the rebellious potentialities that the imaginary might resuscitate in our innermost depths. It is not a time of great works, or perhaps, for us, contemporaries, they remain invisible. Nevertheless, by keeping our intimacy in revolt we can preserve the possibility of their appearance."[49] She seeks in intimate revolt an internal transformation of subjectivity itself and wishes to see this personal and societal revolution visualized in contemporary works of art. In order to address her concern, our task is to understand how these "great works" of revolt may take form and to frame a praxis of radical intimacy in terms of artwork generated in the post-1968 era that leads us out of the hegemony of modernity and into a new philosophical paradigm. Ultimately, my concern is to highlight the subject as a consequence of domination or domestication of internal and external otherness by ideological hegemony, and to suggest the possibility of subversion in the intersection of radical thought and intimate praxis. How can action and object-orientation, in the form of feminist materialist art praxis based in radical intimacy, participate in reframing of philosophy beyond the dreams of the Enlightenment while retaining a spirit of interiority and revolt? This book pairs Kristeva's concern about revolt in the arts, and her discourse on intimacy as an ambivalence of subjectivity, with the dawn of the twenty-first century and the technological and philosophical explosions that point to the possibility of a revolution in the psyche. I suggest that intimacy is a key tool for the coming era, in which subjectivity begins to heavily question itself and perhaps even facilitate its own demise, and that this intimate revolt is already at work in the practice of the selected artists.

The artists in this book are contemporaries, working in and through this rapidly shifting moment of ideological upheaval. They have made themselves vulnerable, personally and professionally, to make work that often challenges and offends. These artists have leveraged their intimate lives—their interior worlds, which remain always already partially hidden even to themselves—to operate on the edge of the symbolic seat of the law, in the poetic rifts of language and illusion. In this book, I examine some of the ways that radical intimacy operates in contemporary art practice, with the aim of expanding possibilities for reading these artworks and those like them, beyond categorical criticism bounded by ideological thinking.

Part I

Leigh Ledare
The Subject on Trial

1

Imagining Intimacy

Your question implies that, as subjects, we've started functioning much more like images, which I believe is true.

—*Leigh Ledare*[1]

I first encountered Leigh Ledare's work at MoMA PS1's Greater New York exhibition in 2010. I remember a narrow space cluttered with people and neat stacks of framed photographs of an attractive middle-aged woman posing in lingerie. I was intrigued by elements that were hidden from view, obscured by collage, and the mysterious brazenness of her pose. The work was sexual, angry, and at moments uncomfortably humorous. It also seemed to deliberately evoke emotionally conflicted readings. In the decade since, I have come to understand that ambivalence and access, as well as a desire to dig through material that has been buried and rejected, fuel Ledare's practice and the intimacy he sparks in those with the courage to see with openness and compassion. I also had an inkling early on that, along with the prurient shock and perhaps even feigned modesty that his work elicits, Ledare is participating in a radical disruption of something much deeper than our collective sense of decency. Ledare's radical intimacy regards the construction of modern subjectivity, faces it courageously, and invites it to dismantle itself from the inside out.

This disruptive gesture in Ledare's work operates in parallel to a broader cultural shift, punctuated and to some extent emblemized by the May 1968 protests. Althusser saw the 1968 uprisings as just the initial murmurings of a bigger, more radical shift to come. He refers to the events as "the commencement of a first dress rehearsal. With, at the end, some day or the other, after a long march, the revolution."[2] What are we looking toward when we look to the future of revolt? How does radicality in the present pave a path for revolt in the future, and how might that future look? These questions have echoed for me in much of my research, both artistic and theoretical, and has brought me back to Ledare.

As a young art student in the late 1990s, Ledare returned home for Christmas to be greeted by his 51-year-old mother standing naked at the door, welcoming her son into the family home under newly intimate circumstances. A former ballerina and model who later in life became a stripper, Ledare's mother began having sexual trysts with young men who she met through personal ads and stripping. Invited by his mother to witness her sexual transformation unfold, Ledare subsequently spent the next eight years documenting her with her lovers, and himself, in a collaborative domestic drama entitled *Pretend You're Actually Alive*. Profoundly vulnerable and moving, Ledare's project tells the personal story of a woman coming to terms with her femininity in a masculine world while at the same time offering a voyeuristic journey into the incest taboo. This complex psychic tapestry invites an inquiry into how the intimacy at the core of Ledare's practice functions, in context to its philosophical implications. This chapter establishes the ideological foundation of Ledare's collaboration with his mother, Tina Peterson, demonstrating the ways that he interpellates himself as a modern subject through a series of material rituals and practices. Through an exposition of his own ideological formation as an individual subject, Ledare makes the construction of modern subjectivity and its institutions visible and open to questioning.

According to Chris Kraus, "disruption lies at the heart of [Ledare's] projects. They are wholly disruptive, not in a strictly transgressive sense—although many of his images can be seen that way—but in their willingness to expose the subtextual exchange that fuels all relationships."[3] Numerous examples abound of Oedipal associations of perversion and lust for the mother figure that land Ledare's work squarely in the Freudian conversation, such as *The Guardian*'s unsubtle headline "Oedipal Exposure."[4] According to Steel Stillman, however, "once you get past Ledare's obvious willingness to confront taboos, you discover that his real subject is far messier: the mostly unconscious intersubjective forces that determine our relationships . . . how we are all—even as viewers—simultaneously subject and object, embedded in webs of projection, transference, and affect."[5] Ledare's work exposes the ideological mechanisms that dominate our intimate lives, including sexual desire, family, and economic relations, and subverts them through radical intimacy. In so doing, he explores both the ideological and politically subversive potential of intimacy.

At the core of Ledare's practice is an investigation of power relations and the performance of subjectivity through the private realm of the family, accompanied by sexual dynamics such as those explored in psychoanalysis. As he explains, "I've never thought of the project as a portrait of [my mother].

Instead, it's a document of our family, centered on the problems she was bringing to the surface." He describes his mother as a woman who lost her livelihood in middle age and "was struggling financially and trying, in her early fifties, to use her sexuality to support herself."[6] Ledare's work has invited criticism from multiple angles regarding his positionality in relation to his mother, including alleged accusations of "exploitation" by Nan Goldin, herself an icon in the field of intimate photography.[7] Ledare defends himself by claiming that the collaborative nature of the project, as well as the performativity exhibited by both him and his mother, amounts to a mutual complicity in the "economy that underwrites the photograph."[8] He also interrogates the nature of image-making and technologies of representation, asking: "Where, for instance, does authority—or indeed authorship—reside in the representation of photographic desires?"[9] Such self-consciousness exhibits an effective distance from the *actual* relationship and establishes the work as a deliberate, structural exposure and intervention into the ideological apparatus that rules it.

Ledare's erotic photographs appear to faithfully reenact the Freudian primal scene; the prodigal son finds himself an unwitting participant in a psychosexual drama of domination, hierarchy, and transgression of taboo incestuous desire. His only recourse is to surrender to his role as voyeur and bearer of the infantile gaze while simultaneously documenting the process of subjectification that takes place in the reciprocity of this gaze. *Mom Fucking in Mirror* (Figure 1) is perhaps the most literal example of such appropriation, as it shows the actual act of penetration into his mother's body by a male lover. The reference to the Lacanian mirror stage is evident in that the photograph was taken through a mirror, with Ledare in the foreground of the reflection, his crotch lined up almost perfectly with the lovers' bodies. Ledare simultaneously witnesses the moment of his own subjective rupture, occurring *through* his mother's body, and the fracture of his own mirrored image. He watches them while watching himself watching. This triangulation is made even more complex by the inversion of the gender positions of the lovers. While the mother in the primal scene was imagined on her knees, penetrated by the father from behind, Ledare's mother lies on top of her lover, legs splayed open with the phallus ambiguously situated between her own legs, and all three of the figures in the photograph shown essentially headless. Ledare's image reveals both his vulnerability as the cuckolded young boy and his power as the beholder to stamp an image of his mother's body both occupying and being occupied by an avatar of himself—one of the nameless young men who, unlike the father in the primal scene, do not gaze back at him.

Figure 1 Leigh Ledare, *Mom Fucking in Mirror* (2002) from *Pretend You're Actually Alive*. Courtesy of the artist.

Ledare's discourse around his work affirms that the imagery is critically and historically informed, and that these gestures are deliberate and self-conscious. He states, "we're constructed as subjects through a dialogical process. We're both staged by the social, and at the same time the social responds to us."[10] By appropriating psychoanalytic vocabulary, Ledare adopts a critical stance that refuses to moralize either the Oedipal Cycle or the Symbolic Order that presumably structures the very intimate relationship at the center of his critique. Such ethical ambiguity destabilizes any system of meaning imagined by these structural paradigms. He explains, "I don't see this as a failure, but as a gap that's opened up where something new is possible."[11] An analysis of *Mom Fucking in Mirror* helps elaborate on the ways that ideology—and sexual intimacy—mutually constitute subjectivity at the same time as they facilitate its destitution.

My inquiry into the ideological realm of sexual intimacy begins with ritual, specifically gestures of mutual recognition of our place in the apparatus we call *reality*. Althusser discusses "actions inserted into *practices* . . . governed by the *rituals* in which these practices are inscribed, within the *material existence of an ideological apparatus.*"[12] The ritual he has in mind is that of mutual recognition, which can operate on the level of the individual as well as on the larger scale of institutionalized practices. These rituals may include minor practices and marginal components of the ISA, such as "a small mass in a small church, a funeral, a minor match at a sports' club, a school day, a political party meeting,"[13] or even, I argue, an art exhibition. Althusser's materialist investigation highlights the dialectical process of subjectification that takes place in an ideological model, proving it relevant to a philosophical inquiry into subjectivity and sexual intimacy. Althusser argues that subjects create the apparatus that reproduces their relations of subjectivity; the apparatus, in turn, reproduces subjects who will reinforce their own modes of subjectification. We do this through rituals and practices, and through a mutual recognition system he terms *interpellation*. The question of whether there is an *outside* of ideology, and the extent to which it is accessible, is key to this investigation of radical intimacy, which operates in the ambivalence of interior and exterior. This inquiry becomes relevant for not only a discussion of exploitation and power dynamics but also the question of the nature of reality itself, and the ways it is imagined and symbolized in sexual intimacy.

Ledare discusses the intersection of the personal and emotional side of his project, with its ideological and structural implications. He explains: "I'm primarily interested in circumstances where everyone, including myself, is forced to recognize that they have skin in the game." He describes his work as "an expanding field of related projects, each addressed to the complexity of human relationships and their visual representation."[14] Ledare's image-making is a ritual of subjectification, but also one of liberation and personal agency in confrontation with the trauma of the real. Ledare describes his initial feelings when confronted by his mother and the use of photography to reimagine his own relationship to his family's conditions:

> My first reactions were anger and frustration. I felt forced to choose between not dealing with those parts of her—which is what my grandparents and brother had done—or finding a way to connect. I had a camera with me and began photographing her that day. By reframing my relationship to the situation, I found a kind of agency, and a working method.[15]

Alongside Ledare's critical practice lies a personal narrative shared in the intimacy of the analytic tradition and the desire for connection. In his work, we see subjectivity established through rituals of mutual recognition and ideology interrogated in acts of repetition. By exploiting the fascinatory and alienating effects of the mirror—the recognition of one's self, as well as the radical exteriority within oneself—Ledare's practice complicates subject-object relations, as well as the subject's relationship to reality.

The Primal Scene

Ledare's taboo act of witnessing his mother having sex echoes the Freudian primal scene, which is central to the psychoanalytic narrative of subject-formation, including its tether to the fear of castration and the splitting that occurs in the subject's initiation into the symbolic authority of language. In the foundational "Wolfman" case study in which Freud theorizes the primal scene, the child is confronted by the image of his mother's body as a receptacle for the phallus—the feminine threatening to subsume the masculine while simultaneously arousing untamed desires. In his interpretation of the fantasy, which he himself constructed on the basis of the notion of *what had to have been* in order for the wolf dream to occur, Freud develops a theory and structure of subjectivity and sexual desire based in misrecognition, castration anxiety, and desire for the lost object. Lacan later identifies the cause of such psychic destabilization as a structural component of language and the drive: "that object around which the drive moves . . . that rises in a bump, like the wooden darning egg in the material which, in analysis, you are darning—the *objet a*."[16] The individual's search for this lost object fuels the symbolic order and ensures its enjoyment—the cycle of desire that perpetually oscillates between image, word, and the unknowable.

Freud claims that memories from infancy are not direct indexes of reality; rather, they are symbolic products of the imagination. Their register in relation to the real increases their value in analysis, thus it is not just one's relationship to desire for the other, nor even one's relationship to one's own subjectivity that is at stake in the subjectification process of the primal scene. According to Ned Lukacher, "[r]ather than signifying the child's observation of sexual intercourse, the primal scene comes to signify an ontologically undecidable intertextual event that is situated in the differential space between historical memory and imaginative construction, between archival verification and interpretive free play."[17] The individual's very relationship to reality is inextricably woven into the imaginary and symbolic fabric of generated meaning that rises from the earliest moment of self-awareness as subject. This manifestation in language is essential to Lacan's extension of Freud's theories into the broader social sphere and to the play of radical thought. Freud's discussions of memories as distinct from reality are echoed in the Lacanian symbolic order, which situates reality and fantasy as codependent, and truth as radically separated from facticity.

In a pivotal moment that occurs in the primal scene, the boy involuntarily defecates, and cries out in arousal and fear, calling himself to his father's attention and creating a disruption of his own act of watching. At the same time, he generates an additional symbol of the distortion and dissolution of his previous, unified sense of self. He realizes that he is, indeed, a separate subject from both his mother and father, and that his sense of exclusive jurisdiction over her body was always an illusion. An originary separation has occurred, and he now stands wholly alone as the fractured observer. From this moment forward, he will attempt to recapture his unity with his mother and his identification with his father. Freud equates the infantile passing of the stool with sexual arousal, implying that the male infant's sexual desire is the ultimate catalyst for making himself known and attracting the gaze of his father, inviting his own intersubjective mirroring. The individual is here shown to be complicit in his own subjectification—on some level he asks to be subjectified, and thereby to be made an intact entity, and he does so through the physicality of his body, through an act of rejection and the production of a new object.

According to the psychoanalytic canon, this confusion around one's unity of form—and therefore one's agency of being—fuels not only individuals' sexual desires but also their entire sense of self. Salvaging the primal scene from the realm of contingency, Lacan removes the need for an actual witnessing of a sexual act and circles back to the subject's wrestling with *subjectivity itself* through one's own self-reflexive gaze. While the Freudian father turns and interrupts the infant's desirous identification with the mother-father body, compartmentalizing it into containers of gender and sexual object choice, the Lacanian *imago* replaces this external authority figure and places the burden of subjective construction back in the eyes of the subject himself. Freud locates the *objet a* in the bodies of the parents, and in the realm of sexual difference and desire for the other; Lacan extends this triangle through the operations of language, into the social sphere and onto the question of subjectivity.

If we understand Althusser's *interpellation* as a function of ideology wherein ideology itself constitutes the subjects that in turn constitute *it*, then we may also assert that the function of the primal scene underpins ideology as well as introduces elements that participate in the disruption by the intimate, including the trauma of castration, and the internalization, repetition, and expression of the drive. According to Slavoj Žižek, the ideological function of recognition is not as simple as Althusser's model indicates because he disregards misrecognition. By reading Althusser through a Lacanian lens, we see the ideological hailing function enacted through the sexual relationship and critiqued in Ledare's ritual performance of these relations. In line with Žižek's assertion, the imaginary construction of the visual realm both operates on the ideological level of recognition and offers a possibility of *working-through* of misrecognition to reveal the truth of the other as the unconscious exteriority within—*extimacy*. Ledare constructs an opportunity not just to mirror the misrecognized ego but also to explore the extimate kernel that characterizes the intimate relationship.

Ledare insists on the "complicity" of the viewer in the ideology of his work, a position consistent with Althusser's, that establishes his work beyond the personal and possessing of social and potentially even political agency. He states: "My hope is that viewers will notice that they are implicated in these and similar situations, notice at the very least that they, too, are part of the story."[18] Beyond individual participation in interpellation, Althusser notes institutional collaborations that render particular spaces and social roles responsible for how citizens are interpellated as subjects. Specifically, Althusser makes a distinction between the repressive and ideological apparatuses, which work together to create and control subjects, and establishes complicity between the artistic culture of a society and the oppression of its subjects by the state. The educational, cultural, and family systems of a society work in collaboration with the legal system, police and military, to perpetuate the repressive social laws that govern individuals' relationship to their reality, including restrictions around sexuality. Patriarchy, for example, is supported and reproduced not only via laws that restrict an individual's gender expression and rights but also through the material rituals of family, pedagogical positions, and institutional practices. Capitalism is secured through the reproduction of modes of production and in the actions of subjects who perform and enforce them. Ledare exposes the patriarchal, capitalist ideologies that have been continually reproduced through three generations of his family and uses radical sexual intimacy as a tool for both mirroring and continually questioning these ideologies.

Ledare's work in *Pretend*, though documentarian in style, is more than mere register of reality and operates on the ideological field via the imaginary and symbolic functions of language. In Althusser's model, ideology does not represent individuals' *real* conditions of existence, rather, their *imaginary relation* to these conditions. The imaginary and symbolic realms offer individuals language to describe their real conditions of existence. The sexual intimacy represented in Ledare's *Pretend* may be understood as having an imaginary function that represents his relationship to the real, in terms of symbols and images that may be decoded, and continually rearticulated through analytic speech and the materiality of art practice. As Lacan reminds us, "[t]he libido is the essential organ in understanding the nature of the drive. This organ is unreal. Unreal is not imaginary. The unreal is defined by articulating itself on the real in a way that eludes us."[19] Our experience of our real, tangible existence is an image projection of that which is not possible onto the fabric of the empirical universe. The imaginary is an illusion, an image we construct of our relationship to the impossibility of the real.

This distinction concerns our investigation of the role of sexual intimacy in subject-formation, as well as the material reenactment of psychical structures through intimate and creative practices. Althusser insists on the manifestation of ideology in physical, material terms. In Ledare's *Pretend*, we see the unfolding of sexual intimacy as the material form of Ledare's imaginary relation to his real conditions of existence. Partaking in the Oedipal drama inherited from the annals of Western civilization, Ledare comments upon ancient psychical landscapes that continue to live on in contemporary subjectivity while engaging the discursive culture that has bred his own self-reflexive strategy. According to Žižek, rituals, "far from being a mere secondary externalization of the inner belief, stand for *the very mechanisms that generate it*."[20] By performing the ritual, the Althusserian subject compels himself to believe. Ledare's repeated ritualistic re-creation of the primal scene may be understood as a subversive repetition of an ideological act that he acknowledges, questions, and creates anew in his own singular discourse. In his act of re-creation, Ledare inserts subversive inversions and revisions, himself immersed in the ideological formations that he simultaneously mocks and critiques.

According to Althusser, interpellation—the ritual of mutual recognition that we, as humans, are always in the process of acting and reenacting—operates from before birth and cannot be extracted from our lives. Just like the Freudian unconscious, Althusser maintains that ideology is eternal. It has no history of its own. Just like the dream, ideology is an illusion; as a distortion of reality, however, it is an allusion to the real and therefore must be interpreted in order to glean truthful knowledge of the real. Ideology thus gives us a screen onto which to project imaginary representations of our relation to our own existence. That which is imagined is only a visual map of the relations between individuals and their reality, not a concrete picture of that reality. Thus, ideology is always a representation, or an abstraction, just as "Freud shows that individuals are always 'abstract' with respect to the subjects they always-already are, simply by noting the ideological ritual that surrounds the expectation of a 'birth.'"[21] By being always already constituted as subjects, we are also always already abstracted and are thus not far removed from the imaginary realm itself.

Sacrifice in the Oedipal Cycle

Ledare employs an imaginary practice, enacted through rituals of performed incest, to examine the ideological structure in which he is steeped and by which he is hailed *subject*. This structure is one of mutual recognition and dual reflection of the individual as subject of ideology and authority. By engaging the ancient mythic structures represented in Sophocles's *Oedipal Cycle*, Ledare reenacts an ancient ritual of subjectivity that shines light on the laws that form us as subjects who have, as Ledare articulates, "started functioning much more like images."[22] Ledare's work addresses an ancient manifestation of the symbolic order, as read through the structural frame of myth. He explains: "Working on 'Pretend,' I discovered that if I could resist judging my mother and treat the images as archetypal information, then viewers would likely be implicated."[23] Ledare therefore deliberately reframes his narrative beyond the localized and the personal to expose mythic subject-formation as theorized by Freud in his construction of the Oedipal model. Sophocles's narratives explicitly link the incest and murder taboo with the imposing structure of ideology and the symbolic order. Ledare presents, via a tragic performance of mythic origins, the sexual mechanisms of subjectification.

Ledare exploits the relationship between tragedy and ideology, and its articulations in the Oedipus myths, to generate disturbing narratives that lure the audience into participating in a tragic double bind. According to Reiner Schürmann, "tragedy always maps out something like a sweep of the eyes. The hero *sees* the conflicting laws, and—at the moment of tragic denial—then blinds himself toward one of them, *fixing his gaze* on the other."[24] This selective blindness allows the subject to make a categorical choice and therefore to take a moral, ideological position in compliance with the law. Oedipus attempts to escape his predetermined fate and in doing so enacts that to which fate has subjected him. When the hero realizes he has broken one law (the prohibition against incest) in favor of another (following the oracular prediction), "an *eye-opening* catastrophe ensues, the moment of tragic truth. The vision of the double bind *catches the eye* (it literally bursts the eyes of Oedipus and those of Tiresias, though in a different way) and singularizes the hero to the point that the city no longer has a place for him."[25] The tragic hero cannot maintain the ambivalence of the double bind,[26] an awareness of which results in either death or exile. This double bind is a function of the symbolic laws that seek to compartmentalize and contain subversive elements. Ledare martyrs himself through his project, seemingly reducing himself to a doomed life of exile in a liminal space between blindness and the inability to unsee what he has already witnessed. According to Schürmann, however, "in fact, there is no double bind unless the *both-and* of the two conflicting laws exhausts the field of possibilities. Blindness is transformed from denial to recognition. Hubristic sightlessness is transformed into visionary blindness. Deprived of eyeballs, Oedipus sees."[27] Oedipus is furnished with intimate sight which eschews binary, categorical, ideological thinking. This interiority destabilizes the double bind, a position that stands in opposition to ideology at the same time that it has been formed by its laws. In confronting his own impossible choice between incestuous sight and blind denial, Ledare shows us that the intimate requires collusion and participation, necessarily resulting in the breaking of prohibitions and operating outside the social law, which remains ever-present and deeply interiorized.

As Sophocles demonstrates, the law is never far away. It operates in intimate proximity, both internalized and in a voice that comes seemingly from outside, or even above us. Creon, Oedipus's brother-in-law who becomes king after Oedipus's exile, operates as the Lacanian "big Other," the symbolic realm of language and the law, as well as an ideological position from which he attempts to *hail* his subjects further into their own subjection, the authority of subjectivity. He is the voice of authority in all matters of the law, the father figure to be obeyed by all subjects, and the steward of divine will. Obedience now is linked to future power and the perpetuation of the symbolic hierarchy, and the ideological apparatus is revealed as a self-perpetuating machine that reproduces its own relations of power and authority. This authority manifests itself in our private institutions, which I add include the family, love, and sexuality. In psychoanalytic terms, the relationship to ideology is not merely one of following orders but one of internalization through devotion and even love for the authority of the law. The big Other operates within the family structure, intimately incorporating state power into private life. Ledare's family members seem to pantomime these interpellated structures of family order while also incorporating subversive, taboo, and disallowed forms of love and intimacy into the imaginary relations represented in Ledare's narrative.

If Ledare as subject of the symbolic order performs the role of Oedipus by symbolically breaking the incest taboo, then Peterson as the figure of Queen Jacosta is both enigmatic and sacrificial. According to Kristeva, Jacosta "is herself Janus-like, ambiguity and reversal in a single being, a single part, a single function. Janus-like perhaps as any woman is, to the extent that any woman is at the same time a desiring being, that is, a speaking being, and a reproductive being, that is, one that separates itself from its child."[28] As Jacosta, Peterson is more than a symbol of Oedipus's shame and a victim of divine prophesy. She acts as his reflection as a fractured subject, caught between speech and the maternal, and representing all that is forbidden to him as a masculine subject of the symbolic. Jacosta's desire is transformed into personal abjection in suicide, while Oedipus's takes form in ejection from the land and purification for the city. Kristeva elaborates on the particularly feminine plight of Jacosta, who exists for the purification function of her son and does not become cleansed herself: "At the limit, if someone personifies abjection without assurance of purification, it is a woman, 'any woman,' the 'woman as a whole'; as far as he is concerned, man exposes abjection by knowing it, and through that very act purifies it. Jocasta is *miasma* and *agos*—that goes without saying. But Oedipus alone is *pharmakos*."[29] Sacrificing himself on behalf of Thebes, Oedipus subsumes his individual humanity to become the ultimate subject, atoning for his sins by blinding and exiling himself. By gouging out his eyes, Oedipus symbolically castrates himself, releases himself of the power of the phallus—the master signifier that sees all, and relegates himself to the abjection of exclusion from the symbolic order.

In his work in *Pretend*, however, and particularly in *Mom Fucking in Mirror*, Ledare perhaps suggests that self-sacrifice can be averted in exchange for poetic seeing, the vision that Oedipus himself gains through his own metamorphosis in exile. Lacan himself elucidates the shift in the modern subject toward the simultaneous construction and annihilation of itself by way of the gaze, which does not function as the recognition function but as the *objet a*, the gaze as object of desire. By sacrificing his ability to see in a literal sense, Oedipus employs his newfound awareness of his own subjectivity to become the object of sight—to *be looked at* without retaining the power of *looking at*. In Lacanian terms, he *photo-graphs*[30] himself by relinquishing his phallic eye, adopting the eye of imagination with which he now represents, through knowledge, his real conditions of existence. Oedipus loses his eyes and gains subjectivity through the gaze, while Jacosta only perishes in shame. In Ledare's storyline, both son and mother operate poetically, and in intimate collaboration, to reject the sacrificial fate seemingly sealed in the eyes of the law. Through Ledare's lens, complicity takes the form of active, creative participation by both gendered positions.

Ledare's practice may be understood as simultaneously ideological and transgressive to the very notion of ideology. Althusser challenges us to withdraw from the ideological apparatus and gain distance in order to understand our position as subjects. He argues that "it is that knowledge that we have to attain if we want, while speaking in ideology and from within ideology, to outline a discourse which tries to break with ideology, and to risk inaugurating a scientific discourse (a discourse without a subject) on ideology."[31] I suggest that artistic practice offers the opportunity for a discourse, without adopting the scientific distance advocated by Althusser. In *Mom Fucking in Mirror*, Ledare stands as the anonymous master of his self-constructed domain. A cigarette juts out from one hand as the other presumably hits the shutter button to capture the symbolically saturated scene. He not only watches himself be constructed as subject of the Oedipal complex, the primal scene and the mirror stage, but seems to almost wink in acknowledgment of his own playful appropriation and subversion. His skillful toggling between subject and scientist reveals a level of facility that threatens to subsume the personal, emotional, and vulnerable components of his relationship with his mother. Is their mutual performance purely an act of intellectual criticism of our collective real conditions of existence? According to Lacan, "the ways of what one must do as man or as woman are entirely abandoned to the drama, to the scenario, which is placed in the field of the Other—which, strictly speaking, is the Oedipus complex."[32] Can such an imaginary practice nevertheless reveal a hint of individualized discovery? According to Žižek, "[t]he pre-ideological 'kernel' of ideology thus consists of the *spectral apparition that fills up the hole of the real.* . . . *What the spectre conceals is not reality but its 'primordially repressed,' the irrepresentable X on whose 'repression' reality itself is founded.*"[33] Ledare's practice plays with this spectral apparition, revealing the unrepresentable pre-ideological kernel of ideology in the constructed fantasy that substitutes for the meaninglessness and anti-symbolic qualities of the Real.

This book suggests that radical intimacy in contemporary art can be a tool for introspection, interiority, and vulnerability, rather than merely automated reenactment and repetition of ideological imperatives. By working through our real conditions of existence in ways that spill out of the boundaries set by the symbolic order into unsymbolized spaces, we enter the realm of the abject, poetry, and revolt and, one may argue, out of the ideological servitude of the symbolic order. We may see Ledare's position as analogous to Tiresias, who sees all but *does* nothing; however, a more visceral sacrifice, and perhaps more tangible responsibility, may be witnessed in the abjection experienced by Oedipus. I extend this revolt, this "[h]orror of darkness enfolding, resistless, unspeakable visitant sped by an ill wind in haste!"[34] to this discussion of sexual intimacy. Lacan emphasizes that the object of the gaze is not the object of desire, rather, that the object of desire is the gaze itself and the desire embedded in the act of looking. Here, we may search for an empowered position as subjects with the tools to construct secondary ideologies, which resist and subvert the primary ideologies that oppress and limit our heterogeneous expression as subjects of desire.

As Ledare's practice demonstrates, we might step outside of ideology and gain awareness as active agents of our own subjectivity by a deliberate intervention into the symbolic order that interpellates subjectivity, via the covalent functioning of the imaginary, the symbolic, and the real. If indeed, individuals may pursue knowledge of their own subjectivity, then Ledare's practice may be seen as an epistemological quest. As we become more conscious of our own position as subjects of ideology, and as we are able (via the enactment of rituals) to step out of ideology long enough to witness its mechanisms, then we have the opportunity to reclaim some degree of agency in the workings of the apparatus that produces us and that *re*-produces our relations. If we take a stance of agency *despite* the workings of the apparatus, we may see Ledare's visual and performative practice as a ritualistic act of resistance against this apparatus, and a provocative attempt to rupture it through the workings, and reworkings, of the symbolic order.

Rupture: Situated Intimacies and Feminist Ethics

Ledare's practice operates as a critical examination of the workings of ideology on himself as subject of the Oedipal cycle. With this knowledge, Ledare presumably attains both agency and potential responsibility in his condition as subject of ideology. I am compelled, however, to examine the relations of the intimacy between Ledare and his mother, a consideration that carries with it not only ethical implications but also questions of meaning and representation, particularly as pertains to intimacy in photography. Ledare elaborates on his rift with Nan Goldin by making a clear distinction between their respective practices:

> I think Nan had this idea that she, more than anyone else, could take the pictures she was taking because she was an insider. She claimed the pictures didn't come from a position of authority, manipulation or judgment, but instead from a space of equality and moral complicity. I think this intimate status she had towards her subjects is where she saw the similarities between our works. But the comparison doesn't hold because I underscore that there is no authentic portrait but rather that it is always a performed one, no authorized picture but instead a game of manipulation, coercion, and power relations, even within family structures. I'm trying to impose a different ethical questioning on the viewer.[35]

Ledare's stance positions his work as an ideological critique of the very structure that gives him his power, lifting it out of the nearness of intimacy between him and his mother, and placing it in context to social, political, and systematic power structures. There remains, however, an intimate thread that operates from these ambivalences in positionality.

In the essay "Aesthetics of 'Intimacy,'" Liz Kotz explores the ways that intimacy is coded in Goldin's *The Ballad of Sexual Dependency*, especially in relation to the more "conceptual" images of artists such as Jack Pierson or Richard Prince. Ledare proposes that the schism between his work and Goldin's centers on the clash between her intent toward authenticity and his choice of constructed performativity. Kotz goes further and argues that the voyeuristic desire to *look* is at the heart of Goldin's practice. She states: "Presented under the guise of an 'intimate' relationship between artist and subject, these images relegitimize the codes and conventions of social documentary, presumably by ridding them of their problematic enmeshment with histories of social surveillance and coercion."[36] While not explicitly challenging *any* notion of authenticity in Goldin's work, Kotz argues that the art establishment has allowed itself to be seduced by the visual language of intimacy, a language that proposes to tell the full, unadulterated truth about the real conditions of existence depicted in Goldin's photographs. By allowing ourselves to consume the image as a direct representation of reality, we lose sight of the ideological apparatus that represents our imaginary relationship to this reality. Rather than, as Kotz warns, "systematically repress the past twenty [now forty] years' critical and artistic work investigating such transactions,"[37] we must understand Ledare's work as commentary that no longer has the luxury of feigning naïvety, as Kotz accuses Goldin of doing. We must therefore understand the intimacy between Ledare and his mother as itself being ideological and proceed with our investigation of the poetics of intimacy through this lens.

The act of situating himself in the midst of his mother's intimate life is itself an ideologically driven act. Operating from the stance of a straight white male holding a technological device of empowered *seeing* (the camera), Ledare bears the authority of the phallus and the gaze, and consciously re-performs the gestures of his own ideological training through repeated reenactments of the primal scene. Through deliberate repetition of what Freud argues is an ancient ritual of subjectivity—the primal scene as exemplified in the Oedipus myth—Ledare shines light on the laws that form us as subjects. Ledare's agency (and perhaps duty) to impact the ideological apparatus from within his artistic practice suggests that rather than simply enacting the terms of patriarchal ideology, it is precisely via performance and subversive acts of repetition that he attempts to rupture the patriarchal, capitalistic ideology of which we are all subjects. Ledare's work is an imaginary construction—a *fantasy* meant to represent to an audience their collective reality or at least their relationship to that reality. Ledare projects the law onto a screen and asks us to see ourselves as the subjects that we are— subjects of patriarchy, modernity, and capitalism. On a more ancient level, through repetition, Ledare and his mother perform a ritual of self-identification in the form of an originating myth of subjectivity. They do not simply reveal the cause of the symptom but employ performance to render such codification impotent. The persistent question of vulnerability, however, exposes potential ethical slippage on Ledare's part, inviting further examination of the intimacy at the core of his practice, notably, in that which is not represented—the "real" as a traumatic kernel untouchable by language.

By situating Ledare's work ideologically, I seek to identify ways that his intimate practice functions as critique and disruption. To do so, it is necessary to complicate Althusser's ideological theories with Lacan's discussions of jouissance and the drive. Žižek critiques the Althusserian model of interpellation as oversimplified because it neglects to address a key question: "how does the Ideological State Apparatus . . . 'internalize' itself; how does it produce the effect of ideological belief in a Cause and the interconnecting effect of subjectivation, of recognition of one's ideological position?"[38] By inquiring into the workings of ideological interpellation, Žižek demonstrates that adding a Lacanian reading to the Marxist model offers a much more nuanced and potentially subversive understanding of the workings of ideology. According to Žižek, by constructing an image-fantasy as semblance of meaning, we avoid coping with our *real* condition of meaninglessness. By applying the Lacanian symbolic order to the problem of ideology, Žižek demonstrates the necessity of ideology, since it "offer[s] us the social reality itself as an escape from some traumatic, real kernel."[39] Most importantly, this escape from the real brings us enjoyment, but it is an impossible enjoyment tied to the impossibility of meaning. Ideology is thus the unavoidable structure we have built to deal with the traumatic lack of meaning in the Real—unavoidable because it is the basic structure of our very own subjectivity.

How might vulnerability manifest in the paradox of self-recognition, as subjected subjects emerge from the prison of ideology conscious but doomed to repetition? According to Žižek, "*jouissance* does not exist, it is impossible, but it produces a number of traumatic effects."[40] Ledare replays his own ideological narrative through the exposed body of his mother presented as a series of images, projected on the ideological screen. Žižek delineates how the reciprocal gesture of interpellation between subject and culture institutes what he calls "*belief before belief*: by following a custom, the subject believes without knowing it, so that the final conversion is merely a formal act by means of which we recognize what we have already believed."[41] Žižek reveals a potential escape hatch from the ideological bubble and an entry point into individual (and collective) agency. According to Žižek, *surplus-jouissance* is generated in the construction of new representations and symbolizations. Fantasy is therefore "*a means for an ideology to take its own failure into account in advance*" (emphasis in original)[42] as we "pass through" and take enjoyment from the images preordained by ideology. In that regard, fantasy may be used as a tool to subvert the seemingly closed Althuserrian model and to use it to produce enjoyment.

Žižek thus locates fantasy and jouissance at the core of ideology and highlights the agency of enjoyment in the construction of even the most subversive images. He argues that the act of subjective interpellation as described by Althusser is always a failure of representation, that

> this "internalization" . . . never fully succeeds, that there is always a residue, a leftover, a stain of traumatic irrationality and senselessness sticking to it, and that *this leftover, far from hindering the full submission of the subject to the ideological command, is the very condition of it*: it is precisely this non-integrated surplus of senseless traumatism which confers on the Law its unconditional authority . . . [and] sustains what we might call the ideological *jouis-sense*, enjoyment-in-sense (enjoy-meant), proper to ideology.[43]

Ideology, therefore, peddles *enjoyment* as a commodity, and the inherent impossibility of full satisfaction keeps the desirous cycle going, fueling enjoyment itself and perpetuating the ideological apparatus. The construction of images is never a fully rational act and can therefore never be a closed loop of ideological subject-formation. *Jouis-sense* and non-sense, the tragic cycle that causes Oedipus to gouge out his eyes, are unavoidable not because of an external source that mandates the sacrifice but because of an internal drive to produce excess jouissance through poetic acts. Fantasy and repetition administer the hold of ideology through enjoyment. Before an ideological interpellation through the symbolic realm takes place, the split subject is caught in the cycle of desire for the unattainable *objet a*, in the realm of fantasy—"the support that gives consistency to what we call 'reality.'"[44] Fantasy is a ritualized performance of the inscribed law, through which the split subject is trapped in a cycle of desire for the *objet a*, "the chimerical object of fantasy, the object causing our desire and at the same time—this is its paradox—posed retroactively by this desire."[45] Instead of attaining the object (an impossibility), the subject constructs an image of "reality" that complies with the symbolic injunction that it affirms through repetition. Does Ledare's fantasy construction simply reify the cycle of desire, affirming his relationship to his mother (and, by extension, women in general) as functioning in line with the Freudian Oedipal model? Or may it be argued that precisely in repeatedly reenacting the fantasy of the primal scene, he disentangles himself from its clutches? Is his work an attempt to free his subjectivity, and does he succeed?

Freud's model of subjectivity and its rearticulation in Butler's theories on gender and performativity are active in Ledare's working process and reflected in his own writings and interviews about his work. I am interested in extending that discourse toward unpacking how the intimacy in his projects operates ideologically and disruptively. Butler's critique of the patriarchal paradigm of heteronormative, procreative sexuality helps identify subversive strategies for undermining ideology and thus dismantling some of the bonds of subjectivity. They assume a position that negates any biological determinism that lingers in Freudian theory, arguing that "[t]he 'real' and the 'sexually factic' are phantasmatic constructions—illusions of substance—that bodies are compelled to approximate, but never can."[46] Pivoting the conversation toward a discourse of *performativity* rather than naturalized genders based in biologically sexed bodies, they argue that "[g]ender ought not to be construed as a stable identity or locus of agency from which various acts follow; rather, gender is an identity tenuously constituted in time, instituted in an exterior space through a *stylized repetition of acts*."[47] Their perspective invites subversion and progress from within ideology; however, as also argued by Žižek, by accounting for its own potential failure by complicity in the ideological cycle, an ideological critique must always pass through fantasy. Butler sees gender as a series of repetitions that reenact and reproduce a continual renewal of experience of social meanings that have been imposed upon individuals, legitimating through the performance of ritual these socially inscribed meanings. By understanding gender as wholly constructed and performative in nature and noting its radical departure from any notion of an originating subjectivity, Butler invites interventions in the form of subversively reconstructed performances of gender and sexuality. They assert that "[t]he task is not whether to repeat, but how to repeat or, indeed, to repeat and, through a radical proliferation of gender, *to displace* the very gender norms that enable the repetition itself."[48] Such displacement, they believe, is the only way to subvert patriarchy in terms that destroy its entrenched mechanisms rather than simply hide them beneath a veil of nostalgia for what is falsely believed to have existed before the emergence of ideology.

Butler refutes the psychoanalytic position on an originating trauma and associated incestuous desire for the mother, which, according to psychoanalytic theory, takes place in infancy and jars the subject into self-consciousness as subject. As long as it remains unchallenged, such a "notion of an 'original' sexuality forever repressed and forbidden thus becomes a production of the law which subsequently functions as its prohibition."[49] Butler does not merely critique patriarchy itself but the broader romanticized notion of a pre-ideological time prior to subjectivation that renders all identifications of gender performative in nature. Butler's critique of patriarchy thus translates into a critique of an *originating subjectivity* and inquires into the agency of individuals wholly constructed—and oppressed—by their own subjectivity. Additionally, by questioning the entire notion of "authentic" femininity, they describe the construction of gender as nostalgic fantasy. They thus highlight a contemporary increase in demand for renunciation of the conservative attachment to dogmatic ideologies of sexuality. Ledare's oft-repeated intention of exposing the performativity of subjectivity and constructed nature of relationships coexists with an emotional vulnerability he shares as he navigates his own emotions and deals with his mother's seeming inability or unwillingness to perform the prescribed maternal roles of caretaking. These responsibilities may be understood as entirely socially prescribed, as in Butler's model, or driven by the bodily and psychical structures of sexual differentiation which are also socially constructed in language, as Kristeva's psychoanalytic discourse suggests.

Butler includes in their reproach what they consider to be essentialist feminist ideologies that privilege a belief in an originating "before" of gender. They critique essentialist feminist positions that privilege the status of *female* in an attempt to reclaim an originary feminine subjectivity, including Kristeva's, for falsely assigning meaning to the maternal body. In their critique of essentialism in feminism, Butler makes the case that "[p]recisely because 'female' no longer appears to be a stable notion, its meaning is as troubled and unfixed as 'woman.'"[50] Butler argues that in the recovery of the maternal body as site of poetic language through which the abject feminine disrupts the paternal law, Kristeva overly relies on the notion of a "before"—that is, before the orginary feminine got subsumed by patriarchy. For Butler, poetic language runs the risk of recodifyng the originary myth of femininity that is in itself a fictitious category created by patriarchy. Such aesthetic rearrangement, in Butler's opinion, is ineffective because it simply masks and replaces the symbolic order with something that may elicit aesthetic pleasure, but that nonetheless only reifies the system it proposes to subvert. Butler's preferred solution involves the conscious repetition of performative gestures of interpellation that, passing through fantasy, expose gender as an oppressive construct.

Is repetition, however, sufficient for rupture? Haraway extends Butler's theories through her calls for a *feminist objectivity* couched in locatability. She challenges the notion of identity as either fixed *or* performative and instead calls for deliberate placement in, and *research through*, marginalized positions, for the attainment of knowledge from the perspective of nondominant subjectivities. Similarly to Butler, Haraway questions the notion of an originating subjectivity by critiquing the subject-object divide as constructed by scientific ideologies of detached objectivity by the empirical subject. This paradigm, she claims, does not hold itself accountable for the damage it imposes upon individuals that do not conform to the demands of a sexist, racist society. Haraway directly addresses the question of methodological integrity with her "argument for situated and embodied knowledges and against various forms of unlocatable, and so irresponsible, knowledge claims," further explicating that "[i]rresponsible means unable to be called into account."[51] She suggests that the scientific "watcher" be situated in a position that closely aligns with the manifestation of the ideology being studied. Thus, a *feminist objectivism*, by situating itself in the lived conditions of ideology, makes itself accountable in ways that *scientific objectivism*, including Althusser's model, does not. Ledare's participation in the primal scene via a deferral of experience retroactively reinscribes the terms of his own subjectivation. His presence directly alongside the sexual act signals some transgression from scientific objectivism into situated knowledge; at the very least, his nearness to his mother's sexual body signals his intention of situated research. Rather than heeding the boundary of Western scientific etiquette, he places himself squarely in the center of the fantasy. Does not the taboo itself, however—that which consecrates the symbolic order by defining its edges—keep Ledare in the safe role of voyeur? According to Kristeva, "separation at the same time as union; taboo and sacrifice partake of the logic that sets up symbolic order."[52] Can the primal scene, by reemerging as a formal structure in Ledare's work, act as a protective mechanism from symbolic ejection, rendering Ledare's performance yet another example of vision deployed within the bounds of patriarchal law?

Haraway argues that the dominant scientific ideology of objectivism has positioned the faculty of vision alongside the all-knowing detached perspective of phallogocentrism, a position that violently separates subject from object. She calls for a return to the body as site of knowledge and an expanded notion of vision that embraces the fullness of holistic experience. She argues:

> I would like to insist on the embodied nature of all vision, and so reclaim the sensory system that has been used to signify a leap out of the marked body and into a conquering gaze from nowhere. This is the gaze that mythically inscribes all the marked bodies, that makes the unmarked category claim the power to see and not be seen, to represent while escaping representation.[53]

Haraway considers scientific objectivism to be a fantasy constructed for the purpose of codifying the dominant ideologies that oppress nonwhite, non-male bodies and calls instead for visual positioning system predicated on location. She argues: "location is about vulnerability; location resists the politics of closure, finality, or, to borrow from Althusser, feminist objectivity resists 'simplification in the last instance.'"[54] Haraway calls for situating one's knowledge in relation to the "conquering gaze" in a way that ruptures it and renders it impotent. Butler suggests that such subversion may be accomplished via embodied performance and repetition of new models of subjectivity, thereby retroactively reinscribing them onto the symbolic order. They ask us to take control of the cycle of interpellation and set it on a new course. Haraway specifically asks for such disruption to occur via the faculty of multisensory vision, in a quest for a new kind of objectivity based on the lived experiences of the un-inscribed. Thus, Haraway actively calls for an aesthetic science that learns and establishes its own symbolic system through vision—a newly reclaimed imaginary realm ruled by the bodies of marginalized and silenced individuals and communities.

Being a straight, white cis-male, Ledare in no way occupies this marginalized position, rendering his performance ambivalent in terms of destabilizing power relations. The power between him and his mother, however, oscillates throughout the eight years of their collaboration on *Pretend*, as well as in subsequent projects. We are unclear as to who is the vulnerable victim of exploitation—the aging mother on the verge of physical and emotional collapse presented as a public spectacle, or the son who survives her sexual advances by turning to the camera as witness? I suggest that it is precisely this ambiguity that renders the intimacy in the project so palpable and anti-ideological, and therefore radical. Ledare's practice leverages the power structures undergirding subject-object relations and both the sociopolitical and emotional stakes involved in occupying these positions, to which he even attributes a certain "masochism."[55] Haraway's position on situated knowledge is consistent with Behar's insistence that "really implicating ourselves as objects is the only chance we have to say anything at all about objects' being."[56] Taking a stance explicitly aligned with Haraway's on the question of situated knowledge, Behar argues that "talking about objects from the perspective of anything other than an object cannot help but foreclose the object's real, independently formulated perspective."[57] Collectively, these approaches help to situate not only Ledare's artistic vision but also Peterson's artistic contributions from her own situated position, in a feminist tradition of performativity and locatability. After all, while Ledare takes ownership of the project in the realm of production and capital, it was Peterson who first opened the door—literally and figuratively—to its creation.

In summary, Ledare is not simply a lone watcher, capturing exploitative images of his mother's vulnerability; he lives, *through his body*, the intimate curse of Oedipus. His status as an unmarked body, however—white, male, Western, educated, publicly straight—and the fact that he retains the power of the gaze, protects him from objectification, as he is always already represented as the empowered subject. In contrast to Butler's stance, Žižek argues that in psychoanalysis, "the status of knowledge at work here is knowledge concerning the most intimate, traumatic being of the subject, knowledge about the particular logic of his enjoyment."[58] Ledare plays with the subversive fantasy of the incest taboo and brings our attention to ideology through conscious repetition, enacted through intimate, poetic jouissance. According to Žižek:

> In psychoanalysis, knowledge is marked by a lethal dimension: the subject must pay the approach to it with his own being. In other words, to abolish the misrecognition means at the same time to abolish, to dissolve, the "substance" which was supposed to hide itself behind the form-illusion of misrecognition. This "substance"—the only one recognized in psychoanalysis—is, according to Lacan, enjoyment [*jouissance*]: access to knowledge is then paid with the loss of enjoyment—enjoyment, in its stupidity, is possible only on the basis of certain non-knowledge, ignorance.[59]

How does the *situated intimacy* at the core of Ledare's practice point to the kernel of the Real— "his most intimate treasure, the kernel of his enjoyment,"[60] a void of meaning that is nevertheless fertile with possibility for self-knowledge?

The Destitute Subject

The ideological mechanisms of intimacy are founded in the mutual recognition function of the process of subjectification. Ledare's employment of subversive repetition from a situated position of intimate enjoyment operates as the radical play of thought and eternal questioning of this *mis*recognition. Ideology, however, is just the starting point of my inquiry on radical intimacy as we move forward into the ways that the artists in this project destabilize ideology in its process of subject-formation, passing through the symbolic order, pressed onwards by jouissance and the drive. The analytic process operates in alliance with the intimacy of speech and desire to effect a subjective transformation that renders the subject capable of self-questioning to the point of ontological self-destruction. Žižek elaborates on the impact of psychoanalysis, "that radical change which, according to Lacan, defines the final stage of the psychoanalytic process: 'subjective destitution.' What is at stake in this 'destitution' is precisely the fact that *the subject no longer presupposes himself as subject.*"[61] As I revolve my investigation moving forward around Kristeva's notions of abjection, revolt, and the intimacy of analysis, I suggest that the radically intimate practices of the artists in this book both expose and disrupt the formation of subjectivity as a function of ideology.

We shall see that the notion of subject-formation can be questioned and challenged via radical intimacy, infusing such practices with an inherently political function. As Butler argues, "the question of 'the subject' is crucial for politics, and for feminist politics in particular, because juridical subjects are invariably produced through certain exclusionary practices that do not 'show' once the juridical structure of politics has been established."[62] In the following chapters, we see how Ledare and the other artists featured in this book enact rituals and practices in the material realm of sexual intimacy by exposing, participating in, and disrupting these processes of subjectification. Baudrillard elaborates on the death of the subject and the implication of this collapse on the ability to represent reality with stable significations. He states, "just because this system of values is coming apart . . . that doesn't mean we are being left in a complete void. On the contrary, we are confronted with a more radical situation."[63] By challenging the entire notion of reality, Baudrillard suggests, the death of the subject allows a more radical world to open up. In the following chapters, I explore the role of radical intimacy in contemporary art practice. I hope to show that beyond the individual practices of the artists featured in this book, new opportunities arise when resistant creative actions center intimacy as their driving force.

2

A Poetics of Abjection

To most people, just the idea of witnessing your mother in the throes of passion is enough to make you spontaneously gag or want to scrub your eyeballs in bleach.

—Charlotte Meredith, Huffpost UK[1]

Clearly it's more comfortable to pathologize an individual than a society that one is a part of, and hence complicit in.

—Leigh Ledare[2]

Intimacy on the Other Side: *Pretend You're Actually Alive*

Leigh Ledare operates as an ideological critic, dissecting the ways relationships are formed through ritualized practices of subjectivation. His eight-year collaboration with his mother Tina Peterson, *Pretend You're Actually Alive* leverages and subverts the psychoanalytic narrative of subject-formation. Ledare's pointed and critically informed practice is provocative, explicit, and sometimes disturbing. A plethora of critical responses that range from the horrified to the adulatory and Ledare's own well-researched articulation of the conceptual bases of his work have contributed to his entrenchment in the art world's upper echelons. His projects subsequent to *Pretend* have continued interrogating many of the same issues of intimacy, consent, and subjectivity. The work with his mother, however, perhaps in part because it was produced before he had the opportunity to fully flesh out his academic discourse, continues to tug at intimate strings that threaten to fray the fragile social fabric. Enjoyment and fantasy play a deep role in both reifying social structures and revealing them as constructs, while horror and disgust continue to resurge in a body of work that many people find unacceptable.

Ledare's poetic play with the language and images that constitute sexual identity, and subjectivity in general, invites a deeper reading through the lens of abjection. Kristeva's early text on abjection interrogates the social and artistic functions of horror, in a treatise that spans religion, literature, and the analytic process. She considers abjection to be "the other facet of religious, moral, and ideological codes" and argues that "such codes are abjection's purification and repression."[3] Abjection, intimately intertwined with ideology, resurges in revolt and disgust. Kristeva asks "on what mechanism of subjectivity (which I believe to be universal) such horror, its meaning as well as its power, is based."[4] This question strikes at the heart of my own motivations for researching the question of radical intimacy and its manifestations in works such as Ledare's. I wish to unpack and understand the meaning and power of art that leverages such uncomfortable spaces as those explored by Ledare in his exposition of his own family's psychosexual dynamics. Horror, Kristeva argues, "far from being a minor, marginal activity in our culture, . . . represents the ultimate coding of our crises, of our most intimate and most serious apocalypses."[5] How does Ledare's work function in this lineage? How does he participate in a culture of revolt, through "not an ultimate resistance to but an unveiling of the abject: an elaboration, a discharge, and a hollowing out of abjection through the Crisis of the Word?" While Kristeva emphasizes the power of literature as a "privileged signifier,"[6] Ledare's multimedia practice operates on many of the same mechanisms, leveraging the uneasy space between image, language, and the real to destabilize and re-signify the intimate crisis of modern subjectivity.

This project begins with yet departs from a structural approach to sexuality as an institution practiced through rituals of mutual recognition and from the Althusserian ideological theory that, according to Žižek, ignores the importance of enjoyment and the drive in the process of subjectivation. As Žižek argues, "'death drive' is not a biological fact but a notion indicating that the human psychic apparatus is subordinated to a blind automatism of repetition beyond pleasure-seeking, self-preservation, accordance between man and his milieu."[7] Just like jouissance, the death drive is intimately connected with both pleasure and pain, and the striving toward negation of being. According to Žižek:

> the "death drive," this dimension of radical negativity, cannot be reduced to an expression of alienated social conditions, it defines *la condition humaine* as such: there is no solution, no escape from it; the thing to do is not to "overcome," to "abolish" it, but to come to terms with it, to learn to recognize it in its terrifying dimension and then, on the basis of this fundamental recognition, to try to articulate a *modus vivendi* with it.[8]

Ledare navigates the terror of destitution—the experience of having one's own notion of "self" dissolve into eternal signification by turning to look at his own condition as destitute subject, in the process of dissolution. By doing so, he recodes the human condition, bringing to light the ideological mechanisms that construct us as subjects while allowing the negativity of the drive to emerge through incestuous jouissance, confrontation with the corpse and the unnameable, and the intimacy of analytic speech.

Ledare broke onto the New York City art scene in 2008 with dual solo exhibitions that debuted his collaboration with Peterson in several forms. The first exhibition, entitled *You Are Nothing to Me, You Are Like Air*, opened at Rivington Arms Gallery. It included the nine-minute film *Shoulder*, a collaborative video he made with Peterson toward the end of his work on *Pretend* in which she cries on his shoulder, initially as a performance and gradually becoming more grounded in authentic, deep pain. According to Ledare, "[t]his film literally performs an ambivalence concerning authenticity, and attempts to destabilize any fixed notion of real versus fictionalized lives, emotions, attachments, and roles."[9] The exhibition also featured a series of photographs produced after the collaboration with Peterson ended, entitled *Personal Commissions*, in which Ledare responded to middle-aged women's personal ads and had them photograph him in their homes according to their specifications.[10] By turning the camera onto himself and ceding power to his collaborators, Ledare explores the vulnerable position of being the object of desire and presents increasingly complex power dynamics that destabilize gender codes. Ledare discusses the project in terms of "economy of intimacy, sexual gratification and material validation,"[11] and the ways that subjectivity is formed through the social and economic constructs of sexuality and relationships. The second exhibition, *Pretend You're Actually Alive*, debuted the project at Andrew Roth Gallery. Roth and PPP Editions were responsible for publishing a limited-edition run of the eponymous monograph. The series was subsequently selected and curated by Nan Goldin for the 2009 Les Rencontres d'Arles Festival in France, a showing which received wide press and critical acclaim and helped put Ledare on the map internationally.[12]

Reviews of Ledare's work since then have been mixed, with some journalists expressing dismay and skepticism, and others admiration for Ledare's boldness and intellectual prowess. In response to Ledare's inclusion in *Home Truths: Photography, Motherhood and Identity* at the Photographers' Gallery in London, Matt Blake of the *Daily Mail* asks: "Is this really art? Artist photographs his MOTHER having sex with young men as part of controversial exhibition."[13] Frankie Mathieson of *Refinery 29* echoes with "Does Photographing Your Mother Having Sex Really Qualify as Art?"[14] Despite an otherwise conceptually rigorous analysis of Ledare's work, Greg Fallis of the Utata network ends his review with the emphatic statement: "Life is complicated. People are complicated. Art is complicated. This one thing ought to be simple: you don't photograph your mother having sex. Even if you're both playing a role. It ought to be simple. Apparently it's not."[15] In the more niche field of published art criticism, some authors responded with reserved intellectualism, seeking to minimize the sexual components of the work and instead focus on its social and emotional content. Thomas Micchelli of the *Brooklyn Rail* argued that the images of Ledare's mother "were shocking more for the ugly truths they revealed about her psychological squalor than for their soft-core sensationalism."[16] In her discussion of the published text, Christy Lange of *Frieze* asserts that "[f]or every nude photograph, there is another, more revealing document,"[17] implicitly asking us to look past the seductive immediacy of Peterson's sexualized body and pay closer attention to the subtexts of her narrative and its sociopolitical content. These critics frame the taboo nature of the relationship between Ledare and Peterson as a distraction from what they deem to be the real content of the work, which is Peterson herself as a tragic heroine and object of the desirous gaze.

These responses demonstrate the extent to which the transgressive positioning of Ledare's *Pretend* has complicated its reception on the level of spectacle and popular media, as well as in the critical discourse of the art world. I suggest that the abjection at the core of Ledare's project is intertwined with its intimate components, through which Ledare lays bare the human condition while evading "the religious and political pretensions that attempt to give meaning to the human adventure. For, facing abjection, meaning has only a scored, rejected, abjected meaning—a comical one."[18] Ledare's work calls forth the absurdity of meaning through his family's grotesque condition, a gesture that disturbs and rattles the public imagination. According to Roland Barthes in his final, tragic book on the ontology of photography, the *studium* in photographic representation "has the extension of a field, which I perceive quite familiarly as a consequence of my knowledge, my culture,"[19] while the *punctum* is that "element which will disturb the *studium* . . . that accident which pricks me (but also bruises me, is poignant to me)."[20] On the level of the *studium*, the prurient content of Ledare's *Pretend* continues to spark disgust in the general public, as evidenced by the revulsion in the previously cited headlines. On the level of the *punctum*, however—that which *pricks* and evokes pain and death—Ledare's project produces a nuanced and philosophically rich poetics of intimacy, experienced in the throes of abjection, rejection, and the unveiling of the emptiness of meaning. By extension, I suggest that the poignancy found in Ledare's delicate balance between poetry and revolt comprises the intimate slippage of his work and its contribution to a discourse of sexuality that extends through but ultimately beyond ideology, sexual difference, and the Oedipal.

As a linear text, Ledare's *Pretend* reads at times like a documentary film, layering images amid an interwoven written text that functions as a voice of narration. Besides Ledare and his mother, the other family members that appear in the story are Peterson's parents George and Roxy, referred to by Ledare as "Grama and Grampa"; Ledare's older brother Cleon; Ledare's girlfriend, who becomes his wife, Meghan; and Cleon's girlfriend and eventual wife, Rhianna. Notably absent from the photographs is Ledare's father Mark Peterson, who is nonetheless referred to in several written texts, including by Peterson who calls him a "sociopath" and accuses him of skimping on his child support.[21] Together, these figures comprise a constellation of interdependent subjectivities that can be read as psychoanalytic in both scope and structure, animating the narrative as an ideological text. The visual imagery of the book ranges from contemporaneous photographs made by Ledare to historical images of the family at various points in time, press clippings, and other documents. Most of the verbal text—both handwritten and typed—operates as a palimpsest, with redactions, cross-outs, and marginalia revealing the editing process in Ledare's recollections. Handwritten lists such as *Childhood heroes* and *Girls I wanted to do*—the latter of which includes the item "My mother"—when juxtaposed with an interspersed typed memoir describing current and past family dramas, situate Ledare's own social and sexual development alongside his family system.

Peterson operates as the text's central figure, alternating between sexual, maternal, and childlike roles. Images such as *Mom with Hand on Bed*, a formal environmental portrait, and a frame from *Entire Roll*, in which Peterson appears to be joyfully masturbating for the camera, highlight her contradictory roles of both mother and sex symbol. In the former image, she seems to pantomime a disapproving parental stance with one hand laid upon her hip as she sternly gazes at the camera, while the other hand rests gently on the bedpost, reminding us of the intimate nature of her environs. Her performance in *Entire Roll* borders on the grotesque, with her bright red hair, wide grin, and heart-shaped fabric playfully concealing her nipples as she pulls aside sheer black panties to display hairless genitalia to her son. Meanwhile, images such as *Mom as Baby Jane* emphasize Peterson's need for attention and caretaking, as she mimes the tragedy of lost youth and stardom. Traversing not only the incest taboo but also cultural taboos against the aging female body, Ledare pictures his mother as a sexual being with desires of her own and a complex set of autobiographical conditions creating her present subjectivity. She is more than a mere exhibitionist, as we see her sexuality unfolding in ways both emotionally moving and aesthetically formal. In *Mom Spread with Red Heels*, Peterson contorts her muscular legs into a diamond, anchored by red patent leather stilettos which point together neatly into a triangle, her genitals pink and exposed as she stares into the camera. The image is formal, sculptural, and alludes to Peterson's past as a ballerina and present as exotic dancer, while her gaze refers to Ledare behind the lens and implies a personal exchange beyond the performative display of her sexualized body.

Perhaps the most radically intimate images in *Pretend* are those that describe Peterson's relationships with younger men, as they both break age taboos and function as visual avatars for an imaginary sexual relationship between Ledare and his mother. The intermittent punctuation of laughter and violence throughout the book highlights the shame and abjection of Ledare's position as the helpless watcher and participant in the tragedy of incest and its enjoyment. According to Kristeva, "the tragic and sublime fate of Oedipus sums up and displaces the mythical defilement that situates impurity on the untouchable 'other side' constituted by the *other* sex, within the *corporeal border*—the thin sheet of desire—and, basically, within the mother woman—the myth of natural fullness."[22] Abjection only arrives once Oedipus becomes aware of his transgressions, at which point he must traverse this horror and transform into the purification factor via self-exile. Ledare, however, does not exile himself; rather, he enters into intimate collaboration and thus destabilizes the law and the double bind.

Ledare maintains an ambivalent position in the structure of the photographs, presenting himself as a simultaneously present and absent figure. Nicolás Guagnini describes Ledare's self-exile as taking form in performance, as he adopts a stylized persona. For example, Ledare's 1970s mustache, which he appropriated during the shooting of *Pretend* and retained ever since, is "a mask, and it's the mustache of the pornographer. But it's also the trademark of the recognizable artist."[23] According to Guagnini, Ledare distances himself using the tools and language of performance and photographic practices, in order to psychologically cope with his conditions. He states:

> For "Leigh Ledare" to make the situation he was submitted to when growing up into an artwork, and an artwork that primarily codifies and maps desires over identities, that documents "scenarios" as repetitive enactments of the primal scene or original trauma, he had to perform a double persona: a sleazy participant, suspended between complicity and bewilderment, and a detached, transgressive artist.[24]

The plurality of Ledare's role in the drama is itself a mark of the ambivalent expressions of radical intimacy that challenge subjectivity, including the duality of the split subject. By constructing multiple reflections through performance and reenactment, as well as the formal choices of his work, Ledare both realizes his subjectivity in the body of his mother and destabilizes it through the intimate workings of abjection and the speech of the other.

The photographs of Peterson with young men are not all necessarily blatantly disturbing. In *Hot Licks*, Peterson is sprawled languidly on the bed wearing only a red bra, her legs spread in view of the camera and in the direction of a long-haired young man crouched at the foot of the bed playing an electric guitar. His feet angling toward her genital region, the man's physical position loosely mimics that of a baby having just emerged from the womb. Peterson's gaze evokes a quiet melancholy, and the scene feels warm and familiar. The rouge of her labia evokes menstruation, birth, and sexual arousal. We are reminded of Peterson's role as mother, having given birth to Ledare himself; the sexual desires she embodies; and the multifaceted quality of the relationships explored in *Pretend*. We are also, perhaps, left to wonder why an expression of human intimacy as moving as the one presented here should be so feared. Kristeva elaborates on the co-presence of abjection and beauty in incest and birth:

> When Celine locates the ultimate of abjection . . . in the birth-giving scene, he makes amply clear which fantasy is involved: something *horrible to see* at the impossible doors of the invisible—the mother's body. The scene of scenes is here not the so-called primal scene but the one of giving birth, incest turned inside out, flayed identity. Giving birth: the height of bloodshed and life, scorching moment of hesitation (between inside and outside, ego and other, life and death), horror and beauty, sexuality and the blunt negation of the sexual.[25]

Peterson both evokes and denies sexual desire, both embodies and satirizes femininity. I suggest that Ledare's project fulfills Kristeva's injunction toward Beauty, in the transformation of sin into jouissance, and the beauty of sacred communion. Rather than functioning as absolute prohibition, Ledare's incestuous jouissance—enjoyment of inappropriate, unsanctioned desire—operates in an unmapped space between complete denial and absolute acceptance, inviting the viewer into an ambivalent cycle of shame and desire, and the intimacy traversed by the artist as borderlander. According to Kristeva, "the border between abjection and the sacred, between desire and knowledge, between death and society, can be faced squarely, uttered without sham innocence or modest self-effacement, provided one sees in it an incidence of man's particularity as *mortal and speaking.*"[26] Ledare and Peterson's tragedy opens up into a poetic expression of human love, intimacy, and sexual desire, as well as the abjection that both holds these constructs together and invites them to continually turn over in eternal signification.

In addition to contemporaneous photo shoots with his mother, Ledare draws from a rich archive of autobiographical material. One historic family photograph, by virtue of its proximity to a text about Peterson's childhood and her father's ministry, may be presumed to depict George, Roxy, a young Tina, and her brother posed in a neat cluster on the steps of a church. The image functions as a foil to the family's departure from the picture-perfect ideal of wholesome family life, as the very next page of the text reveals a dark family secret in the form of George's sexual transgressions. According to Ledare's narrative, Peterson had revealed to him that while a minister, Grampa had supposedly been caught masturbating with two young boys in a church bathroom, causing the family to repeatedly relocate as Grampa tried to outrun his reputation. Ledare further writes that his grandfather admitted to the act, claiming that "he had found two boys masturbating in the restroom and not wanting them to feel too terribly uncomfortable he also began masturbating, to show them that there was nothing [redacted text] {to be ashamed of.}"[27] In contrast to this revelation of improper and likely abusive behavior, intermittent reminders of the grandfather's intellectual clout—such as his personal relationship with Robert Frost and his multiple master's degrees—highlight the standard to which Ledare and his family were held. In Guagnini's words: "It's all too fucked up to be made up. We realize that all of this is true. We'd like it to be fiction; we wish the subjecthood of the author, and our own, were fictional. It is not, nor is it entirely 'ours'—and cannot be, even by force of voyeurism."[28] Ledare's family's structure represents the social complicity of their transgressions and highlights the slippage between fantasy and reality, and their manifestations in memory.

The social rites associated with propriety and family begin to erode under Ledare's scrutiny and through the lens of recollection. Kristeva describes "socially signifying performances where embarrassment, shame, guilt, desire, etc. come into play—the order of the phallus."[29] By exploring the ambivalent territories between shame and propriety, revulsion and arousal, Ledare articulates an approach to intimacy situated in abjection and its associated slippages of meaning, dismantling the order and authority that loosely binds the structure of the family. By juxtaposing the incest prohibition with the death and physical deterioration of his family members, Ledare performs a rite of intimacy—the spatial ambiguity between inside and outside—that extends beyond his relationship with his mother and yet contextualizes that relationship as an intimate practice along the bounds of the law. Ledare follows Kristeva's injunction to define his subjectivity as a mortal and speaking being by submitting himself to the shame of transgression. By abjecting himself, Ledare describes the tension between meaning and non-meaning, life and death, with which the human subject suffers.

In proximity to the narrative of Grampa's confession are scenes of Ledare's brother Cleon's drug addiction and a text about Peterson herself being found "drugged and incoherent"[30] after a date, implying a link between the family's breakdowns and the grandfather's transgressions. A trilogy of images of Peterson's living room full of boxes and clothing hints at Peterson's compulsive collecting, her belongings literally taking over her internal landscape as she constructs a persona and relationship with the world. A series of video still frames of Peterson in a tiara and white satin gown, in the midst of ambiguously sexual gestures, turn out to be stills from a soft-core spanking film. Distorted and grotesque, the images are difficult to decipher and present the viewer with decontextualized fragments of the video, rather than a literal representation of the sexual acts that presumably take place therein. Dream-like in its imagery, only snippets and uncanny gestures hint at the video's contents. Through these images, Peterson emerges as both the central matriarch and discarded daughter of the photographic text, as her sexual body and existential struggles simultaneously unfold to the camera's eye. Ledare presents the deconstruction of his mother's socially acceptable facade as a symptom of Peterson's father's control and disapproval. Installations of the project include sexual images of Peterson alongside the partially redacted memoirs and photos of Ledare's grandfather, highlighting the interweaving of maternal sexuality, abjection, and paternal law.

Peterson's sexuality acts as an undercurrent for the family's story, a narrative that, along with the overriding erotic incestuous thread, traverses family secrets, infighting, drug addiction, illness, death, marriage, and divorce. An additional overriding theme are the economic relationships, both inside the family among family members and to patriarchal, capitalist society at large. In a letter to her parents "and whomever else it may concern"[31] about her son Cleon's decision to sue her over charges she made to his credit card, Peterson rants about the unfairness of having been handed a bad lot in life and her expectation that she be taken care of by her family. She says, "your family has to set you up-hard work and professionalism do not pay off-esp. for women. Everything depends on connections and financing. And luck. And I've had very bad luck. From beginning to end. Period."[32] In her martyrdom, Peterson exposes the marginalized position of women in contemporary capitalism and her own desire to overcome such disadvantages through her reliance on those she perceives as more powerful. Simultaneously, she recuses herself of responsibility for her own downtrodden economic situation, citing it as a result of oppressive socioeconomics and the random luck of the draw.

Ledare triangulates Peterson's subjectivity alongside her own parents, framing her as dependent and rebellious. Ledare's grandfather—Peterson's father—adopts the role of paternal authority, commenting on his daughter's behavior and making his disappointment clear. George's impotence is revealed in his ultimate inability to control the behavior of the women in his life, namely Peterson and her mother. In one typed memoir, Peterson is hospitalized after being "found drugged and incoherent lying supine in the elevator of a downtown apartment building," and "Grampa called grama a spineless fool for driving all the way to the hospital at four in the morning to collect [redacted material] {her. He said she did this, let her get home on her own. She's holding our sanity hostage}."[33] It becomes clear why Ledare first introduces his grandfather through a landscape photograph captioned "View from grandfather's Christmas present to our family: 5 side by side graveplots [sic] in MELBA, Idaho, for $100 apiece."[34] Through the grandfather's foresight, and oversight, Ledare sets a morbid tone for the book and situates the family on a journey toward death.

Grampa's next significant appearance takes place in Ledare's typewritten memoir page detailing his grandfather's frustration with his wife's hoarding and codependence with their daughter, as well as his academic and professional credentials. Ledare writes that his grandfather "{throws fits}and likes everything labeled and in it's [sic] right place,"[35] emphasizing the patriarch's attempt at a rule of law and order. Sandwiched between multiple photographs of Peterson displaying her genitals and a complex set of confrontational gazes to her son's camera, this document situates Peterson's ongoing performance as a rebuke and disruption of paternal domination. All the while, Peterson's own maternal guidepost—her mother Roxy—participates silently from the sidelines, a defunct figure that nevertheless provides emotional sustenance for her daughter. Ledare's grandmother's mental state deteriorates as the book progresses, as she becomes a hoarder and leaves her husband to the task of disposing of a lifetime's worth of junk that she continues to accumulate even as he purges. As Grampa tries to purify the family home, Peterson continues to pollute it, forcing the family to confront its own abjected material. Eventually, Grama falls into a coma at the nursing home and dies. In a final appearance, Grampa expresses hope that his comatose wife may regain consciousness: "You never know, with a little help navigating her ship, still might sail back to port."[36] His optimism falls short as Grama's death is confirmed six pages later, leaving the family struggling to arrange themselves around this new structure. Ledare's family members' subjectivities, when triangulated through the figure of the Father, explicitly embody the Lacanian subject as a consequence of the symbolic and therefore of the paternal law. The maternal position occupied by Peterson and, to some extent, her mother, and the presence of Ledare, his brother, and their partners as the children of the family complete the triadic structure of the family. The cycle of life and death elaborated in *Pretend*—the dying of one generation and maturation of the next—emphasizes the cyclical nature of the Oedipal in its formation of subjectivity.

By including other women in the narrative, Ledare provides telling evidence of Peterson's nonconformity with societal roles, if only by comparison. We view scenes of Ledare and his girlfriend (and soon-to-be bride) Meghan smiling happily for the camera, their normative union put on display in marked contrast to Peterson's abject and solitary narcissism, and to Cleon's partner Rhianna's drug addiction. Meghan appears as an angelic nude on a sunlit bed and as a glowing young bride in a white wedding to which she supposedly "didn't feel comfortable inviting"[37] her future mother-in-law. A dichotomy is formed between the Madonna and the whore, with the new wife taking on the holy maternal role, while the aging mother occupies the position of discarded female, worthy only as abject spectacle. According to Guagnini, "Tina Peterson is perpetually performing for the camera; she's performing her failure to perform as a 'proper mother,' in some kind of redemptive, strategic masochism, topping from the bottom of her life's failure."[38] Meghan, on the other hand, represents both the hope of achieving the feminine ideal and the threat of collapse. By aligning himself between these female characters, Ledare demonstrates his own ambivalent desire and positions himself as the abject observer caught between the bounds of law and incestuous jouissance. Two explicit images in *Pretend* demonstrate the extent to which Ledare positions his mother's sexuality as both parallel in form to his and Meghan's intimacy, and at odds with its ideological content. In one image, Peterson dons an upside-down tiara and jewels as she fellates an anonymous young lover, her costume both echoing and subverting her character from the spanking film. The upright ear of a stuffed rabbit in the foreground of the photograph creates the illusion that she is ingesting a particularly long phallus, a nod to idealized pornographic imagery as well as the icon of the Playboy bunny. Peterson performs the dual role of deconstructed sex goddess undermining societal expectation and seasoned provocateur who is proud of her sexual prowess. By including a child's toy in such an overtly sexual scene, Ledare also gestures to his own status as child, perhaps prematurely witnessing a pornographic act. In contrast to an earlier shot in which Meghan appears playful and nude with her hair thrown in a messy bun, smiling coyly as her mouth grazes Ledare's erection, Peterson's portrayal reads as a cynical commentary on age, femininity, and sexual economics.

Consistently throughout the monograph, Meghan's body is presented as young and fresh, unencumbered by costume or pageantry, with the exception of her bridal attire. She innocently smiles demurely at Ledare's side and only looks on with discomfort as Peterson initiates her into the family with an impromptu outing to a hotel for a private strip performance by a middle-aged man nicknamed "the doctor."[39] According to Ledare's recounting of the family narrative, this was the first and last time that the two women met. In dialogue with this new female, Peterson appears increasingly self-destructive and Ledare's erotic interest in his mother more deeply conflictual with the order of the law and the normativity of his marriage. According to Žižek, Lacanian analysis frames the mother as object of desire, lost object, and object of both fascination and disgust, which complicates fantasy. In fantasy, "mother is *reduced* to a limited set of (symbolic) features; as soon as an object *too close* to the Mother-Thing . . . appears in the fantasy-frame, the desire is suffocated in incestuous claustrophobia."[40] The strict boundaries Ledare maintains between his mother and his wife dissolve as the women reflect one another, each mirroring and sometimes inverting the other. In the intimacy of these scenes—in pain, fear, and desire—Ledare exposes the mythic role of the mother as the wellspring of life and death in one body, degraded as a thing or object to be reviled and rejected, in order to consecrate the integrity of the speaking subject of patriarchy. Apparent throughout *Pretend*, however, is that the myth of the clean and proper self is a fiction and that despite Ledare's attainment of knowledge, there is no purification function available, and his home will continue to suffer from blight. The mother figure is implicated and included in the intimacy, and agency, of the fantasy, rather than being designated monstrous. Throughout the text, Ledare and Meghan's chaste love is juxtaposed with dysfunction in his other family members, with her serving as his tether to order and normalcy. In contrast to his family members' corporeal self-destruction, for Ledare abjection lies not in his own body but in his relation to the maternal body and its transgressions and ambivalences. Ledare and his family members perform both the abjection central to subject-formation and the maintenance of boundaries and roles, and the becoming-abject that signifies a subversion of these very structures.

Central to all family members' journeys is Peterson and her role as the abject and abjected mother and signifier of non-meaning in a patriarchal, capitalist society. Peterson provides the main narrative arc of *Pretend*, as we witness her transformation from child ballet prodigy dancing with the Joffrey, a lifetime of promise ahead of her; to adolescent sex symbol pictured in *Seventeen Magazine*; to middle-aged woman at her sexual peak but on the edge of societal approval; and, finally, to aging mother suffering from mental, physical, and financial breakdown and the progressive loss of her sexualized body. The 248-page tome begins with the foreshadowing of death and decay in the aforementioned grave plot landscape, which appears early in the book's sequence as well as comprises its exterior box cover. The photograph offers a picturesque vista of a brown valley capped by dark green mountains, before the reader flips the page to two images of Peterson that together conceptually bookend the entire narrative. In the left-hand image she is ensconced by the black halo of her fur coat, skin pale and eyes closed as she leans back against a regal headboard. In the facing image, printed smaller on the right-hand page of the book spread, Peterson lies in a synonymous pose, wearing a neck brace and hospital gown, her head propped up on a clinical white pillow, presaging her eventual physical deterioration.

Peterson's devolving bodily condition is key to reading Ledare's text as a poetics of abjection via the movement between the incest taboo and the horrific apparition of the corpse. Through her arc from subject (and object) of the incestuous gaze exchanged with her son to victim of a debilitating car accident that leaves her physically and mentally crippled, Peterson's facade begins to crack, and we are left to witness as she becomes corpse-like, skirting the edges of decay and dissolution. Beginning with the book's cover, a transcription of Peterson's explicit critique of the lack of acknowledgment that models receive for their work and her own feelings of invisibility serves as introduction to the entire project. Peterson laments: "The model is taken for granted. The photographer gets all the credit. Um, as a model I feel wronged by that."[41] Ledare unfolds his mother's story as that of the forgotten artist who never got her big break. She emerges as a codependent, manipulative, and possibly abusive mother preoccupied with her own sexual gratification, creative expression, and finding a man to financially support her. By the end of the text, Peterson is depicted as increasingly ill and depressed, her skin pallid in dark-colored clothing and austere domestic environments. The image series after Grama's death begins with Peterson naked and unadorned, wearing a neck brace while perched on two chairs in her closet/living room. Her body, lacking the enhancement of lingerie and makeup, appears aged and bloated, and her face morose as she stares blankly into the camera. The image seems to signal an ending—the unravelling of a fantasy, perhaps, or the culmination of a performance. Following pages show a close-up self-portrait of Ledare and Peterson in bed; they seem to be fully clothed and possibly in the midst of an intimate moment of emotional bonding, the taboo sexual component of their relationship momentarily omitted in favor of the emotional closeness one may find in a more socially acceptable mother-son relationship. A small image of Grama's empty hospital bed follows, a memento mori circling us back to the beginning of the series and its hearkening toward death.

Peterson's illness grows to dominate her life, as she moves to the suburbs with her newest boyfriend—a 35-year-old virgin until Peterson starts sleeping with him "to get him over the hump of being a virgin."[42] There, she attempts to live off the inheritance from her mother and the cumulative earnings of her romantic and financial entanglements. She stops having sex with her boyfriend because of physical pain and focuses on her injuries and a lawsuit over the accident. Her friends, and even her doctors, begin to doubt the veracity of her claims and, according to Ledare's text, she even begins to question herself. Besides wondering if she has indeed lost touch with reality, Ledare writes that "she says she has no proof of anything positive to show for her life, no real evidence of who she was and all the incredible things she's done."[43] The border between fantasy and reality collapses, situating her subjectivity in the abject territory between the imaginary and the real where even the appearance of meaning is tenuous. Abjection reaches back to a primordial separation before the illusion of misrecognition takes hold and the alienation that necessarily preexists and persists in all subjects. Peterson's femininity occupies the role of the misunderstood hysteric, judged for her unwillingness to comply with societal injunctions, while begging to be heard in her unspoken pain and suffering. Ledare's penultimate image of Peterson depicts her as a shadowy figure in a darkened room, looking at the camera with half her face barely legible due to shadow. Entitled *Mom in New Home*, this image culminates the series with an impression of dashed hopes, dwindling dreams, and a life of solitude ahead.

Fact and fiction, Ledare's photographic text traces a family's abject devolution into addiction and death, with the guiding thread of incestuous desire as its driving condition. After three pages of Peterson's will, which she hand-wrote with flourish on stationery from her alter-ego 'Lady Violette de Courcy,' and in which she leaves all of her belongings to Ledare, the final image of the book appears almost as an epitaph. Four strips of photo booth images depict Ledare and Peterson posing together, toggling between unaffected stares toward the camera and kisses that blur the lines between typical parent-child affection and the passion of lovers (Figure 2). According to Lange, these images of "Ledare and his mother mugging for the camera and making out like teenagers provide glimpses of the pair as willing co-conspirators. Such insertions create a layer of artifice that unsettles the raw, confessional mode that Ledare seems to be emulating."[44] Lange's commentary highlights the conceptual disruption effected by the performative component of the work, a sentiment echoed by Ledare himself, who has explained that the images were taken after a day spent walking around, holding hands and pretending to be a couple, but that they were really about Peterson's obsession with the Factory and Andy Warhol.[45] The final strip of photos from this sequence shows Peterson by herself, posing for the camera and gesturing to her own longing for glamour and fame. This image and its layered backstory seem to remind us that throughout this tragic narrative of a woman and her family on the brink of collapse has lingered a story of intimate desire that often skirts the edges of both reality and fiction, the provocative slippage alluded to in the title of the work.

Ledare's work is a focused commentary on the constructed nature of subjectivity. He employs a performative structure as the mechanism by which facticity is questioned. Placed alongside other image-makers of recent decades who have made work dealing with intimacy—for example, Nan Goldin—Ledare's is a meta-narrative about subjectivity itself, rather than exclusively

Figure 2 Leigh Ledare, *Me and Mom in Photobooth* (2008) from *Pretend You're Actually Alive*. Courtesy of the artist.

an intimate document of a specific family. Such instability can be found throughout the body of work and is crystallized in Ledare's choice of title for the series and book, *Pretend You're Actually Alive*. According to Ledare, this was a phrase repeated by a friend of the family and amateur porn producer from behind the camera while directing Peterson in a soft-core spanking film, a video of which Peterson ultimately gifted to Ledare.[46] By using the borrowed directive as an overarching title for his entire series, Ledare asks us to look at Peterson's life—and, by extension, life in general—as a constructed fiction and performance. According to Ledare, he also asks, "what was this aspect between fact and fiction, and that slippage between the two? . . . *pretend you're alive* . . . you know . . . *pretend you're actually dead* . . . it implies its opposite as well."[47] What does it mean, to *imply* the *performance* of death? Ledare's title leaves open the question of who is targeted by the suggestion—to *pretend* one is actually alive. Is it we, the audience, that Ledare is asking to consider the possibility of our own life and death as performances? Ledare seems to ask us to strongly consider the rich semiotic activity in the borderlands on the edge of accepted territories, where we may witness, and even experience, the instability of signification. Ledare's intimate operation, performed in the gray area between inside and outside that is activated in abjection, challenges the distinction between fantasy and reality, and urges us to reengage the border between the imaginary and the real, pleasure and pain. I suggest that it is precisely in such semiotic ambiguity that the intimacy of Ledare's practice lies—in his discomfiting proximity to taboo desire, he both rejects and performs the oracular injunction of ideology, through which the symbolic and subjectivity are destabilized. In the words of *Artforum*'s David Velasco: "Is a life pretended one more fully lived? Pretend you're actually alive, Ledare pleads, and shortens the tether of the simulacrum."[48] We may posit that it is also Ledare himself who tries to outrun the pull of the simulacrum—the illusion with no referent—through the pinprick of the *punctum*, that surprising little accident that occurs while one is busy performing expected roles, reminding us of our own mortality. The title takes the project into a liminal space straddling life and death, being and nonbeing, subject and object; the title alone takes us into the realm of the abject.

Intimacy and Instability

By radicalizing intimacy through the abject, artists can effect a subjective, temporal, and spatial rupture from within a seemingly intersubjective framework—and thereby develop new pathways toward the deployment of radical intimacy as poetic and critical speech. Ledare's approach to sexual intimacy locates the intimate body as a poetic site or what Kristeva terms the *semiotic*, "a primal mapping of the body"[49] and a key component of poetic language. Kristeva clarifies that "while being the precondition of language, it is dependent upon meaning, but in a way that is not that of *linguistic* signs nor of the *symbolic* order they found."[50] In her discourse on abjection, Kristeva demonstrates that through the horrific, revolting, and inappropriate, subjectivity is revealed to be a construct that stifles and misdirects an originary nondifferentiation that she identifies as maternal—and therefore feminine—in origin. Through his intimate engagement with this suppressed maternal femininity, as embodied in his mother in *Pretend*, Ledare performs a radical, abject poetic, thus both exposing and challenging the workings of ideology, subjectivity, and patriarchal sexual relations.

Often speaking in terms of performance theory and the constructed nature of subjectivity, Ledare aligns himself with critical theories, such as Butler's, that reveal psychoanalysis itself as an ideological apparatus wielding power and control over our subjectivity. Why, then, contextualize his work within the very framework he appears to be critiquing? Does the work itself not nullify its very foundation by bringing to light the power structures that underlie societal relations and the subjectivities interpellated by those very same apparatuses? Rather than rejection, however, Ledare's critique of ideology comes packaged in what appears to be an ongoing engagement with a variety of analytic and psychological models. According to Micchelli, for example, Ledare's debut exhibition at Rivington Arms included as part of the installation "dutifully positioned artifacts like a copy of Melanie Klein's *Love, Guilt and Reparation* and an unspooled videotape of an amateur fetish film starring the artist's mother,"[51] suggesting that Ledare formally engaged psychoanalysis in his research during the time of his work with Peterson. More recently, Ledare's 2017 exhibition at the Art Institute of Chicago—consisting of a documentary film entitled *The Task* and installation of related ephemera—examined group psychology in an experimental setting, further revealing Ledare's persistent consideration of psychoanalysis and its offshoots.[52] Far from being proof of his commitment to such formulations, Ledare's employment of the language of analysis as part of his visual vocabulary functions as a series of citations through which he builds his critique on the edge between the symbolic and the semiotic. By creating situations that amplify and re-symbolize these structures, Ledare invites reflection into how we as humans are constructed by them and also generates the surplus signification—new languages, images, and affects—produced through and by discourse.

    Ledare claims to address desire as a dialogical process, situated inside of a dialectical personal relation; however, he simultaneously demonstrates the *fragility* of the Oedipal model and its prohibitions. When asked about his frequent use of the term "intersubjectivity," Ledare responds, "I guess it's . . . counter to this idea of the autonomous subject, in some ways, so, understanding that we are who we are in relationship to the situation . . . and in relationship to the Other."[53] I am interested in exposing the semiotic aspect of Ledare's practice as a challenge and counterpoint to its symbolic surface, thereby situating his work—and the work of intimacy—as a poetics of abjection. Kristeva makes apparent that the abject is not simply a deconstruction of meaning but a bright, radiant coming-to-be in what she calls "incandescent states of a boundary-subjectivity."[54] By existing as a shimmering boundary state, abjection *embodies* the paradox of intimacy rather than simply *effecting* it. According to Kristeva, the *abject* is "radically excluded and draws me toward the place where meaning collapses,"[55] therefore, by definition, the abject is "always already" cut off from discourse and constantly asking to be reconsidered. In parallel, she describes the *intimate* as a site of questioning prescribed meanings and ideologies. She thus introduces a poetic approach to a relation whose object is neither beauty nor coherence but a radical dissolution of boundaries. Intimacy may thus be understood as an infinitely unfolding process of poetic reconfiguration from which meaning continually escapes.

    Kristeva offers pathways between the ideology of psychoanalysis and the semiotics of poetic speech via jouissance. She asks us to pay attention to the structure of language itself, including the places where it breaks down, and to experience jouissance as a consequence of our own split subjectivity. She states:

> Our eyes can remain open provided we recognize ourselves as always already altered by the symbolic—by language. Provided we hear in language—and not in the other, nor in the other sex—the gouged-out eye, the wound, the basic incompleteness that conditions the indefinite quest of signifying concatenations. That amounts to joying in the truth of self-division (abjection/sacred). Here two paths open out: sublimation and perversion.[56]

Kristeva asks that we derive satisfaction not from the projections of our suffering, aggression, and internal divisions onto others but from the poetic mechanisms of language and from responsibility for our own aggression. The analytic format allows individuals to partake in enjoyment, as well as to generate additional enjoyment from the construction of new languages and discourses derived from our split selves. Kristeva states, "there is nothing either objective or objectal to the abject. It is simply a frontier, a repulsive gift that the Other, having become *alter ego*, drops so that 'I' does not disappear in it but finds, in that sublime alienation, a forfeited existence."[57] As Hal Foster states in his discussion of Kristeva's abjection, "'Obscene' does not mean 'against the scene,' but it suggests an attack on the scene of representation, on the image-screen."[58] By destabilizing representation and thereby evading signification, our own obscene intimate desires, collisions, and failures to reach unity become sites of poetic non-meaning.

On the surface, Kristeva's discussion of disgust may be directly translatable to the repulsion reaction that Ledare's work has at times garnered. What could be more revolting to the bourgeois Western sensibility, invested in the notion of "civilization," than sex with one's mother? According to Kristeva, "the abject is perverse because it neither gives up nor assumes a prohibition, a rule, or a law; but turns them aside, misleads, corrupts; uses them, takes advantage of them, the better to deny them."[59] Taboos play a role in the establishment of the symbolic order and paternal law. Ledare and Peterson's collaboration pierces the veil of fantasy constructed by the Oedipal model and questions our attachment to the taboos that mark our conformity to the law. Simultaneously, it presents an intimately ingrained mythology of consanguinity, balanced between the rigors of representation, semiotics of drives, and the agitation of poetics.

Intimacy situates itself in a discourse of abjection that is, perhaps, the reverse side of the ideological coin. Kristeva describes the effect of the abject on the burgeoning subject, how expelling objects from the body both sets the boundaries between the self and outside the self, and continually denies that which is inside itself, its identity in selfhood. The infantile subject performs its rebellion in acts of abjection, rejecting the maternal and paternal offerings at the same time as it rejects the construction of its own self. Through rigorous research into the dynamics at play in human relationships, does Ledare discover a radical stream of intimacy that questions the boundary between self and other, subject and object, inside and outside, and the very notion of subjectivity itself? Kristeva offers us such a way of thinking about subject-object formation of identity and, by extension, sexuality. By *becoming abject*, by expelling the self from itself, poetic language performs an obscene shattering of representation and exposes a pre-symbolic core of meaning and consciousness that refuses encapsulation by the codes of the law. If intimacy can be understood as a function and manifestation of ideology, then how can radical intimacy, couched in a poetics of abjection, function as its rupture?

The Phantasmatic Mother

By directly engaging the psychoanalytic model of subject-formation, Ledare traverses the symbolic realm of social propriety and immerses in the abject—the discarded, ejected border traces of jouissance that both undergird and destabilize the symbolic. According to Kristeva:

> A certain sexuality, which does not have in Greek tragedy the meaning it has for modern man, which does not even adorn itself with pleasure but with *sovereignty* and *knowledge*, is the equivalent of disease and death. Defilement blends into it: practically, it amounts to tampering with the mother. Defilement is incest considered as transgression of the boundaries of what is clean and proper.[60]

Ledare transgresses maternal boundaries through a representational system which allows fragments of the abject to continually break its surface, both formally in the construction of images and via the sensual, bodily reactions of both arousal and disgust that he repeatedly confronts and elicits. Peterson both personifies the mythic Jacosta, the abjected sacrificial figure marginalized in her own suffering, and breaks expectations by asserting her own subjectivity and desire. Ledare's willingness to occupy the liminal space constructed by his mother, operating in intimate collaboration with her, facilitates a dissolution of the fantasy mother and by extension the fantasy of the object and of subjectivity.

According to Kristeva, biblical injunction attempts to tame the maternal function—the pre-symbolic, visceral, uncontrollable *feminine*—via the implementation of regulatory laws against the impurity of incest. Paradoxically, the mother, despite being the embodiment of such wild forces, is also the constructor of the subject in its differentiated, subjectified form. She performs the rites that prepare the body for initiation into the realm of law, finalizing its separation from her body—for example, feeding, cleaning, and preparing the child for circumcision, which "would thus separate one from maternal, feminine impurity and defilement . . . a sign of the alliance with God."[61] In his work in *Pretend*, and particularly in *Mom Fucking in Mirror*, Ledare incorporates the maternal into the subjectivity and desire that ideology attempts to control. When questioned by *The Guardian* about his own sexual feelings while working with his mother, Ledare replied, "there are many ways to be excited. Towards a sexual object, towards direct honesty and openess [sic]. I think already in the background there were some foggy boundary issues. What people talk about as being Oedipal—there's a flirtation with that, but the boundaries were never actually crossed."[62] By insisting that the incest in *Pretend* remains in the realm of fantasy, Ledare asks us to read the work as performance—and, ultimately, mediated by language, the law, and artistic practice.

Through a confrontation with his mother via the fantasy of incest, Ledare explicitly challenges the symbolic order, the paternal law, and his own status as a speaking being. He subsumes himself in a prelinguistic state of nondifferentiation—through mirroring and displacement—that illuminates the *chora*, a psycho-geographic location outside of the bounds of consciousness and the law that is also continually repressed by language. According to Kristeva, "[t]he sign represses the *chora* and its eternal return. Desire alone will henceforth be witness to that 'primal' pulsation."[63] The radicality of intimacy allows for the constant and instant commutation of signs in abjection, which rejects the stability of meaning, but nevertheless lives in the social sphere. Ledare opens up a doorway, not simply into unconscious spaces that Western society has supposedly repressed but into the beyond of poetic language in conversation with that social landscape. According to Kristeva, the biblical injunctions against taboos serve to protect the speaking subject from a return to the pre-monotheistic maternal cults. The maternal is cast out as a primitive forebearer of the symbolic order and incest, together with other taboos, labeled an abominable sin against religious, paternal authority. Ledare complicates these divisions by showing that participation in the taboo through the deeply interior configuration of the family system disrupts and produces new languages and along with them, surplus-jouissance. This surplus enjoyment may be derived both from following the law and from breaking it, as well as from the formation of new significations to describe this process. In *Mom Fucking in Mirror*, this poetic resignification operates through obscenity in the disturbance of the surface of representation.

In *Mom Fucking in Mirror*, Ledare uses the surface of the mirror to conflate identity and distort spatial distance. While Peterson has sex with a young man close to her son's age, Ledare performs both the Freudian primal scene and the Lacanian mirror stage in one gesture. This is clearly articulated on the surface of this photograph; however, what can also be discovered is the way that the mirror becomes an invisible border between Ledare's physical body, and the bodies of his mother and her lover. His crotch almost perfectly lined up with their genitals, Ledare exposes his own desire to insert himself into the frame, his mother's desire to replace her lover with her son, and the ambiguous relations that result.

This is a very different photograph than would have resulted from a straight shot of the two lovers, even with Ledare in the foreground. The insertion of the mirror surface speaks both to ideological interpellation in the reflection of the gaze and to the blurring of differentiation between subjects and resistance to the law that takes place in the primordial relationship to the mother's body. Perhaps also noteworthy is that *Mom Fucking in Mirror*, though displayed in traditional format in formal exhibitions of Ledare's work, is one of several photographs that appear in the printed monograph turned on their side, bisected by the book's gutter. Ledare's scopophilic position is distorted and displaced by the book's physicality, as a cigarette dangles nonchalantly from his hand, adding to his rebellious affect. He thus appropriates, and to some extent *mocks*, the Freudian-Lacanian position while still acknowledging his own formation as subject of its ideology.

As previously cited, Kristeva considers abjection to be "the other side of ideology" thus situating her own work as a counterpoint to the dominant psychoanalytic structures and theories to which she nonetheless remains committed. A follower of Melanie Klein's school of psychoanalysis, Kristeva believes that it is possible to reference a pre-symbolic being before language and the law took hold and formed our subjectivity. While Lacan criticizes the "Kleinian attempts . . . at symbolic repair of the imaginary lesions that have occurred to the fundamental image of the maternal body,"[64] for Kristeva, "abjection is in fact recognition of the *want* on which any being, meaning, language, or desire is founded."[65] This *want* has primordial qualities, bodily sensations that arise in connection—and disconnection—with the lost object, the mother. The conflicting desire to reunify while establishing one's self in the realm of language is a vestige of this pre-symbolic nondifferentiated state. Unlike Lacan, who insists on the totality of the symbolic order, Kristeva situates her theoretical universe outside of and *before* ideology—as well as obverse to it as a coexistent, yet disruptive, element.

Kristeva derives her theory of abjection from Klein's pre-Oedipal *paranoid-schizoid* position, a psychic space of "uncertain identities of the protagonists"[66] and ambivalent, yet interwoven, relations. Refusing to cede selfhood entirely to the Oedipal, both Klein and Kristeva carve out a niche in which I situate the potential for an infinite unfolding of identity in intimate exchange. Kristeva articulates the way that the paranoid-schizoid position informs her own theories on abjection and literature: "Like a band in a Möbius strip that is characterized by its limitlessness, the future subject is forever transported toward the 'ab-ject' (on the side of the mother) and toward 'primary identification' with the 'father of personal prehistory' (on the side of the loved and loving pre-oedipal father, who displays the traits of both parents)."[67] The subject is propelled into the infinite loop of ambivalent desire for both mother and father. The limit states signified by both the prohibition of taboo and the promise of transcendence through the word of divine law also point toward what lies beyond them. Abjection challenges the constructs represented by the limits of taboo and the sublime, destabilizing the divide between pure and impure, holy and desecrated, representation and the unrepresentable. These unstable boundaries also manifest in art, where questions of truth, identity, and symbolization collide with the eruptions of the unconscious into unrecognizable, and sometimes, horrific signs.

As a departure from the Freudian-Lacanian dominant emphasis on paternal law, Kristeva positions the mother as the keeper of the body, its inner and outer states regulated and prepared by her. She describes an *archaic*, perhaps primordial relationship of the mother to the child's body, as it is prepared for induction into the realm of language. This relationship is contingent upon the law but operates in its borders and edges, in the places where the law establishes orders but does not perform the *intimate* work of transgressing the body's boundaries. The mother quite literally wipes away the abjected material from the child's body, facilitating the individual's maturation into society. By doing so, she herself is unable to escape her status of perceived producer (in the form of menstrual blood) and receptacle of filth and defilement, making the maternal role both essential and reviled, respected and rejected, in the eyes of the sexist regulations of patriarchy. As Kristeva describes:

> Through frustrations and prohibitions, this [maternal] authority shapes the body into a *territory* having areas, orifices, points and lines, surfaces and hollows, where the archaic power of mastery and neglect, of the differentiation of proper-clean and improper-dirty, possible and impossible, is impressed and exerted.... Maternal authority is the trustee of that mapping of the self's clean and proper body; it is distinguished from paternal laws within which, with the phallic phase and acquisition of language, the destiny of man will take shape.[68]

If we continue to explore intimacy as a spatial contradiction and paradox of subjectivity, then the maternal function—the cleaning of the orifices—becomes a physical, psychical, and fantasmatic embodiment of this particular aspect of intimate exchange. According to Kristeva's analysis of Western society's religious roots, the transition into language, ushered by maternal care, shapes the destiny of the modern subject. Ledare may now be understood as performing a traversal of his own masculinity, and his own subjectivity to language and the law, which I suggest is an inherently transgressive position because it both generates visibility around a condition naturalized by ideology and destabilizes its foundations. This gesture, performed in concert with his mother's rebellious devolution, begins to rupture and disrupt the Oedipal, and patriarchy by extension. Beyond the spectacular unraveling we witness through Peterson's traumatic acting out, her abjection interwoven with Ledare's own descent into the unrepresentable reveals a deeply intimate engagement with the maternal in both its primordial and its social states. The intimacy and abjection embodied in Ledare's practice cannot themselves be unraveled from one another.

In addition to incest and the taboo of maternal sexuality, the corpse for Kristeva is a key site of abjection. She states, "the corpse (or cadaver: *cadere*, to fall), that which has irremediably come a cropper, is cesspool, and death; it upsets even more violently the one who confronts it as fragile and fallacious chance."[69] In revisiting *Mom Fucking in Mirror* from this perspective, we notice that Peterson's position on top of her lover appears limp and inactive. Her legs splay out to the sides as one foot dangles slightly off the edge of the bed, and the fullness of her weight presses down on her lover's body, which sinks into the surface of the mattress. This image differs significantly from another penetration image, in which Peterson actively straddles her partner, muscles flexed and golden skin taut. The colorful surface of the warm-hued photograph animates the scene with passion and desire, and functions in great contrast to the grainy black-and-white mirror image with its lifeless undertones. According to Kristeva: "The corpse, seen without God and outside of science, is the utmost of abjection. It is death infecting life. Abject. It is something rejected from which one does not part, from which one does not protect oneself as from an object. Imaginary uncanniness and real threat, it beckons to us and ends up engulfing us."[70] *Mom Fucking in Mirror* represents an intimate ambivalence at the core of subjectivity, founded in desire. Peterson as a figure of both lust and decay thus straddles life and death, the desire for the lost object, and the disgust with which we are socialized to orient ourselves toward maternal sexuality.

Particularly when examined side by side with this parallel image, *Mom Fucking in Mirror* does more than simply re-perform the primal scene, underlining Ledare's position as ideological subject. Ledare's intimacy, his intense closeness to the scene of his mother's penetration and his simultaneous proximity to her condition as corpse, begins to erode the edges of ideology and subjectivity. Kristeva tells us that "refuse and corpses *show me* what I permanently thrust aside in order to live.... There, I am at the border of my condition as a living being."[71] Unlike a word or symbol—such as Kristeva's example of a "flat encephalograph"[72]—the corpse has bodily presence that forces one's own body to react in revulsion and horror. It forces witnesses into confrontation with the involuntary mechanisms of their own body, which, by abjecting itself in convulsive retching, erases the boundary between inside and outside. By presenting his mother's sexuality as occupying a liminal space between life and death, Ledare himself engages not only with the maternal taboo of incestuous relations but with the taboo of close, intimate contact with the corpse, thus complicating his own subjective position as regards to ideology.

The purpose of my inquiry is not to deconstruct the actual sexual relations that take place in *Mom Fucking in Mirror* but to reveal the imaginary workings in the precise moments of sexual intimacy that Ledare chooses to encapsulate in *Pretend* and the philosophical narrative that he ultimately weaves with these representations. Ledare's work may be seen as a continual recycling of ideologies in performative gestures that eventually wear away and break down language, and in the process, formulate a poetic reconsideration of intimacy. How does this gesture open up our philosophical discourse on sexuality and its radical poetic potentiality? According to Kristeva, the abject, the reconfiguration of language and law, and the erotic, all collide in jouissance and comprise the artist's unique position as *borderlander*. While the hysteric suffers from the return of the repressed in the form of symptoms, the abject in artistic practice, hovering on the edge of the primary repression, reconfigures language by producing new significations, participating in the production of meanings. Abjection both fuels and is fueled by incestuous jouissance that is neither prohibited nor allowed but rendered revolting. I contend that both Ledare and Peterson participate in its productive capacities from their respective gendered positions that they expose and destabilize. Kristeva states: "In abjection, revolt is completely within being. Within the being of language. Contrary to hysteria, which brings about, ignores, or seduces the symbolic but does not produce it, the subject of abjection is eminently productive of culture. Its symptom is the rejection and reconstruction of languages."[73] With this statement, Kristeva emphasizes her own career-long thesis—that the power of revolt lies in literature and the arts, the imaginary realm that constructs and deconstructs itself through its own mechanisms of representation and symbolization.

It may be argued that for Kristeva, artists are always already continually abjecting themselves through the poetic process itself. She states: "The nondistinctiveness of inside and outside would thus be unnamable, a border passable in both directions by pleasure and pain. . . . And yet, there would be witnesses to the perviousness of the limit, artisans after a fashion who would try to tap that pre-verbal 'beginning' within a word that is flush with pleasure and pain."[74] She describes the poetic space preceding language and the only people she believes have access to that level of instability without becoming psychotic: "They are *primitive man* through his ambivalences and the *poet* through the personification of his opposing states of feeling—but also perhaps through the rhetorical recasting of language that he effects."[75] The oppositions and contradictions confronted by the artist contribute to the intimacy of art practice and generate surplus-jouissance in the process of signification.

Kristeva's description of the borderlander is tinged with admiration and respect for the dangers he will encounter while mining the semiotic frontier for new poetic languages. Rather than being spared symbolic castration, "he in fact runs a far greater risk than others do. It is not a part of himself, vital though it may be, that he is threatened with losing, but his whole life. To preserve himself from severance, he is ready for more—flow, discharge, hemorrhage. All mortal."[76] What does Ledare accomplish in *Pretend* that makes his practice especially radical and particularly worthy of consideration in a theory of intimacy? The answer may lie in jouissance and Ledare's explicit employment—and poetic *enjoyment*—of the incest taboo. Here, we may consider jouissance as the perverse joy one takes in annihilating one's ego and understand Ledare's erotic content as essential to its radicality. Kristeva argues that "the eroticization of abjection, and perhaps any abjection to the extent that it is already eroticized, is an attempt at stopping the hemorrhage: a threshold before death, a halt or a respite?"[77] By extending his imagination beyond the territorial boundary of the symbolic and toeing the line of the supreme sexual taboo, Ledare abandons the false hope of the clean and proper, and its promise of salvation.

Abjection acknowledges that which inspires revolt by the purifying act of expelling it and differs from *repression* which will return in the form of neurotic symptoms. Abjection employs the body in a process of purgation of unwanted material and functions at the site of the orifices—the mouth, the genitals, the anus—and the skin as ultimate border of the body, permeable and vulnerable to puncture. Kristeva states, "the abjection of those flows from within suddenly become the sole 'object' of sexual desire—a true 'ab-ject' where man, frightened, crosses over the horrors of maternal bowels and, in an immersion that enables him to avoid coming face to face with an other, spares himself the risk of castration."[78] The sexual component of Ledare's work, rather than exclusively the intimacy of emotional proximity circulating among the family members, is essential to understanding its radicality. Lacan states that "the orifices of the body... are linked to the opening/closing of the gap of the unconscious," noting that "[t]he erogenous zones are linked to the unconscious because it is there that the presence of the living being becomes fixed."[79] It is through the ambiguous border between inside and outside, embodied by the opening and closing of the orifices, that we may uncover hidden significations and memories, and engage in the infinitude of signifying chains. Libidinal desire becomes a formal *punctum*, a horizon that marks our entry into the realm of the unconscious—an unmappable space of vulnerability and transgression. By highlighting the porousness of inside and outside, as experienced in sexual intercourse involving the orifices, we may better understand the added intimate weight of a relationship with sexual components and Ledare's explicit choice of imagery. The breaching of physical boundaries that takes place at the locale of the orifices is present in sexual intimacy, in birth, and in the purification function of the maternal, situating Ledare's project at the crossroads of intimacy and abjection.

We may reexamine the aforementioned image of Peterson with the young guitar player, her genitals splayed and exposed. Neither fully open nor in the act of being penetrated, her female orifice points to an ambiguous blurring of the borders of inside and outside, being and nonbeing, life and death. The scene feels melancholy and its musical component evocative of the myth of Orpheus—the mythological musician who tries, and fails, to bring his lover back from the land of the dead. In concert with Peterson's own life and death unfolding throughout *Pretend*, her lover appears to both emanate from and be reabsorbed back into her sexed maternal body. In combination with what appears to be a tenderness Ledare shares with his mother, and his ambivalent sexual desire toward her, Ledare refuses the reduction of abjection to mere disgust. Instead, he asks us to consider the implication of returning to the pre-symbolic state of nondifferentiation, at the border between the imaginary and the real. Lacan's extimacy engages the unstable division of inner and outer space and the unknowability of the unconscious as radical exteriority. It is through the pathway of incestuous jouissance that Ledare incorporates sexual desire into his poetic and asks us to reconsider the radical potentiality of intimacy at the helm of the abject.

Transference/Countertransference: Poetic Rifts in Discourse

As an intimate engagement, Ledare's *Pretend* is conceived in the lineage of the analytic process—the unearthing of memory in intimate collaboration with an other and with speech—that invites the abject to emerge from the porous boundaries of the socially bound subject. This language which is other represents the extimacy of speech—the radical otherness within subjectivity. Kristeva contends that such an instability in intimate engagement also manifests itself in the analytic session through transference and countertransference—the mutual love and desire between analyst and analysand. It is through this relationship that we may find a key to the deferral of meaning that takes place in a poetics of abjection—in the slippage between the symbolic space of subjective identification and the semiotic realm that helps define (and reject) its borders. Ledare and Peterson's collaboration is one built, at least in part, upon the familial love relationship. Ledare's dedication for the monograph reads: "This book is dedicated to my mother, without whose love, generosity and immense creativity it would not have been possible."[80] Along with the abjection at the core of their collaboration, their work cannot be detached from its intimate structure, which is itself grounded in the love relationship. Love and intimacy should not be conflated; according to Lacan, however, "the transference is what manifests in experience the enacting of the reality of the unconscious, in so far as that reality is sexuality," which in turn can be "manifested in the open in the form of love."[81] The analytic relationship is marked by desire and the emergence of the unconscious drives of sexuality through the intimacy of analytic speech.

Though the basic analytic structure involves discourse between two individuals, it offers additional elements, projected from the unconscious in the form of images and symbolic representations, that complicate the manifestly intersubjective relationship. Kristeva specifically addresses what she feels is the fallacy of categorizing the analytic experience as dialogical: what she calls "the diversion of intersubjectivity . . . the reduction of transference to a simple dialogue between two psyches."[82] Kristeva also notes that this framing of the analytic relationship ignores a much deeper function of psychoanalysis, which is "a poiëtic formulation that has nothing to do with explication and communication between two consciousnesses. On the contrary, this *par-don* draws its efficacy from reuniting with affect through the metaphorical and metonymical rifts of discourse."[83] Therefore, the dialogical component of psychoanalysis, intimacy, and intersubjective interpellation is challenged by what Kristeva considers to be a poetic temporal rift that takes place in transference, through the mechanism of language and recollection. In the metonymic rift, one association leads into the next in an infinite chain of signifiers; in metaphor, we make leaps from one chain to another by substituting elements for each other, generating meanings and associations that eclipse linear time and space. Through free association of memories, thoughts, and images, the analytic process produces a new set of poetic interpretations that eschew linear narratives and instead reveal underlying psychical connections. By *par-don*, Kristeva refers to the forgiveness mechanism of analytic speech, dependent on the analyst's ability to identify with the analysand and defer guilt. This *par-don* is key to understanding how Ledare's discourse on intimacy functions analytically, challenging intersubjective models of the sexual relationship and revealing it instead to be founded on metonymic and metaphorical *poeisis*, pursued in forgiveness. Further, it allows for Ledare's exploration of complicity in relationships while maintaining the innocence of libidinal fascination. Through the use of memory as a device, Ledare presents the point of view of the child, mining the history of his own subjectivity. The analytic relationship, based in love, is dependent on the temporal displacement of memory to get to the roots of subjectivity and its myriad expressions.

Ledare's *Pretend* draws on memory, through a series of documents that pepper the photographic text, including photographs from the family's past, ephemera such as notes and lists, and typed memoirs interspersed with crossed-out redactions, corrections, and marginalia. In one such document, Ledare describes being a seventh-grader, his mother regularly inviting him into her room to keep her company and soothe her loneliness, sometimes even paying him to do so which initiates him early into a practice of emotional and sexual labor. He reveals his own burgeoning sexual curiosity, fueled by his mother's apparent awareness of her power to titillate her pubescent child. He describes a scene during which she exits the shower naked:

> When the water stops I pretend to be asleep. I hear the shower door shut behind her. My eyes are open just a slit but I see her walk straight back to the room and lie on the bed. She is entirely naked. Her hair is wet and her legs are stretched out and covered with droplets. Her eyes are closed but I can tell she knows I'm watching her. Her nipples are hard. The mound of red hair at her crotch is starting to dry and get fluffy. [Redacted material]. A few minutes later she stretches out and lets out a sigh. "I thought it would feel nice to airdry," she says.[84]

This excerpt disrupts temporality when viewed as an object of visual representation and not only read as a linear text. The physicality of the text, and its deferral of precise interpretation, mirrors the analytic *après-coup*—retroactive signification—demonstrating the ways that Ledare's ordering of his present subjectivity refers back to childhood experience. Miller emphasizes that "[t]he retroactive schema of sense—envisaging the future from a certain point in the present in order to give again a sense to the past—is absolutely at the core of the Wolf Man case such as Freud presents to us."[85] Just like Freud's attempt at theorizing subjectivity from the significations of the Wolf Man's unconscious expressions, the facticity of Ledare's story remains ambiguous as we surrender to his chosen recollection and interpretive authority. Repeated cross-outs remind us of the storyteller's power to defy and reject interpretation, relying instead on the reader's erotic imagination to fill in the gaps of Ledare and Peterson's play of desire.

By establishing chains of potential meanings from fragments of emotion and recollection, analysis invites individuals to experience their histories in new and transformative ways, generating new poetic versions of their memories. Kristeva's formulation of the *par-don*—the forgiving, or gift-giving, characteristic of analysis as a form of interpretation—requires countertransference by the analyst in the form of empathy, identification, and desire. Embedded in this analytic function is the suspension of moral judgment and the eradication of guilt. In the previous example, for instance, we may adjudicate Ledare's recollection and place moral value on Peterson's sexuality and its effects on her young son, or we may take an analytic stance of *forgiveness* in interpretation. To do so would be to engage intimacy at its most fragile—in the places where it is vulnerable to ethical considerations—as a poetic occurrence akin to the analytic experience, without falling prey to didactic moral imperatives. Thus, the interlocking axes of metaphor and metonymy that are found in such discourse manifest themselves in Ledare's *Pretend*, generating poetic pathways and new meanings that eschew clear categories. The intimacy between Ledare and his mother thus becomes a poetic narrative interweaving metonymic leaps of signification, and metaphoric condensations and associations, as opposed to a more symmetrical intersubjective relation. Through Ledare's deliberately layered images and writings, the original event recedes into the past and the new inscriptions effect a reprocessing of those very same occurrences in a quasi-analytic discursive structure. By confronting the Oedipal model through a framework that mimics the analytic session, Ledare transmutes seemingly intersubjective experiences (analysis and sexual intimacy) into a practice that deliberately plays with temporality and subjectivity through poetics. Similarly, analytic discourse is never unified and always generates surplus-jouissance through speech and the conjuring of representations and symbols of self-constructed tableaus of heterogeneous significations. Ledare performs this process not simply as a formal engagement but as a reflection on our society and the complicity and enjoyment subjects share across time and culture. According to Kristeva, "[h]owever abject these desires may be, which threaten the integrity of individual and society, they are nonetheless sovereign.

Such is the blinding light cast by Freud, following Oedipus, on abjection, as he invites us to recognize ourselves in it without gouging out our eyes."[86] By introducing the analytic structure into his relationship with his mother, Ledare subverts the clinical nature of analysis and inserts the ambiguously bounded intimate into the play of subjectivity. In revealing subjectivity, Ledare reveals himself as a subject-in-process, a subject on trial, continually in flux, and both implicates and forgives us all along with him.

Recoding Modernity

As an artist, scholar, and researcher of the human condition, Ledare offers an immense contribution to a discourse of radical intimacy. From his strategic and intentioned ideological play to the vulnerability of abjection, Ledare exposes and recodes the crises of modern subjectivity, including patriarchal notions of gender, the economy of sexuality, and the movement of the unconscious through the intimate family relation. By generating a poetics of abjection, Ledare boldly traverses horror and pain, as well as beauty. Kristeva states: "If one wished to proceed farther still along the approaches to abjection, one would find neither narrative nor theme but a recasting of syntax and vocabulary—the violence of poetry, and silence."[87] By silencing the chatter of symbolic edicts, and fragmenting the illusory cohesion of beauty, the abject violently ejects us from the order of the law. Ledare's practice violently shakes us out of our blindness, forcing us to see our own condition mirrored in his work.

Part II

Genesis P-Orridge
Radical Sensibility

3

Ritual and Revolt

Life Art Sex Magick

In the 1976 performance *Cease to Exist no. 4*, which took place at the Los Angeles Institute for Contemporary Art (LAICA),[1] Genesis P-Orridge and Cosey Fanni Tutti of the English performance art collective COUM Transmissions enacted a "ritual purification,"[2] the fourth of five performances executed in the United States. Involving extreme acts including the injection and extraction of bodily fluids from genitalia with hypodermic needles, ingestion of these fluids, vomit, defecation, masturbation, live maggots, bodily mutilation with rusty razor blades, and a host of other actions, the performances and the formation of the group behind them originated, according to the artists, in "an attempt to erase security."[3] The performance was apparently so disturbing that one witness described a mass exodus of people and that "[p]erhaps one-fifth of the audience found some element of the act impossible to accept mentally."[4] Ford relates that, according to P-Orridge, "[a]mongst those unable to withstand the intensity of the show at LAICA . . . was the performance artist Chris Burden and the conceptual artist John Baldessari. Apparently they left after just fifteen minutes saying 'it's sickening and disgusting and it's not art.'"[5] For Burden and Baldessari, giants of the American conceptual art movement, P-Orridge and Tutti's action reportedly did not find, to use Kristeva's words, "the harmony likely to give it the dignity of Beauty."[6] The performance concluded with P-Orridge and Tutti sliding toward each other through the revolting mess, to finally meet at the genitals where, in P-Orridge's words, "[t]hey meet in a pool of vomit and join together cunt to cock, legs entwined, on thee wet floor."[7] How might we understand this moment of contact, and the revulsion reactions that preceded it, within a discourse of radical intimacy? Furthermore, how might we position this performance, and subsequent works produced by P-Orridge, within a discourse of intimate artistic practice that functions along the periphery of the symbolic, on the porous border between the imaginary and the real—that is, the *abject*?

With P-Orridge and Tutti's action and its erotic content as backdrop, I continue my investigation of artistic practices that repel, revolt, and disturb Western sensibilities and trample across cultural taboos. Simultaneously, I continue to deepen our exploration of abjection in sexual intimacy, which I argue is both poetic and politically active. Exploring the nuances of radicality through the notion of *revolt*, as Kristeva frames it, "a sub-version, a re-volt in the etymological sense of the word (a return toward the invisible, a refusal and displacement),"[8] I suggest that form can become active through intimacy. P-Orridge and Tutti's performance may have constructed a visual symbol of sexual intimacy; however, the performance's impact involved an intimacy with the audience that we see present in much of P-Orridge's lifelong practice, as well as an ambivalence between inner and outer space, life and death, self and other. In this chapter, I examine P-Orridge's work with Tutti and COUM, as well as other intimate collaborators including Thee Temple ov Psychick Youth and Lady Jaye Breyer P-Orridge, to address Kristeva's concerns about the lack of an aesthetic culture of revolt. The practices explored in this chapter deploy the sexually intimate, erotic body in an attempt to destroy convention and challenge societal control over the individual. These practices intend to effect a metaphysical reordering of subjectivity and individuals' imaginary relationship to the real, employing abjection, revolt, and disgust as disruptive, yet poetic mechanisms. According to Kristeva, after the decline of religion, "psychoanalysis restored to men and women the heterogeneous continuity between body-soul-mind, and the experience of this heterogeneous continuity now appears to us as the essence of the intimate."[9] In parallel, artists working in radical intimacy continually dissolve and redraw the borders between the body and its environment, inviting a reengagement with sexual intimacy and its potential for revolt.

While continuing to reference Kristeva's 1982 *Powers of Horror*, I also delve deeper into *The Sense and Non-Sense of Revolt*, first published in 1996. Therein, Kristeva indicates dissatisfaction with the contemporaneous state of the art movements and the dearth of revolutionary forces as the twenty-first-century approaches. She argues that "[t]he great moments of twentieth-century art and culture are moments of formal and metaphysical revolt,"[10] referring to the surrealist art and literature to which she devotes much of her criticism. In contrast, faced with the dual specter of post-industrialization and the loss of religion in favor of the spectacle, she believes that contemporary society is threatened by automation, simulation, and violence. She calls for a newfound culture of revolt in the arts and insists that "[t]his is a matter of the survival of our civilizations and their freest and most enlightened components."[11] What might a culture of revolt look like today? How might art practices that deliberately mine the realm of sex and intimacy operate as radical mechanisms on the level of ideology and subjectivity?

P-Orridge's performative practices incorporate the physical body, its fluids, and its modifications over time and, on a very tangible level, operate as embodied philosophical discourse. P-Orridge destroys the physical, bodily manifestations of ideology—specifically, that of gender, sexual differentiation, and subjectivity—via the vehicles of sexual orgasm and intimacy. P-Orridge's body and the bodies of their collaborators become active participants and radical agents of transgression in an abject poetic.

We cannot speak of sex without speaking of the body. From the biological realities, and associated ambiguities of sexual difference, to the incontrovertibly embodied nature of the sexual relationship, sexuality lives and breathes in the body. Sex manifests itself in and through our physical flesh, buttressed by language, deployed in politics, and reimagined in revolt. How can we address the intimate body without further cementing the artificial divide between mind and matter that exists in much of Western philosophy? If we conceive of the body as a larger organism than what is seemingly contained inside the contours of our skins, then what are the implications of such an inquiry to a philosophical discourse on sexual intimacy? In this chapter, I will introduce ideas from Brian Massumi's *Semblance and Event* and propose that his renewed attention to "the event of the sense-relation,"[12] coupled with Kristeva's discourse, invites a reconsideration of the intimate body as a site of revolt. I suggest a framework for *thinking-feeling* the intimacy of *ritual* that helps expand our understanding of intimacy by renegotiating our relationship to the sensual body. In parallel, Kristeva's psychoanalytic discourse on abjection introduces a poetic operation that invites a framing of sexual intimacy as a poetic methodology. In *The Sense and Non-Sense of Revolt*, Kristeva further extrapolates the relationship of physical and psychical revolt to acts of social and political resistance. Within this context of non-dualistic approaches to the body, I suggest that P-Orridge's practices over the last half-century represent significant contributions to our thinking about sexual intimacy and radical intimacy in contemporary art.

P-Orridge, self-proclaimed "artist, cultural engineer, and wrecker of civilization,"[13] spent a lifetime devising interceptive strategies to undermine societal conditioning and facilitate a radical overhaul of how human beings think, live, and love. From their early performance works and influence on rock and industrial music in the UK in the 1970s to their extensive writings and their integration into the visual art canon such as solo exhibitions at the Rubin Museum of Art and the Invisible Exports Gallery toward the end of their life, P-Orridge's role as a cultural producer is well documented. Nevertheless, their presence has historically been anarchic and underground, and their works are only recently being integrated into institutional discourse. According to Simon Ford, author of *Wreckers of Civilisation: The Story of COUM Transmissions and Throbbing Gristle*, "Genesis P-Orridge was born Neil Andrew Megson on 22 February 1950"[14] in England and attended religious school as a boy, during which he was frequently ridiculed for being small and sickly.[15] In Marie Losier's documentary *The Ballad of Genesis and Lady Jaye*, P-Orridge cites these early experiences with the Catholic Church as contributing to their personal culture of revolt and as "places where you either submit, or you decide that you'll fight. Guess what we chose?"[16] P-Orridge has taken this fight to its metaphysical limits and beyond, with their art combining deeply interior work with the psyche, along with physical trials and practices meant to break down subjectivity and rebuild it in continual metamorphosis.

One of P-Orridge's earliest collaborations was a rock band and art collective called COUM Transmissions that P-Orridge founded in 1969 after a mystical vision during which the name COUM and an insignia of the band came to them inexplicably.[17] The group began as a rock band, but eventually, with the addition of P-Orridge's then partner Cosey Fanni Tutti abandoned the instruments and turned its attention to performance art.[18] In their autobiography, P-Orridge extrapolates on the vision and the name, explaining that COUM "stands for 'Cosmic Organicism of the Universal Molecular.' Which basically means that everything is particles and everything is part of everything else; there's no separation between what makes everything. We're all space and we're all dust."[19] The lack of differentiation intended in the name of the group reflects the abject currents of their practices, including the mixing of body fluids and blurring of identities and classifications embodied in their performances. Artistically, the group was in dialogue with other movements of the time, including Fluxus and the Vienna Actionists.[20] According to Ford, however, "the main stylistic influence remained the Dadaists, especially in the distrust of specialists and the belief in chance, intuition and improvisation as techniques for producing art."[21] The techniques were not limited to physical performances, as P-Orridge's practice of changing the spellings of common words can be seen as early as 1971 in a letter to *Friendz* (no. 28, 1971) that invites the reader "[t]o coum to something via intuition" and "invent your own vocabulary and leak your secrets slowly."[22]

Rather than aligning themselves with the "radical art movements" of the time and focusing predominantly on direct political activism, COUM was interested in a poetic reordering of perception and interaction.

COUM Transmissions eventually evolved into the band Throbbing Gristle (TG) in 1975, returning to musical performance and spearheading the industrial music scene in the UK.[23] In 1981, TG announced its mission "terminated" and disbanded.[24] P-Orridge would go on to found Thee Temple ov Psychick Youth (a.k.a. TOPY), an anarchist art collective performing inter- and *intra*-relational interventions on the body, subjectivity, and ideology; and the associated electronic music and video art group Psychic TV. They would also meet Lady Jaye Breyer P-Orridge, who became their partner and collaborator. Subsequent to Lady Jaye's death in 2007, P-Orridge continued to produce musical, performative, visual, and written artworks that explored the intersections of sexuality, spirituality, and ideology until their own death in 2020. In this chapter, I explore three distinct moments in P-Orridge's practice that engage the intimacy of abjection, specifically in relation to sensibility and revolt. I will begin by exploring COUM Transmissions's 1976 performances *Cease to Exist 1-5*, executed by P-Orridge and Tutti in Chicago and Los Angeles. I will then introduce the orgasmic practices of Thee Temple ov Psychick Youth, including the canonical tome *Thee Psychick Bible*, which includes writings from various members of the collective, and object-based artworks produced in context to the practice of the orgasmic sigil. Finally, I will explore the Pandrogeny project, a collaboration with Lady Jaye Breyer P-Orridge. The arc drawn by these three moments demonstrates the extent to which P-Orridge destabilizes meaning, subjectivity, and reality through practices grounded in sexual intimacy, abjection, and the poetics of revolt.

COUM Transmissions/*Cease to Exist*

COUM Transmissions existed from 1969 until 1975 and consisted of a rotating group of collaborators, including the founding members of Throbbing Gristle—Peter "Sleazy" Christopherson, Chris Carter, and Cosey Fanni Tutti[25] (né Christine Carol Newby), the last of whom joined the group after meeting P-Orridge at an Acid Test Party[26] and becoming their live-in partner.[27] Sexuality was already central in P-Orridge's practice during this time, and COUM Transmissions expressly addressed the instability of borders between and among bodies in communal intimate space. COUM's employment of bodily fluids, public nudity, and flagrant transgression of taboos contributed to their performances' disruptive effect. According to Richard Metzger, "COUM's shamanic improvisations involving enemas, blood, roses, wire, feathers, sexual intercourse, milk, urine, licking up vomit, crucifixion, maggots and self-mutilation were . . . about freeing themselves (and the spectators) of their own taboos by performing benign exorcisms of a sick society's malignancies."[28] Abjection, as I have already explored in the previous chapter, can be understood as the obverse to ideology, dependent upon the boundaries of the law, yet operating as a radical mechanism for disrupting oppressive systems of meaning, power, and authority from a position of radical exteriority.

COUM also challenged norms of representation and dominant ideologies, such as the sexual power structures depicted in pornographic material. The performance *Studio of Lust* (1975), for example, featured P-Orridge, Christopherson, and Tutti engaged in a three-way sex act, forming a triangle between their bodies with Tutti appearing to perform fellatio on P-Orridge, who was locked in a kiss with Christopherson. On the surface, COUM's nonconformity to gender and sex norms is immediately apparent in the multiplicity and non-heteronormativity of the act itself. On a deeper level, however, COUM challenged not only patriarchy but also knowledge and meaning, through the disordering of language and representation. In fact, as Wilson explains, this particular performance was enacted for the camera and precisely for the purpose of photographic indexing. Visible wounds on Christopherson's and Tutti's skins, for example, were produced by makeup and not real blood, creating a schism between how the live performance operated and how the documentation of the performance operates half a century later, decontextualized from the performativity and physicality of the sex acts themselves. The poses construct an image of nonconformity to gender norms through the performance of live bodies in intimate exchange; however, the images do not directly reflect the exchange itself.

COUM's public performances involving bodily fluids, extreme physical stress, and public nudity are quite relevant to our conversation on the radicality of abjection, but the work produced by intimate partners P-Orridge and Tutti particularly concerns my investigation of sexual intimacy. One particularly notable set of performances took place at the Los Angeles Institute of Contemporary Arts (LAICA) and IDEA Gallery in Santa Monica in 1976. Working off of the foundation set by COUM, whose actions were meant to disrupt and destabilize borders, P-Orridge and Tutti traveled to the United States for a series of performances entitled *Cease to Exist 1-5* that explored this dissolution via their collaborative partnered exchange. I will focus on *Cease to Exist 4*, which took place at LAICA.[29] Ford states:

> According to P-Orridge's account the action involved the enactment of a catalogue of taboo acts using bodily fluids such as urine, blood, vomit and milk, combined with abject acts of defecation, urination, self-mutilation and masturbation. COUM focused attention on the body as bearer of pain and mutilation, a body the boundaries of which were violated by needle and thread and syringe.[30]

The title of the piece(s), which came from a Charles Manson song later adapted by the Beach Boys, alone points to a dissipation of subjectivity and accepted notions of reality, implying that through a deliberate mining of physical and psychical taboos, one may achieve a disintegration of self.[31] COUM's choice of these particular lyrics underlies their interest in the annihilation of both self and other, their frequent provocative allusions to toxic corners of society, and P-Orridge's oft-articulated desire to destroy societal conditioning of the individual.[32]

Aside from abjection of bodily fluids by casting out, or forcibly discarding them from the body, the very notion of "self" is abjected when these materials are attempted to be re-assimilated. According to Zappe, "this radical exploration of physical boundaries in its auratic materiality inevitably raises the general question of the permeability of identity constructs. The complete collapse of the inside/outside logic of the culturally coded system of normalized corporeality retroacts with the subjectivity of both the performer and the viewer."[33] The abjection of the body confronts the artist and audience with their own fragility as sensual and social subjects. This abjection may be understood as radical in scope, in its embodied public gestures that disturb oppressive ideologies such as patriarchy and capitalism, but more so, it disturbs subjectivity via close and intimate contact, and the disruption of the body's borders. By doing so, intimacy becomes implicated in a cycle of abjection that questions the social bonds of ideological subject-formation and therefore operates politically. Wilson wishes to "address [COUM's] transgression as a violation of the law" and "an antisocial mode of queer aesthetics,"[34] attributing a queer form of activist aesthetic to COUM's performances and contextualizing sexuality within patriarchal constructs of sexual difference and gender. She also, however, introduces a line of inquiry much broader than questions of gender, identifying the semiotic rearrangement that occurs as COUM transgress boundaries as literal as the body's organs—skin, orifices, fluids. According to the group's writing, "Coum demonstrate that there are NO boundaries in any form."[35] It is precisely this semiotic rearrangement—this poetic function of abjection—that I argue points to the radical potential of sexual intimacy.

P-Orridge's lifelong practice of intimate collaboration with their lovers provides ample opportunity for an exploration of intimacy as an intersubjective occurrence; however, their practices also reveal an engagement with a poetics of abjection that radicalizes sexual intimacy by extending it beyond the bounds of the intersubjective relationship and toward a confrontation with the unknowable and unnamable. As Ford writes, quoting P-Orridge:

> COUM resembled sex: "Sex is sensual, delirium, escape, key to magick, joy, excitement." Sexuality was also subjected to the most repressive forms of conditioning within society. The body was a battlefield, a territory that was fought over and often broken in the process: "We expand ourselves to boundaries, even destroying, condemning ourselves to forms of madness and isolation, to damnation in evil forms. . . . We need each other, hate each other, hate is nothing."[36]

COUM's performances and writings explore sexuality as both partnered and communal activity, and as private, individual activity such as masturbation. As a personal practice, sex was leveraged to elevate the individual to a greater connection with themselves, the divine and their own power in the universe. As a communal activity of transcendence and magic, sex and its enjoyment became a social and political practice for the group, inviting people to discard old notions of themselves and rebuild through sexual pleasure. According to Ford, "[i]n a world of underachievement and self-evasion, COUM offered self-realisation and the opportunity to know one's true self: 'We want people to be themselves, and thee price of that is to abandon thee false ideas one has of oneself.'"[37] Noteworthy is P-Orridge's early reliance on sexual difference, as evidenced in their emphasis on sperm and phallic penetration as defining elements of orgasm. COUM's logo, designed by P-Orridge, consisted of "a post-coital, limp, sperm-dripping penis formed from the word 'COUM'"[38] and implies a constantly exhausted, yet freshly used, source of pleasure and phallic enjoyment. As I continue to explore the trajectory of P-Orridge's practice, I suggest that the appropriation of the phallic symbolic is a strategy of subversion against identity and authority, as much as it reflects narcissistic attachment to the masculine symbol of power.

As COUM Transmissions evolved into Throbbing Gristle (according to Tutti, "Yorkshire slang for an erection") in 1975,[39] sexuality remained a central thread in the group's practices. According to Ford,

> P-Orridge's most extensive discussion of the name was published by Red Ronnie in 1979:

> Throbbing Gristle: Thee involuntary muscular spasms of death perhaps, sound throbbing, body, blood, air, cunt, throbbing air conveying sound, affecting thee metabolism. Throbbing, pulsing, rhythmic direct. Throbbing of pain, bruising, injury of existence, throbbing with excitement too. Gristle. Hard, tough, neither skin nor muscle, a paradox, on thee boundary. Gristle, rejected by everyday consumers when they buy meat at butchers: meat, sign of human animalism, death to feed life, of our assumption to have right to genocide of other species that we might live. Gristle, cock, sexuality, fuck. Gristle, reject matter, unwanted, separated from good. Throbbing gristle, thee moment of orgasm, penetration of male into another body, joining of two people in most vulnerable moment, moment of immortality, sperm and thee moment of life injected. Possibility of birth, or masturbation and wastage. Throbbing gristle; crude colloquialism, working class street culture, ordinariness made unusual, something common place sex/fuck made oblique, subtle seen another way. Regional slang, parochial joke, rough humour of vision. Uncouth. TG. TG.[40]

Besides merely representing the phallus as a symbol of power and authority, however, the statement also acknowledges the disposability of the organ, through the association its nickname makes to the discarded part of a piece of meat, rejected from the mouths of the masses. Returning to a framework of intimacy as an instability of borders, I suggest that mainstream society is unwilling to interiorize the sexuality represented by COUM Transmissions and Throbbing Gristle. By creating a taboo against the real aroused organ, instead symbolizing its authority and power through abstraction, society makes intimacy itself taboo outside of sanctioned spaces and relationships. Furthermore, the infiltration of the phallic symbol and its assertion of dominance perpetuate the ideological components of sexual intimacy. By bringing the organ and the jouissance it embodies into the open (quite literally, the public spaces in which COUM and TG performed), P-Orridge demands attention for the phallus.[41]

P-Orridge's focus on the phallus may be understood in context to their interest in the sacred and ritual, and elucidated by Kristeva in her discussion of the religious functions of art. In *The Sense and Non-Sense of Revolt* Kristeva analyses three Italian baroque sculptures that feature personified religious virtues and the face of Christ beneath the translucency of sheer fabric rendered in marble. Noting that "all forms of the sacred, all ritual celebrations can be traced back to a phallic cult"[42] and that "the initiation rites of the Dionysian mysteries and phallic cults were celebrated with the veiling and unveiling of the phallus,"[43] she further asserts that "[a]ll art, all innovation . . . is translated by work on the veiling and unveiling of tradition."[44] Here, she somewhat paradoxically links the practice of art with rituals that establish language and culture—the seat of the symbolic realm—so how does this support my notion of radicality and subversion in ritual practice? Kristeva emphasizes that these veiled figures "do not represent anything besides representation itself and its possible failure."[45] These three sculptures represent a "veritable revolution of thought"[46] because "to hide/show, to examine what is showable, to veil it, to make the visible appear through that which obscures it, to center attention on the possibility of monstrance itself: this is an inquiry into the roots of phallic meaning and simultaneously into power and the sacred, which are its apotheosis."[47] This chapter suggests that P-Orridge's practices reach toward the sacred through the veiling and unveiling of language and symbols, and by inquiring into the roots of meaning and power via the abjection of radical intimacy. By doing so, P-Orridge locates in contemporary art practice the incarnation that Kristeva identifies in religious traditions, by which she means a full sensory and spiritual experience, an experience of something real.[48]

Embedded in the intimate is a communal experience with the sacred, which operates as an overturning of the ideological mechanisms of institutionalized religions while retaining religion's emphasis on interiority and transformation. P-Orridge spent their life exploring the intricacies of human experience in the sexual, creative, and spiritual realms, striving for meaningful experience over commercial success. In an interview, they discuss the eating of flesh in the context of ritual sacrifice, as opposed to the commodification of meat-eating at contemporary Western religious celebrations. Referring to the practitioners of such institutionalized religions, they argue, "they've divorced themselves from the meaning of their own rituals."[49] As I explore in this chapter, P-Orridge's relationship to ritual and interiority, as well as their commitment to integrating the body and spirit in intimate practice, reveals their contribution not only to a discourse of sexual intimacy but to one of intimacy as a vital part of human existence that has been lost to the controlling forces of ideology and social control. According to P-Orridge, "the only way forward for art is for it to become spiritual and devotional and mystical again,"[50] a position that closely aligns with Kristeva's notion of revolt.

TOPY: Orgasm as Occurrent Art

After the breakup of Throbbing Gristle in 1981 and P-Orridge's breakup with Tutti as a romantic partner,[51] P-Orridge's work continued to draw on their history with intimate collaborations with friends and lovers. Along with a core group of like-minded artists and anarchists, P-Orridge founded Thee Temple ov Psychick Youth (TOPY), a set of localized communes and global network of individuals with a shared desire to circumvent rigid societal expectations and develop uniquely singular subjectivities, operating in collective unison. The group's stated goal and intention of much of their practices was to "defeat 'control' and seek ways to consciously take command of our behaviour and our identity" in a "collective system of focused orgasm within ritualized living and gender RE-EVOLUTIONARY exploration."[52] P-Orridge's practices, enacted for many years under the auspices of TOPY, involve experimental actions with sexuality, performance, language, and ritual in the pursuit of a new model for human evolution, or "Re-Evolution," as they call it.[53] Through creative and spiritual interventions that challenge constructs of sovereign subjectivity while simultaneously celebrating the power and potential of the individual, P-Orridge has consistently aimed to deconstruct prescribed identity and expand consciousness, leading to expanded, even limitless, personal freedom.

How might intimacy take us to "the sublime point at which the abject collapses in a burst of beauty that overwhelms us"?[54] TOPY's signature practice is the orgasmic sigil, a ritualized, meditative practice which can be enacted either individually or with a partner to leverage what may be seen as a core component of sexuality—orgasm—in the pursuit of personal and collective happiness. Here, the intimate body is given space to exist independently of the catalysis that occurs in moments of exchange between individuals and emphasizes individuals' relationships with themselves and the universe. In addition, orgasm is deployed not just as an individual practice but in the context of a communal practice meant to bring a community of individuals together in a collective gesture of societal resistance. By devising a framework for the orgasmic body as site of deconstruction—of patriarchy, capitalism, the oppression of Western religions, and the limitations of Western notions of subjectivity—we may come to see the communal component of the sigil as an essential gesture toward situating sexual intimacy within a political discourse of subversion. We may come to agree with P-Orridge's suggestion that "the entire universe is breathing in a sexual way"[55] and that engagement with this universal process through radical intimacy can be understood as a practice of revolt and a return to the sacred. We may thus understand the need to liberate the orgasmic body from the constraints of the law and honor its life beyond the borders of subjectivity, in order to glimpse the radical, poetic mechanisms at the core of sexual intimacy.

P-Orridge's work with TOPY led to a document that promotes precisely these propositions. Shortly following the disbandment of the commune in 1991, Breyer P-Orridge compiled *Thee Psychick Bible: Thee Apocryphal*

Scriptures Ov Genesis Breyer P-Orridge and Thee Third Mind Ov Thee Temple Ov Psychick Youth. The volume is in parts manifesto, instruction manual, memoir of both individual and collective origin, historical archive, essay collection, and dialogical debate on the nature of TOPY as an organization, ideological model, and creative project, as well as a detailed examination of orgasm as a "magickal" practice. A key component of P-Orridge's oeuvre is the transformation of the magical sigil—a sign or mark meant to enact a magical purpose—into an integrated system of private creative performance employing sexual orgasm as its key ingredient for effecting tangible change on both the individual and collective levels. According to Abrahamsson's Foreword to *Thee Psychick Bible*, the art produced at TOPY "is in many ways an anti-art. It's not art made specifically for other people to see, and thereby it doesn't fit in with the contemporary ideals of pleasing an art market."[56] In these rituals, orgasm is deployed as a mechanism of resistance to dominant modes of knowledge, identity, and behavior. In an orgasmic sigil, the subject *as subject of ideology* is broken down through the body's surrender to its own enjoyment and deliberate and focused loss of bodily control. As a poetic practice, the orgasmic sigil activates the intimate body as site of challenge to ideology and, therefore, subjectivity. By harnessing the power of jouissance, the never-satisfied enjoyment that both fuels and disrupts language and the law, P-Orridge expands our understanding of the philosophical scope, and poetic function, of sexual enjoyment.

The orgasmic sigil is an event during which the initiate meditates on a desire, wish, or intention while bringing themselves to orgasm, either alone or with a partner. The moment of orgasmic release is believed to have special powers to focus the will and is made into material form via the production of a physical object that the initiate anoints with three bodily fluids (blood, saliva, and ejaculate) and to which they attach two hair types (head and pubic). During the years that TOPY was active, these objects were sent to TOPY headquarters ("the Temple") to be archived.[57] Regarding the use of sexual orgasm as a key to expanded states of consciousness, and by extension, the development of a reconditioned self, P-Orridge argues that "sexual experience can bring more than simply physical pleasure . . . in some mysterious, 'magical' way it could intensify the consciousness, expand . . . awareness and heighten the body beyond its physical form."[58] P-Orridge extends their conception of consciousness outside the rational mind, into and through the mechanisms of the body, a process that I suggest destabilizes subjectivity beyond a sense of self bounded by societally sanctioned identity.

A discourse of orgasm unfolds in *Thee Psychick Bible* as a methodology for the assertion of selves outside of dominant ideologies and even, perhaps, beyond the modern ideological subject. Throughout the text, orgasm is consistently described as a liberating force that, when accessed, fuels the individual with freedom and power. Dominating powers attempt to, but cannot, control orgasm. In the section entitled *Thee Grey Book*, P-Orridge outlines the reason for the use of orgasm as a resistant mechanism, arguing that "[o]f all the things people do . . . sex alone is subject to extraordinary interference and control from outside forces. This is no accident. They recognize its power."[59] P-Orridge goes on to explain that orgasm is a private pleasure impervious to social control. In an ode to the powers of pleasure, they explain:

> Even if only for a few moments, Individuals can release a power and energy from within that renders any system of society, or regime, meaningless. It is a liberator. Even an Individual in solitary confinement can indulge in it and in their fantasies travel into any situation and possibility unfettered, and, at the moment of orgasm itself, be both blissfully vulnerable and undeniably free, elsewhere, filled by energy.[60]

The freedom to access one's unlimited imagination is more than a momentary illusory escape from the constraints of one's physical circumstances. P-Orridge's discourse suggests that a rigorous, deliberate, and disciplined orgasmic practice, in the lineage of TOPY's "magickal" system, generates revolutionary power by funneling imagination through the body and sensuous experience, endowing it with the power to break down thought systems poetically. It is important to note that while we may speak of poetics as an approach to language, it is perhaps even more relevant to speak of poetic *activity* that functions in precisely the same way—deconditioning and designification via the sensuous.

The orgasmic sigil is intended as an action that powers the imagination to conceive of realities outside the realm of the senses, beyond existing experience. Following is an excerpt from one of many documents intended to communicate the message and mission of TOPY:

> *We have reached a crisis point . . .*
> *We are faced with dissolution far more complex than death. A New Dark Ages.*
> *We have been conditioned, encouraged and blackmailed into self-restriction, into a narrower and narrower perception of ourselves, our importance and our potential . . .*
> *Resistance is dangerous and unpredictable but for those who realize the totality of defeat, resistance must be thee only option conceivable.*[61]

The idea of dissolution is essential to the orgasmic sigil in its emphasis on defying borders and resisting form, and helps to situate the TOPY orgasmic sigil as a strategy for facilitating resistance to subjectivity in the individual. In the earlier statement, dissolution occurs as a result of oppressive ideologies—the destruction of a "real" self—and can be combatted by the expansion of consciousness facilitated by the orgasmic process. In my examination of orgasmic sigils, I suggest that by focusing the imagination through the body—through the sensuous—the orgasmic state facilitates comprehension of perspectives of magnitude previously unavailable to the rational mind. The individual discovers a world of pluralistic possibility and expanded consciousness. TOPY initiate Coyote 37 observes that "[w]orking without reference to self cannot occur without a living experience of the ephemeral nature of the self."[62] By inviting a momentary loss of reason, followed by rapture, we may find in the orgasmic a pathway to the loss of the self and its reconstitution in the form of embodied infinity. As Coyote 37 concludes, "[w]e are reminded of our nonexistence from working with concrete situations."[63] In P-Orridge and their collaborators' materialist praxis, the subject's autonomy and power are challenged and the conditioned self is destabilized. By activating the infinite capacity of the mind through the experiences and sensations of the body, the self is subsequently reconstructed as a newly integrated and whole being, but one that has been untethered from the imposing design of dominant ideologies and Western conditioning. Stripping the conditioning in the mind to allow bodily desires to flow and manifest, the orgasmic body becomes an agent of change, effecting a shift in consciousness and in the individual's relationship to reality.

A key point in a poetics of the orgasmic is that it promotes action and in itself facilitates an active destruction and rebuilding of the self. Brother Words, an initiate in TOPY, offers an interpretation of how the orgasmic sigil may contribute to an active poetics of resistance via a "process of constructive deconstruction."[64] In his essay "Even Further: The Metaphysics of Sigils," Words explains that "[t]he sigils [P-Orridge] presents to us are intentionally 'active'; that is, embedded within them is a principle of mediated agency."[65] Words positions the sigil as a "full-fledged intersubjective dialogue," in which artist and artwork become indistinguishable due to both the performative aspect of its creation and the use of bodily fluids by which the artist "becomes genetically joined to the sigil."[66] This integration of action, ideas, and artwork leads to what Words refers to as "a radical disruption of the spatial and temporal modes of being"[67] and transforms the physical artwork into not just a representation but an *agent* of change. In what may seem like a bold declaration, Words claims that the "work does not so much change the way in which we see the world, but rather, 'changes the world in which we see.'"[68] While this sentiment may reflect intention more than action, or wish as opposed to reality, the orgasmic sigil is just one aspect of a unified expression of deconditioning and ritualized lifestyle that, taken as a whole, operates as a radical affront to church, state, and the limitations of sanctioned behavior.

The sigil operates not just on the level of the human body but also in the functionality of the formal object produced as a result of the action. P-Orridge is heavily influenced by the cut-up method developed by William Burroughs and Bryon Gysin, as well as the occult practices of Austin Osman Spare.[69] The cut-up process involves an intuitive and quasi-accidental reconfiguration of items, such as randomly cut-up newspaper pages pasted back together to form poetry, often fueled by various types of mind-altering trance states and believed to result in a significant revelation or magical change. An orgasmic sigil functions in much the same way, working through the body's enjoyment, concentration, and surrender. Words argues that the production of the artwork—which on the surface appears as a "simple collage"[70]—functions in a mode beyond simply being the formalized detritus of orgasmic activity. Rather, he says, "each sigil is essentially functional, centred on the initiation of agentive activity.... They are thus much more than mere representations of what magic might look like, and their existence constitutes a direct challenge to our understanding of the world and to normative models of causality, meaning and creativity."[71] The production of a physical artwork as the culmination of the performance of an orgasmic sigil leaves behind a trace of the intimate body in the process of reconfiguration. For example, *B-Right-On* depicts imagery as disparate as wolves, performance stills, dolphins, women in lingerie and the psychic cross, and is listed as being made of C-prints, black-and-white photographs, photocopies, antique postcards, Polaroids, acrylic, wolf fur, snakeskin, semen, blood, wax, and paint pen. As functional art, the sigil is a performative structure, imbued with action and change. One must pass through a process of flux and endure a measure of transformation, in order for the work to be completed. A poetics of catharsis and dissolution works its way through the orgasmic body—both physically and psychically—into the material form of the artwork, and the artwork is believed to then signify, and continuously reactivate, the perpetual process of transformation taking place via the initiate-artist's intention.

Here, we return to Kristeva's concern about harmony and beauty, and her desire for an aesthetic heritage to operate on this level. Words's analysis focuses on the functionality of P-Orridge's objects, rather than their visual aesthetic form alone. Words warns against adopting a more traditional modernist formalist stance when approaching P-Orridge's artworks critically. He argues:

> [T]o consider these sigils in terms of conventional art-criticism, in terms of aesthetics and form, would thus be to remove them from the context in which they were created and to place them in a frame antithetical to their purpose. Art for P-Orridge serves a sacred role: the integration of consciousness with the fluxion of universal pattern. Art is not simply to be looked at, dissected, and critiqued; but to be experienced.[72]

How might we reconcile Words's caution with a desire to integrate P-Orridge's visual and object-based artworks into a discourse of sexual intimacy and its radical potential? How does the resulting object operate in this constellation?

P-Orridge's sigils operate as semiotic spaces that reconfigure languages, dissolve boundaries of subjectivity, and vacillate between inner and outer space. They also function as facilitators of a new symbolic landscape, drawing from dreams, myths, and the unconscious. While piercing the edges of sexual boundaries, P-Orridge demonstrates the fluidity of gender and the quest toward the attainment of higher spiritual consciousness and unity with a universal force beyond the immanent world. P-Orridge is quoted as stating that "the real purpose of sex is to believe in the possibility of union with the divine. That it's a magical and spiritual metaphysical act. In a sense, it's poetry. Poetry is about leapfrogging consensus reality to some more incredible place where the world is revitalized and the vision is renewed."[73] How do P-Orridge's artworks manifest this renewed vision, fueled by the jouissance of orgasm?

P-Orridge's particular mode of representation extends the private, ritualized practice of orgasm into a metaphysical expansion of the mind. The notion of holiness arises when situating P-Orridge's practice inside of a discourse of abjection. Kristeva specifies that *pure/impure* "pertains to setting in order, dependent on a covenant with God. That opposition, even though it is not absolute, is inscribed in the biblical text's basic concern with separating, with constituting strict identities without intermixture."[74] P-Orridge explicitly demands the intermixture of bodily fluids in the performance and construction of an orgasmic sigil, thereby complicating the biblical injunction of separation. They provide insight into the poetics of resistance embedded in their sexual and aesthetic practices when they explain:

> And that's why they [referring to the powers of the law] control and manipulate and inhibit people's sexual expressions, because they are very aware of the hidden power of the knowing use of the potential of sexuality. And one of the

greatest services we could do for mankind would be to push them towards a place where they had a candid spiritual respect for the incredible potential and power of sexuality.[75]

Therefore, it is not only in the utilization of particular fluids or substances, or explicit mechanisms of "disgust" that P-Orridge's abjection takes its form, but through the hybridization of meanings and construction of movable borders that provide a horizon of metamorphosis that is by its very nature subversive in practice.

P-Orridge's practice, however, is far from strictly ideological, as it operates in the psychical interiority—the extimate otherness that Kristeva feels has been compromised by the society of the spectacle. Specifically, Kristeva believes that modern Western society has lost its connection to sacred rites and rituals, historically contained within religious practices. While herself espousing atheism, she remains nostalgic for the beauty of the sacred. She explains:

> This sacred isn't the stability of religion nor the institution that inhibits it to some degree or other, but something that cuts across all that and allows our most imperative bodily needs to access symbolic representations that could be shared and that are sometimes sublime. This transition from the body to meaning, from the most intimate to the most binding happens via sexual desire. And a lot of religions recognize in sexual climax the core of their conceptions of the sacred.[76]

P-Orridge's practices are not mere practical strategies for self-actualization into an elevated, and stable, subjectivity. They are aesthetic rituals enacted to question and destabilize subjectivity, the mind-body-spirit divide, and the relationship between artist, object, and environment. I contend that despite Kristeva's concerns, intimate revolt is well underway in the artworks of the artists selected for this project. The works of P-Orridge and their collaborators reflect the blurring of subjectivity and the metaphysical divide that my current research suggests is inherent to radical sexual intimacy and its manifestations in contemporary art. P-Orridge's works support my contention that by radicalizing intimacy, we may challenge the Western philosophical canon that Kristeva argues has split the mind, the body, and the sacred. Furthermore, P-Orridge's somatic practices introduce a radical language of the body as activist philosophy, which, according to Massumi, "does not presuppose a subject, only 'something' going on."[77] P-Orridge's work exemplifies strategies that radically intimate art practice utilizes to carry out the very metaphysical transformations Kristeva values in analytic and literary processes, otherwise experienced in religious apotheosis.

While Massumi's text *Semblance and Event* does not explicitly address intimacy or sexuality, his interrogation of abstract form and the event proves helpful to unraveling the slippage of the subject-object divide in radical intimacy as an occurrence unfolding as a process. Along with the sacred, we may also situate P-Orridge's use of ritual as a formal, aesthetic intervention into how contemporary artmaking and consumption are experienced. The reframing of subjectivity that takes place via P-Orridge's practices and performances questions and destabilizes the subject-object divide, generating fluidity and unity between individual, artwork, and environment. Massumi promotes what he calls an activist philosophy based on events of durational becoming—change taking place over time. He proposes that events create themselves through the synergy of all elements, including all events prior, a model which is neither objectivist nor subjectivist, thus challenging the subject-object divide. Because artworks operate on the level of relationality and community, as well as qualitatively in the individual's self-enjoyment, the character of such an event is what Massumi refers to as "*aesthetico-political.*"[78] Massumi tells us that "process as becoming is not just creative activity, it turns out. It is *self-creation*. More than that, the self-creation is 'enjoyed.'"[79] By exploring this enjoyment as a form of jouissance, we may draw an important connection between Massumi's emphasis on "the *politicality* of process"[80] and the simultaneously generative and degenerative enjoyment of orgasm in P-Orridge's practices. By doing so, we link to Kristeva's theories on abjection, jouissance, ritual, and revolt, which also rely on the destabilization of the subject-object divide, and thus position radical intimacy in contemporary art in a lineage of radical practice.

The notion of the *event*, central to Massumi's discourse, is echoed in P-Orridge's works and writings, specifically in the orgasmic sigil, in that the sigil activates the multisensory feeling body and calls forth future possibilities. P-Orridge themselves is influenced by Whitehead's "process philosophy," the subject of Massumi's text, which P-Orridge claims "offers a view of reality in which process is the true stuff of reality, and in which 'matter' is little more than the documentation resulting from the activity and process of continuous becoming."[81] Likewise, Massumi tells us that "a thinking-feeling, without the actual feeling, is the semblance of an event."[82] An *evental* art practice is one that compels the sensory body to engage in continual flux between itself and other objects in the world, as well as internally in its own form. Thus, the boundary between subject and object is challenged and ruptured through sense itself. Further, Massumi defines *ritual* as "a way of *performing* thought. . . . Ritual gestures forth virtual events from the horizon of thought."[83] Massumi conceives of *sense* as an event that activates movement and multiplicity in perception, destabilizing the concreteness of subjectivity and instead preserving the durational existence of living beings. He states, "[t]he senses only ever function together, fusionally, in differential contrast and coming-together."[84] By extension, his argument asks us to redefine *form*, not as a concrete dimension of materiality but as an active agent of experience; and *sense* as a process of activation and reformulation through the body. In this way, "the artwork becomes *the subject of its own pure act*,"[85] rather than an idle object of the human subject's gaze. While experience could be conceived as originating in the embodied subject via perception, Massumi argues that the sensuousness of perception is only one component of a much larger, broader, and infinite set of relations in lived reality. By understanding life itself as an abstraction, we become *one* with the form of a work of art and see the object as inseparable from our own physical body. Here, we heed Massumi's caution, borrowed from Whitehead, to understand *one-ness* not as a formal unity but as "the thinking-feeling 'singularity' of an occasion occurring to itself."[86] Massumi salvages the abstraction of mid-twentieth-century modernism from conceptual death, its ideal concepts vertically removed from the content of lived reality, and reintegrates it into the world of the living body. By meditating *on* and *through* a work of art, our senses merge with its form, and we are launched into lived abstraction. In parallel, "[t]he art that interests P-Orridge is functional—'art that makes things happen,' as s/he puts it. Art made not for aesthetic judgements, or because it looks good hanging in a penthouse, but designed to make something happen—whether that is to heal someone or show the impermanence of existence."[87] P-Orridge's practices thus echo Massumi's activist philosophy as both relational and qualitative, aesthetic and political.

P-Orridge's works operate on this level of potentiality, leveraging enjoyment to *constructively deconstruct* and create pathways into new futures unbound by ideology. The art practices that Massumi refers to as *occurrent art* are predicated on techniques that emphasize process as the object of the art practice. These techniques "make no gesture of claiming 'objectivity,' nor do they pride themselves on their grasp of common sense. At the same time, they reject being characterized as 'merely' subjective. They are *inventive* of subjective forms in the activist sense: dynamic unities of events unfolding."[88] This is exactly how sigils operate, offering us a bridge from the abstracted discourse of analytic speech to the embodied sensibility of sexual intimacy in material art practices. Rejecting the Platonic notion of *mimesis*, Massumi opts instead for the notion of *semblance*, "the being of the virtual as lived abstraction."[89] Massumi shifts our thinking from conceiving of a fully formed artwork as an object that abstracts reality into representational, illusory form, toward a different kind of abstraction akin to Barthes's *punctum* as a vanishing point, which "is how the scene's continuing into its own distance appears."[90] This momentary visual encounter—a hidden subtext in a photograph or the horizon in a landscape painting, for example—arrests the gaze and compels it to travel beyond the surface of the image into a realm of infinite and ever-expanding meaning, what Massumi describes as "the dynamic wholeness of a life-world including its own afterlife."[91] Just like the skull in Lacan's reading of Holbein's painting, the *punctum* punctures consciousness, inserting memory, imagination, and an infinite poetic field that transcends representation.

Massumi's analogy of the horizon line mimics the operations of analytic speech—taking us into *the beyond* of language and desire. Lacan elaborates upon the process endured by the analysand of recounting memories and associations, and the position of the analyst as witness to, and facilitator of, the analysand's realization of the truth of their own desire. Lacan sees interpretation as a necessary mechanism of analysis but one that ultimately operates on the level of fantasy. He explains:

> The emptier [the subject's] discourse is, the more I too am led to catch hold of the other, that is to say . . . led into seeking out the beyond of his discourse—a beyond . . . which is nowhere, the beyond that the subject has to realise, but which he hasn't, and that's the point, realised, and which is in consequence made up of my own projection, on the level on which the subject is realising it at that moment.[92]

Analyst and analysand engage in a mutual, collaborative reordering of form—formal language, storytelling, and visual representation—to construct a realm of fantasy and desire beyond the container of given significations. This very same mechanism is employed by P-Orridge and their partners, as they reconfigure subjectivity and explore the ambivalence between unity and multiplicity. Through intimate engagement—in analysis and in the occurrent arts—individuals transcend their own conditioning, break up the visual and symbolic field of their own bodies, and transcend the horizon of representational language systems to continually re-signify the self.

Intimacy may be seen as an evental or relational practice, rather than an interactive one based on the subject-object divide or even an intersubjective practice that concretizes the notion of discreet, yet interconnected, individuals. P-Orridge's work may be framed as an intimate practice with aesthetico-political potentiality, as according to Massumi, "[p]ractices we call doing politics and practices we call doing art are all integrally aesthetico-political."[93] The embodied practices and theoretical contribution of P-Orridge and their collective of collaborators exemplify such intentionality. According to Massumi, "the world of change is *made* of self-creative expression. This has obvious advantages for an aesthetico-political activist philosophy oriented toward a creative autonomy of forms of life."[94] An *evental* art practice compels the sensory body to engage in continual flux between itself and other objects in the world, as well as internally to its own form; the boundary between subject and object is ruptured through sense. In Massumi's words: "Neither object nor subject: event."[95] P-Orridge explicitly employs sexuality as both content and medium, through the use of sexual fluids for the creation of artworks in the performance of embodied rituals, deliberate deconstructions of the gendered body via medical and shamanic interventions, and collaborative practices that challenge subjectivity through intimate exchange. Massumi poses the following challenge to activist practice: "it is a given that no event can lay down the law in a way that essentially predefines its succession. But are there still ways in which an experience can *orient* what comes? In what way can an event constructively include formative potential for what lies beyond in its own constitution?"[96] For Massumi, an artwork or a moment of experience is never isolated from the moments that came before and the moments that are to come. Seen as a series of events, artistic practice becomes a formative strategy for integrating the past, present, and future in a movement toward possibilities that may be.

On the surface, Kristeva's discourse on abjection and her discussion of body fluids, broken signifying chains and ruptures of subjectivity appear to be eloquently embodied in the works of artists such as P-Orridge, who exploit the taboo nature of such substances in an integrated aesthetic resistance to social and political orders. Kristeva distinguishes between the poetic defilement situated in excrement and menstrual blood, and the symbolic function of sperm and urine, while P-Orridge elevates the sexual fluids of both sexes to a divine provenance. Can shifting borders, in and of themselves, effect a deconstruction of the subjective self? In order to recognize the poetic potentiality at play in a system of rites and rituals that establishes the speaking subject as subject of the law, we may understand Kristeva's interplay of the symbolic and the semiotic as a horizon, akin to Barthes's and Massumi's *punctum*, that establishes a territory in the *beyond* of meaning and signification. Biblical and tribal law protects itself through the same transgressions that threaten its collapse, and these mechanisms are infiltrated and appropriated in an orgasmic sigil.

While drawing from the mysticism of cross-cultural and historical practices, P-Orridge's practice, in the lineage of the modern texts explicated by Kristeva, "resides in the revolt against identity: the identity of sex and meaning, of ideas and politics, of being and the other."[97] Deconstruction and rejection, however, are not sufficient for embodying Kristeva's revolt, and the abject facilitates regeneration as well. As Kristeva makes apparent, the abject is not simply a destruction of meaning but a newly radiant creation. Here we may return to Massumi's notion of the evental art practice and the body as "*[b]are activity*: the just-beginning-to-stir of the event coming into its newness out of the soon to be prior background activity it will have left creatively behind."[98] Reading Massumi, Kristeva, and P-Orridge in concert with one another helps thwart a traditional aesthetic reading of these artworks as simply visual representations of the orgasmic sigil. We may understand the artwork *as* a body, functioning as bare activity in the semiotic realm—the poetry of coming into its own newness again and again.

P-Orridge's creation of a ritual space in which the body, the mind, and the sacred join in making something happen operates as a radical form of resistance to religious, capitalist, and patriarchal regimes, as well as to the authority of language. Kristeva is less interested in a complete annihilation of modern subjectivity and a nostalgic return to a utopian past than she is in exploring the interplay between the symbolic and the semiotic. Kristeva asks:

> Could the sacred be, whatever its variants, a two-sided formation? One aspect founded by murder and the social bond made up of murder's guilt-ridden atonement, with all the projective mechanisms and obsessive rituals that accompany it; and another aspect, like a lining, more secret still and invisible, non-representable, oriented toward those uncertain spaces of unstable identity, toward the fragility—both threatening and fusional—of the archaic dyad, toward the non-separation of subject/object, on which language has no hold but one woven of fright and repulsion?[99]

In this question, which she identifies as her "point of departure," Kristeva invites a reading of *ritual*—or, to be specific, ritual deemed "sacred" by its practitioners—as having two functions, the first being the construction of society and the second being a secret and invisible "lining" that operates in both constructive and destructive capacities. Her message is less an injunction to destroy culture and move backwards in history to a purer state of being than an invitation to move through law and regulation via the unmapped, unspeakable interstitial lining that both threatens and fuses subjectivity. To traverse these ambivalent spaces of memory, the imagination, and love, one must operate in tandem with the other in the lineage of analytic speech.

Pandrogeny

The intimate may be understood as a futile attempt at fusion of the multiple into the singular. Intimacy may also contain the friction and movement generated in acts of revolt and the attempt to unearth the unknown, revealed unto the world of symbols and representations. How does such revolt manifest through the intimate love relationship, and how is the impossibility of meaning suggested in the poetic language of P-Orridge's practice? From their disturbing performances with Tutti to the ritualistic use of orgasm and body fluids, we may follow the arc of P-Orridge's aesthetico-political practice, to their more recent life work with their wife Jacqueline Breyer, a.k.a. Lady Jaye Breyer P-Orridge. Such an inquiry suggests that the intimate exchange with their lovers provides P-Orridge with what may be understood through a Lacanian framework as "speech"—"a third dimension, the space, or rather the volume, of human relations in the symbolic relation,"[100] a third entity between two individuals that also changes those individuals. As I argue throughout this book, intimacy initiates a slippage between inner and outer space and destabilizes ideological subject-formation. To truly break into the realm of radicality and disrupt ideology, I suggest that actors must traverse through the poetic realm of abjection, and the instability of boundaries, and that this traversal is echoed in sexually intimate art practices. The artwork of Genesis and Lady Jaye Breyer P-Orridge (collectively, Breyer P-Orridge) demonstrates the depth to which sexual intimacy and love can be leveraged to destabilize ideology and constitute newly porous subjectivity as a space that activates the unconscious. By activating speech, memory, and the eternal questioning of subjectivity, Breyer P-Orridge's relationship participates in a culture of intimate revolt.

Breyer P-Orridge's lifelong (and after-lifelong) quest to establish a new identity, a new gender, and a new self/other relationship through their every action, choice, and experience is expressed most tangibly through an extensive series of plastic surgeries and other physical transformations aimed at merging to create a new person. This non-gendered entity defined by multiplicity and dissolved subjectivity is a being they call the *pandrogyne*. According to Holly Connolly of *Dazed*, the couple "began a process of mirroring each other's physical forms, undergoing $200,000 worth of plastic surgery (including matching breast implants on Valentine's Day 2003) and briefly experimenting with hormones."[101] Between the time of Lady Jaye's death and Genesis's own succumbing to leukemia in 2020, Genesis sustained the project in the belief that their "other half" is still present in nonphysical form and continued to refer to themselves in the plural to indicate the multiplicity of their subjective position. The 2010 edition of *Thee Psychick Bible* offers the following dedication: "DEDICATED TO MY 'OTHER HALF' / THEE ANGELIC BEING / LADY JAYE BREYER P-ORRIDGE / 1969-2007 / S/HE IS (STILL) HER/E."[102] In the documentary film about their relationship, *The Ballad of Genesis and Lady Jaye*, P-Orridge describes the origins of the project and its roots in the "cut up" method:

> It began as very romantic, about love and about wanting to be as much like each other as we could... but as we thought about it and explored it more, we realized that we were including some of the William Burroughs and Brion Gysin ideas of the *cut up*... Burroughs and Gysin said that when they cut up writing and remixed it, that they were no longer the writer, it was the creation of what they called a *third mind*. So with Lady Jaye and I cutting up our bodies, we say that we are creating a third being, a third entity, and we call that the *pandrogyne*. When we began to explore that, we realized that it was really about evolution and the future of the human species. So pandrogeny in the end is a cry for survival.[103]

Pandrogeny therefore not only interrogates the boundaries of subjectivity, and the limits of love and intimacy, but it is also a distinctly feminist creative practice that exposes the fantasmatic qualities of gender, as defined by Jacqueline Rose as "[a]n artistic practice which sets itself the dual task of disrupting visual form and questioning the sexual certainties and stereotypes of our culture."[104] Sexual identity, confidence in language, and security in our image, according to Rose's reading of Freud and Lacan, are all fantasies, "[h]ence one of the chief drives of an art which today addresses the presence of the sexual in representation [is] to expose the fixed nature of sexual identity as a fantasy and, in the same gesture, to trouble, break up, or rupture the visual field before our eyes."[105] Pandrogeny, while founded in what may be considered an outwardly heteronormative union between individuals who were assigned male and female at birth, nevertheless strives to destabilize the categories of masculine and feminine that accompany these distinctions. Their wedding featured Genesis as the bride in a white wedding dress and Lady Jaye as the groom in tuxedo as they playfully swap social roles.[106] Their practice taken as a whole, however, refuses these binary designations as anything more than social and political performance (Figure 3).

Ritual and Revolt

Figure 3 Laure A. Leber, *Jackie and Genesis, November 5, 2006.* © Laure A. Leber.

Pandrogeny takes the ideas developed in P-Orridge's practice in the prior decades—challenging the conditioned self, upending gender constructs, and destabilizing ideological thinking—and extends them into the love relationship. By turning their coupledom into an intentional physical practice, Breyer P-Orridge seek to embody unity as a gesture toward the future of humankind. Through this practice, they contend, "'WE ARE BUT ONE . . .' becomes less about individual gnosis and more about the unfolding of an entirely new, open-source, 21st-century myth of creation."[107] Calling themselves "ultra-genetic terrorists,"[108] this new mythic being eschews biological imperatives handed down by science, just as much as it resists ideological injunctions imposed by state authority. According to the artists, "Breyer P-Orridge believe that the binary systems embedded in society, culture and biology are the root cause of conflict, and aggression which in turn justify and maintain oppressive control systems and divisive hierarchies."[109] By turning life, love, and sexual intimacy into a performative stance meant to enact change in the individual and society, Breyer P-Orridge destroy their ideologically conditioned selves and present a new ontology of radical intimacy for future human beings.

Breyer P-Orridge's interest in altered states and the unconscious mirror the early camaraderie between the surrealists and the Freudian-Lacanian school of psychoanalysis. P-Orridge describes the first time they met Lady

Jaye as a hallucinatory vision that occurred while napping in a New York City sadomasochism dungeon:

> I was lying on the floor in the death pose with a white sheet over me [laughs] and then, I heard these noises, and I woke up, and I could see through the doorway of the room this incredibly tall, slim—to me, very beautiful—woman walk across the doorway dressed in all authentic sixties clothing. And she was smoking a cigarette, of course, very elegantly. And she started walking backwards and forwards across this doorway and I was just entranced. "This is great." You know, what a nice way to wake up. And then she started to shed her sixties clothing, and she gradually got dressed in all this incredible fetish clothing.... It was very unlike me, but I do remember very clearly closing my eyes, and it was almost like a prayer. I basically said, "Dear Universe, if you find a way for me to be with this woman, that's all I want. I'll stay with her forever."[110]

P-Orridge draws from the world of dreams and the unconscious to describe their desire for Lady Jaye, and their willingness to subsume their sense of individual, autonomous subjectivity to have the feeling of unity—of being *most inside* the other, *intimus*. The radical exteriority of the intimate manifests in recollection welling up from the unconscious, always out of reach. According to Breyer P-Orridge's text S/HE IS HER/E (3/23/03), "(CHANGE THE WAY TO PERCEIVE AND CHANGE ALL MEMORY,"[111] revealing their practice as a poetic intervention into all systems of thought, meaning, and recollection. Out of the intimacy generated in the instability between conscious and unconscious spaces, even after her death, Lady Jaye continued to manifest through P-Orridge's imagination, ready to assume mystic and phantasmatic qualities. The third being generated via their intimacy—the Pandrogyne—embodies the simultaneous unity and fragmentation, as well as the timelessness of the unconscious.

It is also most tangibly in Breyer P-Orridge's Pandrogeny project that P-Orridge openly begins to integrate the feminine into their practice, embracing a fluid gender identity and plurality of subjectivity. Breyer P-Orridge proclaim that "EVERY MAN AND WOMAN IS A MAN AND WOMAN" and urge us to

> Destroy Gender.
> Destroy the control of DNA and the expected. [112]

Pandrogeny, however, deconstructs much more than gender, offering a vision of the future in which the humanist subject is destabilized through the merging of self and other. P-Orridge explains:

> We came to the conclusion that it's not about gender, it's about a much deeper form of identity that's not binary. It's about evolution, the reclamation of our own physical, mental and behavioural self, and it has nothing to do with either or at all, but just what are the possibilities of what we can become, do we even have to think in terms of even human?[113]

Though the initial impetus of the project was to "become enough of a mirror of each other to say that you've dissolved the previous being,"[114] the move to question and de-signify the subject through intimate exchange is evocative of Lacan's extimacy—the radical exteriority within, the interior presence of the Other operating like the cries of the unconscious, disrupting the stability of identity. According to Miller: "If we use the term extimacy in this way, we can consequently make it be equivalent to the unconscious itself. In this sense, the extimacy of the subject is the Other . . . where the extimacy of the Other is tied to the vacillation of the subject's identity to himself."[115] In death, Lady Jaye not only became the extimate other *in* the unconscious of Genesis but actually began to *become the unconscious*, further destabilizing Genesis's subjectivity. By developing a practice around their intimate relationship, dissolving the distinctions between their identities in pursuit of self-recognition in the other, Breyer P-Orridge mines for the extimate—radically intimate—unknown in the other that manifests in the interiority of the self.

Pandrogeny also invokes Kristeva's interest in the return to the maternal as a site of nondifferentiation, prior to identification and integration into the symbolic realm of law and ideology. Breyer P-Orridge exclaim:

> *You were in your mother's womb for forty-nine days an androgyne.*
>   *Who chose your gender? GOD?*
>
> *Society? Family?*
>   *Only by YOU ending this separation, returning to*
>   *that first pure state can real freedom begin.*
>   *When all are but one sex, one species.*
>   *This is not about becoming an Other,*
>   *This is about returning to a state of perfect union.*[116]

In the short film *The Pandrogeny Manifesto*, Breyer P-Orridge wear matching striped shirts, blonde hairdos, makeup, and accessories, and recite the manifesto: "In the beginning all were perfect. The first man was the first woman, the first woman was the first man . . . until the whispering began."[117] As the camera angle changes from shot to shot, defying conventional cinematic strategies of continuity, the identities of the individuals become subsumed in one another, just as the sense of space within the room becomes confused on the screen. Genesis reads: "Lady Jaye calls the human body a cheap suitcase that we carry around our consciousness, our self, in."[118] Lady Jaye recites: "Genesis Breyer P-Orridge likens it to a coral reef, a sophisticated biosystem that allows our consciousness to be mobile."[119] Breyer P-Orridge toggle between the movement toward unity and the desire for multiplicity and metamorphosis.

As an aesthetico-political practice, Breyer P-Orridge position their work as social and political resistance, arguing that it serves as an antidote or foil to the control of media and the distraction of the spectacle also criticized by Kristeva. Breyer P-Orridge explain the nature of their performative works as a blurring of subjective boundaries that identify the autonomous self: "Consciousness, passion, intimacy, and identity are important in a world that has become so cynical and addicting to consuming."[120] Both P-Orridge and Kristeva point to the ideological noise that conditions individuals and blocks them from looking inwards and experiencing something sacred, something deeply and strangely interior. While disappointed with "the current political state and the lack of revolt that characterizes it,"[121] as well as the ability of art to participate in such revolt, Kristeva nevertheless believes that art has the capacity to salvage ritual and the experience of communion that religion once offered. She states, "the ultimate goal of art is perhaps what was once celebrated as incarnation. I mean by that the desire to make one feel—through abstraction, form, color, volume, sensation—a real experience."[122] Breyer P-Orridge's collective practice and life as lived abstraction exemplify the potential impact of radical intimacy on the human relationship to the sacred, in a commodified and overconnected world.

Is Beauty Still Possible?

Radically intimate art challenges our assumptions about love, gender, socially sanctioned relations, and even beauty in art. It tramples upon expectations, generates discomfort, and can repel and revolt. For Kristeva, the loss of the intimate in contemporary society is a serious concern that needs to be addressed by artists and poets willing to reveal this abjection through a return to the sacredness of ritual. She expresses admiration for the interiority offered by religion and wishes for the silence of poetry and the quieting of ideology that she believes can lead us there. She explicitly calls out the threat of automation, bringing to mind both the dangers of technological alienation and the systemic control of human behavior linked to tyrannical ideologies, governments, and social systems.

Despite her general skepticism of the image over the word, Kristeva is most concerned with the effects of the media and spectacle in distracting us from developing our innermost experience. With the decline of religion in the West, she worries that we have lost our connection to the sacred and sense of incarnation that accompanies religious apotheosis. One art form she finds particularly impactful on her search for Beauty, however, is the contemporary art installation which she describes as an invitation "to tell our story, to participate, through it and our sensation, in a communion with being."[123] As a full-bodied sensory experience of dissolution and fragmentation, the contemporary art installation "also produces an unsettling complicity with our regressions, for when faced with these fragments, these flashes of sensations, these disseminated objects, you no longer know who you are. You are on the verge of vertigo, a black hole, a fragmentation of psychical life."[124] As this project suggests, in order for the intimate to be understood as a potentially radical part of life and art, we must acknowledge and develop access to the abject at work in the sexual body—the dissolution and rejection that continually forms and rejects the body's borders and the injunction of subjectivity. As we grapple with modernity, Kristeva asks, "[i]s it not the fearsome privilege of contemporary art to accompany us in these new maladies of the soul?"[125] She worries that "we are experiencing a low period,"[126] but that "we all need an experience, by which I mean something unknown, surprise, pain, or delight, and then comprehension of this impact. Is it still possible?"[127] By approaching art as an event of lived experience, and life as an aesthetic event, I believe that P-Orridge's practices meet Kristeva's call for a return to the sacred in intimate revolt and in love.

How, then, might an aesthetic culture of revolt operate through the mediation of sexual intimacy? Kristeva argues that contemporaneous culture is caught between the loss of religious ideology and the rise of the spectacle in the form of media. As a result, she states, "[w]hen the excluded have no culture of revolt and must content themselves with regressive ideologies, with shows and entertainments that far from satisfy the demand of pleasure, they become rioters."[128] P-Orridge's use of literal mechanisms of disgust—vomit, blood, the ingestion of body fluids—operates through the mechanism of abjection, creating a repulsive confrontation with the porous borders of the body. Kristeva reframes revolt as return to the self, a consistent thread that runs through P-Orridge's lifelong practice. P-Orridge's performances with body fluids in the *Cease to Exist* performances and the orgasmic sigil, combined with the subjective destabilization enacted in Pandrogeny, may be juxtaposed to reveal a philosophy of intimacy couched in a poetics of abjection, ritual, and jouissance, as well as love. By reinventing a relationship to the divine that rejects Christian constructs and celebrating the fluidity of human intimacy, P-Orridge participates in a culture of beauty and revolt. Kristeva asks: "Is the Beautiful still possible? Does Beauty still exist? . . . (for what other antidote to the collapse of fantastic ideologies, what other antidote to death, than Beauty?)"[129]

By warning of the fragility of revolt, Kristeva encourages us to continuously repeat, in the swaying and circular motion of the historical epoch, our initiatives that lead us toward ultimate revolution. She issues the following invitation: "Rather than falling asleep in the new normalizing order, let us try to rekindle the flame (easily extinguishable) of the culture of revolt."[130] Our investigation of P-Orridge's life work demonstrates one way in which artistic practices deploy radical intimacy to challenge the mind-body-spirit divide, calling forth the harmony and dignity of the sacred. Kristeva states: "One of the insights of Christianity, and not the least one, is to have gathered in a single move perversion and beauty as the lining and the cloth of one and the same economy."[131] P-Orridge's works access the sacred, in intimate revolt, while refusing institutionalized religious ideology. As Kristeva asks: "Infinite jouissance for each person at the intersection of happiness for all . . . is it anything else but the sacred?"[132]

Plate 1 Genesis P-Orridge, *B-Right-On* (2002), C-prints, black-and-white photographs, photocopies, antique postcards, Polaroids, acrylic, wolf fur, snakeskin, semen, blood, wax, paint pen 20 x 14.75 in (50.8 x 37.5 cm) GPO09 148. Courtesy of the Estate of Genesis Breyer P-Orridge and New Discretions

Plate 2 Ellen Jong, *Lily NYC* (taken between 2006 and 2010) from *Getting To Know My Husband's Cock* 2010. Courtesy of the artist

Plate 3 Leigh Ledare, *Mom with Hand on Bed* (2006) from *Pretend You're Actually Alive*. Courtesy of the artist

Plate 4 Leigh Ledare, *Mom's Profile in Seventeen Magazine* (1968) from *Pretend You're Actually Alive*. Courtesy of the artist

Plate 5 Leigh Ledare, *Untitled (Entire Roll)* (2008) from *Pretend You're Actually Alive*. Courtesy of the artist

Plate 6 Leigh Ledare, *Hot Licks* (2002) from *Pretend You're Actually Alive*. Courtesy of the artist

Plate 7 Leigh Ledare, *Mom in New Home* (2007) from *Pretend You're Actually Alive*. Courtesy of the artist

Plate 8 Breyer P-Orridge, *You Are My Other Half* (2007). Courtesy of the Estate of Genesis Breyer P-Orridge and New Discretions

Plate 9 Leigh Ledare, *Mom with Neck Brace* (2004) from *Pretend You're Actually* Alive. Courtesy of the artist

Plate 10 Ellen Jong, *Two Chairs Two Coffees* (taken between 2006 and 2010) from *Getting To Know My Husband's Cock* 2010. NYC

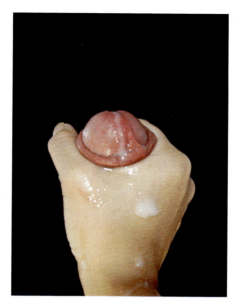

Plate 11 Ellen Jong, *Cum NYC* (taken between 2006 and 2010) from *Getting To Know My Husband's Cock* 2010. Courtesy of the artist

Plate 12 Ellen Jong, *In the Window NYC* (taken between 2006 and 2010) from *Getting To Know My Husband's Cock* 2010. Courtesy of the artist

Plate 13 Ellen Jong, *Red Door NYC* (taken between 2006 and 2010) from *Getting To Know My Husband's Cock* 2010. Courtesy of the artist

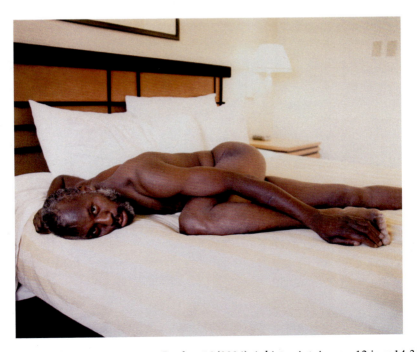

Plate 14 Barbara DeGenevieve, *Gordon #6* (2004), inkjet print, image: 12 in x 14 3/8 in, paper: 14 in x 20 in. Courtesy of the Museum of Contemporary Photography at Columbia College, Chicago

Part III

Ellen Jong
The Object in Revolt

4

Sex and the Symbolic

> Now normally or habitually, "I love you" is said to an enigma: "an other." An other body, an other sex. I love you: but I don't quite know who or what. "I love" slips away, it is swallowed up, drowns, burns, disappears into nothingness. We must wait for the return of "I love." Perhaps for a long time, perhaps forever.
>
> —*Luce Irigaray, When Our Lips Speak Together*[1]

The Poetics of Objecthood

I was first introduced to Ellen Jong's work through a curator who cited our mutual interest in intimate photography. Jong had recently self-published a photographic monograph called *Getting to Know My Husband's Cock*, which was a bold and surprisingly direct exploration of the early stages of her relationship and subsequent marriage to her husband. The art world at the time was, as it often is, conservative and unaccommodating to such graphic depictions, but Jong had managed to garner some positive attention for her work, and I was fascinated. We had lunch at a café in New York City, and I was stirred by her confident humility. She had a story to tell, and she would tell it in her own visual language. In the subsequent years, as I have learned more about Jong and her practice, I have come to realize that despite the personal scale of her project, she is consciously and intentionally a trailblazer, rebel, and practitioner of intimate revolt. Her work operates as an important intersectional feminist intervention into subjectivity, objecthood, and the politics of sexual representation. On a fundamental level, it challenges the heart of identity, intimacy, and love.

What happens when the ambivalence of inside and outside, self and other, collapse in the attempt to represent love and the intimate sexual relation at the edge of the impossibility of jouissance? How might the bounds of subjectivity be further eroded through a feminist practice that recognizes both the poetics and politics of the object, operating intimately alongside and within the eroding subject? In her monograph *Getting to Know My Husband's Cock*, Jong directly confronts the male organ, lovingly and intimately, through the indexical representational system of photography. This formal and conceptual choice places Jong's project in direct conversation with questions of the "pornographic" and suggests a challenging and destabilizing of such categories. According to Baudrillard, "pornography is but the paradoxical limit of the sexual,"[2] producing the desire aimed toward it and which also reifies and reproduces it. Echoing Kristeva's concerns about a culture overtaken by ideology and spectacle, Baudrillard argues that "[o]ur center of gravity has been displaced towards a libidinal economy concerned with only the naturalization of desire, a desire dedicated to drives, or to a machine-like functioning, but above all, to the imaginary of repression and liberation."[3] This chapter examines Jong's use of the language of "love" to interrogate its impact on our discourse of radical intimacy. I suggest that Jong appropriates the phallus and stages it as the object of desire, operating in solidarity with this object and leveling the hegemony between the master signifier and the *objet a*. I suggest that Jong takes us to the paradoxical limits of sexuality, and into a realm of intimacy and feminine jouissance, appropriating not only the phallus but also the gaze as object of desire.

I frame this chapter against the backdrop of Lacan's infamous twentieth seminar, *Encore: On Feminine Sexuality: The Limits of Love and Knowledge*, and his repeated assertion that there is no sexual relation—*il n'ya pas de rapport sexuel*. Lacan leaves open the question of intimacy in the wake of the failed sexual relation and seems to preclude the possibility of including an other—specifically a *feminine* other—into any kind of meaningful discourse. Lacan's view is predicated on the idea that there is no signifier in the symbolic realm for Woman, supporting his claim that Woman does not exist except as a void in meaning. His discussions of *feminine jouissance*, however, provide an opportunity to elaborate on Jong's contribution to a discourse of radical intimacy in feminist praxis. According to Rose's reading of Lacan:

> Woman is excluded *by* the nature of words, meaning that the definition poses her as exclusion. Note that this is not the same thing as saying that woman is excluded *from* the nature of words, a misreading which leads to the recasting of the whole problem in terms of woman's place outside language, the idea that women might have of themselves an entirely different speech.[4]

For Rose, and for us, this distinction is key to addressing Lacan's central question in *Seminar XX*, which, according to Mitchell and Rose, "is that of woman's relation to *jouissance*. It is a question which can easily lapse into a mystification of woman as the site of truth."[5] Jong's practice explicitly addresses sexuality, femininity, and the body, and borrows from much of the vocabulary of psychoanalysis, without lapsing into the mystification of which Mitchell and Rose warn. I place Jong's work alongside Lacan's, Irigaray's, and Kristeva's writings to elaborate my own discussion of radical intimacy and its manifestations and operations in contemporary art practice, as well as to situate her discourse among contemporary feminist theory and praxis. Specifically, I examine Jong's engagement with jouissance, "that moment of sexuality which is always in excess, something over and above the phallic term which is the mark of sexual identity."[6] As a feminist response to patriarchal ideology, Jong does more than simply flip the direction of the gaze or appropriate masculine subjectivity—both of which she does; she situates herself in the ambivalent space between masculine and feminine, self and other, subject and object.

The fields of feminist thought and practice are vast and active with debate. I first engage Jong's work in context to the writings of Irigaray, one of Lacan's most outspoken critics, who fiercely attacks his ideas on feminine sexuality in her essay "Cosi Fan Tutti." With this direct response to *Encore*, along with other writings that both outline and perform her position, Irigaray challenges Lacan's patriarchal views on the sexual relationship and instead celebrates feminine sexuality as a site of meaningful intimacy. In the following chapter, I continue to respond to Kristeva's call for a culture of revolt and suggest that Jong's work be considered as part of an aesthetic heritage of "artistic practices that redistribute the phallic signifying order by causing the preoedipal register to intervene, with its procession of sensoriality, echolalia, and ambiguous meaning."[7] Both Irigaray and Kristeva advocate situating intimacy—and love—within the ambivalence of inside/outside, subject/object, to reconstruct subjectivity into poetic, ever-evolving multiplicities of meaning that generate jouissance and surplus-jouissance. Emphasizing Jong's unique approach to the object of desire, and her contribution to a shift in ontological thinking, I elaborate on object-oriented feminism, situating Jong's "experimental and process driven art practice"[8] in a discourse that I suggest may operate as a more radical, contemporary intervention into ideologies of sexuality and the body, than re-situating or expanding the idea of subjectivity. I ask how Jong's visual, poetic form may activate the politics of objecthood, a question that will lead into the book's conclusion.

Il n'ya pas de rapport sexuel: Sex and the Symbolic

I begin with *Encore*, Lacan's twentieth seminar in which he repeatedly claims that "there is no sexual relation." Recognizing an as-yet sparsely mined territory in Freudian theory, Lacan attempted to elaborate his own thoughts on the sexual relation while taking the feminine position into account.[9] Lacan's premise remains firmly rooted in not just a social relationship between men and women but also the physical act of sexual intercourse. He describes the sexual act as "what remains veiled in law, namely, what we do in that bed—squeeze each other tight (*s'etreindre*),"[10] with the metaphorical bed as a tangible extension of the laws that govern the relations between men and women. While the "sexual relation," on some level, is understood to mean the physical act of sex, a translator's note early on in *Encore* tells us that "*[r]apport* also means 'ratio,' 'proportion,' 'formula,' 'relation,' 'connection,' etc."[11] According to Lacan's formulation, if there is no proportion between men and women, then sexual intimacy between them offers no connection and no knowledge. Miller explains Lacan's position:

> The unconscious knows nothing of the relation of man to woman or of woman to man . . . the two sexes are strangers to one another, exiled from each other. But the symmetry implied by this statement is slightly misleading. In fact, the missing sexual knowledge concerns only the female. If nothing is known of the other sex, it is primarily because the unconscious knows nothing of woman.[12]

Miller makes it clear that the discussion Lacan opens up is absolutely gendered and that there is no entry for the female—"The Other sex, meaning the sex which is Other, and absolutely so"[13]—into the sexual relationship, because she is un-signified and invisible. This position is untenable for feminist theory and praxis because of its erasure of femininity from the unconscious, its insistence on heteronormative structures of desire, and a gender binary that excludes gender-nonconforming people. Furthermore, it creates a block to intimacy by maintaining strict boundaries between subjects supposedly lacking knowledge of one another in the unconscious. Intimacy, as we are discovering throughout the trajectory of this book, is dependent upon the blurring of boundaries and identities.

Extrapolating on Lacan's discourse on the object in the nonexistent sexual relation, Miller emphasizes that the nonexistence of the relation and its manifestation in the form of fantasy are produced and perpetuated by the object of desire. He states: "It is not the object that obstructs the emergence of the sexual relation, as the expectation of its eventual coming might lead one to believe. On the contrary, the object is that which stops up the relation that does not exist, thereby giving it the consistency of the fantasy."[14] How might we understand the agency of the object of desire in the context of intimacy, and how might a feminist praxis of radical intimacy provide an alternative model for the sexual relation? According to Lacan, "everything revolves around phallic jouissance, in that woman is defined by a position that I have indicated as 'not whole' (*pas-tout*) with respect to phallic jouissance."[15] Since the feminine position in Lacanian discourse remains empty and desire aimed at an empty space between two positions, *jouissance* may be understood as an attempt to derive meaning and unity for the male Ego. For the Lacanian split subject, this wholeness remains unattainable and both the masculine and feminine positions incomplete. Lacan argues that there is no relationship between jouissance and the sexual relationship:

> It's a question of metaphor. Regarding the status of jouissance, we must situate the false finality as corresponding to the pure fallacy of a jouissance that would supposedly correspond to the sexual relationship. In this respect all of the jouissances are but rivals of the finality that would be constituted if jouissance had the slightest relationship with the sexual relationship.[16]

In other words, just as jouissance does not result in satisfaction, the sexual relation does not result in unity or finality. The pleasure or joy that one feels when reaching climax may be diametrically opposed to jouissance, which compels the subject to keep returning to the *objet petit a* in a self-perpetuating cycle of desire and release. This excess—this surplus-jouissance—ensures that the cycle will continue, as there will continuously be enjoyment in the process of failure to signify.

Lacan argues that the sexual relation, rather than striving toward unification, actually operates on the level of failure. He asks, "is love about making one (*faire un*)? Is Eros a tension toward the One?"[17] Jouissance cannot be satisfied and comes with a mix of pleasure and pain. It self-generates at the culmination of an act that has ostensibly satisfied the biological need but has refused to fully satiate desire. Jouissance is the fuel that keeps the cycle of desire and the force of the drive going. Lacan questions the role of jouissance in the disconnection he observes between the masculine and feminine positions: "Now then, this *jouissance* of the body. If there is no sexual relation, we need to see, in that relation, what purpose it might serve."[18] Further clarifying his position on the impossibility of the sexual relation, he argues that "[p]hallic jouissance is the obstacle owing to which man does not come (*n'arrive pas*), I would say, to enjoy woman's body, precisely because what he enjoys is the jouissance of the organ."[19] In other words, not only is feminine sexuality inadequate for engaging in the exchange of knowledge of the Symbolic realm, but she is also unavailable for *mutual* jouissance, as her body (and subjectivity) is incapable of competing with the primacy of the phallus. How can intimacy, if it is based on shared (if incompletely so) interiority, ever be expected to emerge from that excluded space?

How can feminists leverage the cultural criticism in Lacan's limiting formulation to develop theories and praxes of intimacy that both acknowledge the patriarchal structures embedded in language and free women and other marginalized groups from the constraints of this historically silenced position? A frequent critic of psychoanalysis, Baudrillard also criticizes feminist movements that are "ashamed of seduction, as implying an artificial presentation of the body, or a life of vassalage and prostitution. They do not understand *that seduction represents mastery over the symbolic universe, while power represents only mastery of the real universe.*"[20] This position is also limiting and places women in the romanticized role of seducer while ignoring the need for agency in the real conditions endured by oppressed and exploited people. How can feminists claim mastery over symbolic *and* real conditions while simultaneously deconstructing these ideologies, including the mysticism around women perpetuated by both Lacan's and Baudrillard's discourses? According to Mitchell and Rose, Lacan's writings on feminine sexuality,

> which show "Woman" as a category constructed around the phallic term at the same time as they slip into the question of her essence—underline the problem which has dominated the psychoanalytic debate on feminine sexuality to date: how to hold on to Freud's most radical insight that sexual difference is a symbolic construct; how to retrieve femininity from a total subordination to the effects of that construction.[21]

Mitchell and Rose's reading of Lacan, along with a consideration of Jong's monograph, initiates a discourse of radical intimacy that destabilizes the symbolic while retaining its grounding in feminist materiality. In the following chapters, I frame Jong's work as a feminist response to Lacan's statement alongside Irigaray's and Kristeva's poetic approaches, as well as Behar's, Morton's, and Lunning's object-oriented strategies, positioning radical intimacy as a tool for ideological critique and instability.

Ellen Jong: Radical Objectification

Jong describes *Getting to Know My Husband's Cock*, her 150-page monograph, self-published in 2010, as "a love song in photos and text . . . a collection of #bts [behind-the-scenes] photographs over the first three years of love and first year of marriage."[22] According to Jong, "the pictures help tell a story of how I fell in love."[23] Its scale measures 6 x 8.5"—small enough to invite a close, intimate immersion for the viewer and offers an individual experience of Jong and her husband's erotic love story. At first look, the book's cover and bold title establish the aim of Jong's inquiry—to gain knowledge of an object that signifies her husband but simultaneously exists externally to him as an object unto itself. By selecting the word "cock"—rather than "penis" or "dick," for example—Jong highlights the sexual desire at the core of her project and her "passionate and tumultuous relationship"[24] with her husband. She deliberately selects a word persistent in pornography at the outset of her visually explicit sexual narrative, setting up a highly charged erotic space that also engages the social construction of language. Also embedded in the title is a direct reference to state-sanctioned marriage and a heteronormative union, in her reference to "her husband." Besides being a personal ode to her marriage, I suggest that she does this both to flout the rules of propriety that accompany the ideal of marriage and to soften the explicitness of the forthcoming images and bring the experience of the work back to love. Jong thus keeps the series grounded in the attributes of contemporary Western marriage; implied within these pages are love, commitment, monogamy, and sexual desire.

In her foreword to Jong's series, sex activist Cindy Gallop uses the word "love" and its derivatives sixteen times, referring to the volume as "sexual scrapbooking of the highest order."[25] Gallop's ideological contribution to the project may be inferred from her own activist stance. She is founder and CEO of makelovenotporn.com, a website that claims to be "the world's first user-generated, human-curated social sex video-sharing platform, celebrating #realworldsex as a counterpoint to porn, with the aim of socializing sex—making it easier for everyone to talk about, in order to promote good sexual values and good sexual behavior."[26] The "highest order" Gallop references in her foreword may be understood as the moral high ground of love and goodness, in counterpoint to patriarchal pornographic representation, which she deems harmful in its constructions of fantasy. I suggest that the concept of love sanitizes what may be seen by the mainstream public as merely pornographic, adding a social and political component to Jong's intimate praxis.

This chapter will engage the acknowledged social aims of Jong's project, as articulated by Gallop, as Jong has presumably aligned herself with Gallop's stated mission of "re-education, re-habilitation and re-orientation"[27] of the visual field of sexuality. If women have been historically excluded from the symbolic universe, how might Jong's work reorient and rehabilitate the representation of female sexuality? Sontag tells us that "[t]o photograph people is to violate them, by seeing them as they never see themselves, by having knowledge of them they can never have; it turns people into objects that can be symbolically possessed."[28] Jong uses the imaginary as a tool to not only reclaim subjectivity—a position of mastery in the symbolic universe—but also re-situate the status of the object from inert and passive object of desire to an active agent in the relational field that is more aligned with, and yet exceeds, the psychoanalytic *objet a*. Reading Jong's work through Kristeva's and Irigaray's poetic theories reveals Jong's radical intimacy, operating in the field of language and employing poetics, feminine jouissance, and objecthood as conceptual tools. Jong's project disrupts and reorients modern ideologies of sexuality, love, and subjectivity through the lens of radical intimacy.

Jong's use of poetics, and the physical, materialist experience of jouissance, situates her work in the realm of the intimate; by extension it brings us close to death, decay, and abjection. Jong's engagement with abjection and the death drive is evident as early as the cover of her monograph, via the image emanating from behind the printed title of the book. Her introductory gesture contextualizes our discussion within the discourse of abjection and the eternal presence of the corpse. The image selected by Jong for her book cover depicts a cemetery and one tall gravestone emerging from between the splayed limbs of a bifurcated tree trunk. The image speaks of sexual penetration and sexual difference, in its usage of a phallic symbol emerging from—or penetrating into—a "V" shaped crevice. It also operates as a memento mori—a reminder of death—embedded within the ideal of marriage as well as in the medium of photography. According to Sontag: "All photographs are *memento mori*. To take a photograph is to participate in another person's (or thing's) mortality, vulnerability, mutability. Precisely by slicing out this moment and freezing it, all photographs testify to time's relentless melt."[29] The title of the photograph, and the final line of the poem that Jong uses to punctuate her visual series, is also the final line of the Western Christian marriage vow—*till death do us part*. This line appears handwritten on a square of toilet paper in the image just before the cemetery photograph and is followed first by a blurry image in the mirror of the couple in bed, then by a sunset, and finally by an image of Jong's husband's backside naked on a white bed—the final image of the monograph. Jong thus begins and ends her series with an homage to the lifelong commitment she has made in marriage, to the abjection at the core of intimacy, and to the death at the core of both sex and photography.

In addition to the book's examination of abjection and revolt, Jong's positioning of her husband's sexual organ as an object of desire serves as a useful foundation for my inquiry into object-orientation as feminist praxis. According to Behar, "[f]eminist politics might also arise from outward orientation, from looking to the abounding realm of inanimate, inert, nonhuman objects. In this case, the call for solidarity should be to rally around objects, not subjects."[30] While Jong's husband's sexual organ undoubtedly stands in for a real human being, whom Jong loves as a fellow subject, her playfulness with the notion of the object invites a consideration of her work through object-oriented feminism's proposal for radical objecthood. Jong's book dedication reads simply "*For you*," identifying an explicit object of her visual research and sexual desire—the unnamed *You*. One may assume the *You* referenced, and simultaneously positioned as the object of the *Me-You* dichotomy, is Jong's husband. *You* may also refer to the cock as the Other—the *objet petit a* or even the big Other of patriarchy—that is the object-cause of Jong's desire and epistemological search. Lacan's object of desire, according to Mitchell, "only comes into existence *as an object* when it is lost to the baby or infant. Thus any satisfaction that might subsequently be attained will always contain this loss within it. Lacan refers to this dimension as 'desire.'"[31] This symbolic loss of the phallus—a concept that in Freudian and Lacanian theory is central to sexual differentiation, wherein "the girl will desire to have the phallus and the boy will struggle to represent it"[32]—is continually reflected in Jong's projects and discourse. Jong and her husband perform this struggle of representation and power while at the same time subverting and questioning it through acts of intimacy. Finally, *You* may be understood as the reader of the monograph's pages, the consumer of the love, sex, and loss that accompany Jong's search, highlighting the complicity and intimacy between artist and audience.

Complicity and participation are key to understanding the ideological context of Jong's work, as well as both her employment and rejection of ideological constructs. She re-situates femininity in sexual relationships—in both private and public spaces, and in the sociopolitical sphere. Jong's feminist intention is evidenced in her website masthead: "IDENTITY, FEMALENESS AND MY PLACE IN THIS WORLD";[33] as well as her platform Peeness Envy, which is both an online shop for products such as her "GIRL caps" meant to support the stories of women and girls, as well as a conceptual project in which she superimposes the cap on celebrities and iconic figures.[34] Peeness Envy is an outgrowth of Jong's photographic series *Pees on Earth*, in which Jong documents herself urinating in public places as "a statement about the ownership of self, of sensuality, of humanity, and of womanhood."[35] Noteworthy is Jong's selection of Annie Sprinkle, "a prostitute/porn star turned performance artist/sexologist"[36] as coauthor for the book, in the form of a conversation between the two women in acknowledgment of the feminist discourse and praxis with which her work is engaged. Throughout my investigation of Jong's work, I remain in dialogue with Lacan's assertion, articulated by Miller, that there is "just one symbol for the libido, and this symbol is masculine; the signifier for the female is lost."[37] These references help to re-situate Jong's documentation of love and intimacy both as claiming the phallus as signifier of power and as a feminist act of solidarity with the object of desire.

Getting to Know My Husband's Cock, while deeply personal in scale, is visible and intentioned as an art practice and therefore has ideological implications. Reflecting the arc of this book, Jong opens the monograph with a gesture on intersubjectivity as interpellated through the intimate gaze. We are reminded of the co-presence of intimacy and ideology, and the construction of subjectivity in the imaginary and symbolic. The very first image inside the monograph depicts Jong's husband standing naked in what appears to be a living room, his cock positioned center frame, slightly obscured by the hanging strap of an old twin-lens reflex camera through which he gazes back at Jong and her camera. His head is bowed as he squints through the viewfinder into the prism inside the machine, which he points straight at his partner. His right leg casually crossed over his left, he seems at ease in his body and yet delicately balanced. In the foreground is a low table and two mostly finished cups of coffee in saucers, presumed remnants of the couple's morning ritual. This image describes domesticity and comfort, as well as the ideological interpellation taking place within the intimate relationship. Jong makes it clear from the first visual reference that knowledge is being obtained bilaterally, by both her and her husband, via the mediums of his cock and the camera eye.

The images that follow affirm the Freudian and Lacanian references of Jong's project, as well as lead into Kristeva's discourse on abjection, key to our investigation of radical intimacy. An adjacent image surveys the same room and features the same coffee cups and magazines as the opening image, but this time the camera has been turned toward the rumpled futon previously out of the frame, on which is perched a dark orange cat. The animal's head is turned in repose, with the lighter portions of its ear and face mimicking a pair of eyes staring back at Jong. The low technical quality of Jong's original digital photograph, coupled with its relatively small scale on the printed page, makes it difficult to read and contributes to its mysterious effect. On the coffee table lays a magazine featuring a bespectacled caricature resembling Sigmund Freud, staring upside-down toward the frame. This photograph carries multiple references to *looking* and hearkens back to the ideological function of the primal scene—a scene in which marriage, sex, vision, and knowledge collide to both construct and imperil the subject-in-formation. In the third photograph of the volume, we encounter Jong's husband splayed out on the very same couch previously revealed, his head slightly tilted back and mouth agape. He has one hand inserted into his pocket and the other tucked into the front of his jeans, reaching toward his own genitals in the delirium of sleep. We are reminded of his vulnerability and his closeness to his own flesh toward which intimacy strives. With this initial trilogy of images, Jong establishes the interiority of the couple's domestic sphere, in which the camera and numerous fields of vision coexist. We are also reminded of the starting and ending points of the book—that of the cemetery and the ever-presence of death, embodied in the figure's reclined position and open mouth. In my exploration of abjection as the representational limit where subject-object divisions dissolve, I also situate the intimacy explored by Jong and her husband beyond the ideological bounds of sexual difference, modern marriage, and the subject-object binary.

The series of images that follows this introductory sequence continues to circle around the male figure in the domestic sphere. The first depicts Jong's husband clad in a bright blue tee-shirt, sitting bottomless on a bed with the top of his buttocks exposed as he takes a sip of a drink. Out of the top-right corner peeks a shadowy face of a blond woman wearing heavy eye makeup, gazing out of a poster or photograph on the wall, continuing the theme of the gaze in a domestic environment. Elements of the domestic sphere emerge from the background and set the stage for a still-life of flowers that comes next in the series, illuminating Jong's focus on the quotidian beauty of the banal. At this point in the monograph, Jong introduces the poem that will continue to punctuate the monograph in bursts of rhythmic stanzas interspersed among the figurative photographs. "Your Cock," reads the first of the poem images—a photograph of a sheet of toilet paper, with these two words handwritten in pencil in casually rendered block lettering. The next image displays Jong's husband's crotch, slightly un-zipped out of dark jeans, revealing a landscape of dark body hair on his arms and lower belly as he holds a white lily—a potential signifier of death, virginity, and the sacred—in front of his still-dressed genitals. From the poem opening to the photograph, his cock is rendered poetic, beautiful, and perhaps even tragic, portending the specter of death embedded in the marriage vow.

As the book proceeds, we see images of beaches, windswept palm trees, his backside on a sandy towel, and other signifiers of leisure and intimacy. We see a close-up of his eyelashes amid skin peppered with grains of sand. Jong's lens studies her lover's contours, his textures, and their shared surroundings, creating a private, interior space in a public arena. The next stanza of the poem appears—"Smells like me, smells like you, Inside"—introducing the olfactory realm of intimacy and the mixture of fluids that comprises a breakdown of the boundary between inside and outside, self and other. The confounding of subjectivity within the ambivalence of interiority/exteriority grounds Jong's practice within a discourse of intimacy, as I have explored it through abjection, revolt, and in the ambivalent relation to the object. The remainder of the monograph meanders through still-lifes, close-ups of Jong's husband's cock in various states of arousal and images of the couple in the midst of sexual activity, often photographed in and through reflective surfaces. The poem operates as a rhythmic structure and love song to Jong's husband and his cock. It reminds us that the intimacy between them is littered with "pleasure and pain, in every vein,"[38] and that their sex operates beyond the pleasure principle, in the realm of the death drive. In Lacan's words, "*jouissance* appears not purely and simply as the satisfaction of a need but as the satisfaction of a drive."[39] This jouissance, from a feminist standpoint, challenges the binaries associated with sexuality and its pleasures. According to photography critic Vince Aletti of *The New Yorker*, "Jong has said that her pictures . . . are about falling in love, but it's her unapologetic lust that comes across most appealingly here."[40] The separation Aletti suggests between love and lust is reflective of the ideological barriers placed on feminine sexuality—the binary of love/lust corresponds to the binary of pure/impure—and invites a feminist discourse of intimacy that refuses these distinctions.

The photographs of Jong's husband's sexual organ punctuating the monograph are striking in their descriptiveness. Aletti states that "[p]ictures of a beach littered with fruit, of ripe bananas and shells atop a microwave, and of pink peonies in full bloom provide sensuous contexts, but none are as rapturous or as startling as the closeups of erections."[41] We see the head of Jong's husband's cock center frame, gleaming white from the camera flash. It juts crookedly out of the opening of dark pants, the slit of its head pointed almost directly into the camera eye. In the very next image, we see just its red tip, emerging from inside of Jong's fist, covered in glistening white semen against a black background—a formal still-life of sexual orgasm and catharsis. According to Kristeva, "[p]oetic catharsis, which for more than two thousand years behaved as an underage sister of philosophy, face to face and incompatible with it, takes us away from purity."[42] Jong's use of humor and absurdity breaks the ideals of the purity of love, and the rapture of sexual orgasm, presenting a wilder and more complex sexual relation. A faux mound of pubic hair emerges absurdly from the waistband of her husband's jeans in a seemingly self-mocking gesture that serves to anthropomorphize his cock; the image, at first glance, evokes a man with a handlebar mustache or funny wig. A side-view of his erect penis, pointed upwards toward the padlock of a red door, exaggerates his arousal and turns it into an absurd performance of phallic agency—the phallus as a character in a tragicomedy. According to Susan Sontag, "[a]ll images that display the violation of an attractive body are, to a certain degree, pornographic. But images of the repulsive can also allure."[43] Jong utilizes her husband's sexual organ to engage the idea of objecthood, and to reposition herself and her subjectivity in relation to the allure of the object of her desire.

Jong consistently directs the camera as an apparatus of power. Her project can therefore be understood as chronicling *her* subjective experience of desire, as her husband's face is often obscured or cut off at the edges of the photographs. Jong's approach, however, is far from being merely a binary model based on subject-object relations of power and agency. Though the power relation remains intact in its reversal, we may *simultaneously* consider the collaboration implied in both the imagery and the discourse surrounding the work. Jong's husband's missing visage can just as easily represent respectful anonymity agreed upon by the couple, as it could an objectification of the male body. Jong's work seems to operate as a representation of rapport and collaboration between herself and her husband, in solidarity with the object of desire. As part of her 2012 solo exhibition *The Invisible Line* at Allegra la Viola Gallery in New York City, the photographs from Jong's monograph were displayed along with a video of the couple having sex in the ocean at a beach in Puerto Rico. Simply titled *Naked Beach Day*, the video depicts the couple frolicking in the shallow blue waters and presumably consummating sexual desire through intercourse, though the actual coital activity remains veiled beneath the water. In the video, Jong's husband repeatedly turns to look at the camera, highlighting his awareness of the recording apparatus. His gesture removes any ambiguity, in the event that the obviousness of the camera's presence on what must have been a sparsely populated beach is lost. He pulls his lover toward him, playing a coy game of cat and mouse as he glances over his own shoulder, breaking the invisible fourth wall between himself and the camera-viewer machine and revealing the performative aspect of the work. While his actual intention remains unknown, the effect is one of complicity and collaboration in his role producing a representation of his and Jong's intimacy. Despite the satisfaction of consummation implied in *Naked Beach Day*, and the unity called forth in the term "falling in love," there remains an alterity at the heart of Jong's series, an acknowledgment of separateness and distance between herself and her partner that compels her to turn her gaze, almost obsessively, onto her husband's body. His male organ triggers awareness of the physical differences between them, but also of a deeper strangeness than biological sexual difference supposedly signifies—something that operates independently of sexual difference and yet is informed by its socializations. We may be reminded of Lacan's *extimacy* as "an existence that stands apart, which insists as it were from the outside, something not included on the inside."[44] This exteriority, hidden deep within the psyche, is both innermost—*intimus*—and radically unassimilated. The phallus is thus appropriated to represent the extimate object of desire, and mutual jouissance, rather than simply *phallic* jouissance or even the jouissance of the Other. Jong's gaze itself becomes the *objet a*, the object of desire experienced as the enjoyment of looking, "the mysterious object, the most concealed object, that of the scopic drive."[45] Does Jong's approach comprise an object-oriented position, as proposed by Behar, toward a feminist aesthetic practice? Or does she merely reverse the male gaze and disrupt the hegemony of subject-object relations by inserting a feminine subjectivity? How can a range of feminist approaches, both psychoanalytic and object-oriented, help us situate Jong's work within a feminist discourse of radical intimacy and contemporary art practice?

Irigaray's Materialism: Jamming the Machinery

In Lacan's discourse, an unavoidable division between the sexes occurs at the moment that we are initiated into the realm of sexuality and language—indeed, initiated into sexuality *through* language. At this moment, the boy and girl realize that they are different, that one has a biological phallus (the penis) and the other does not, and that this biological difference is transmuted into symbolic difference. Lacan explains the difference between a *masculine* jouissance that follows the structures set up for it by the phallic discourse and a *feminine* jouissance that functions as an active void that reveals a limitlessness to her desire: "When I say that woman is not-whole and that that is why I cannot say Woman, it is precisely because I raise the question (*je mets en question*) of a jouissance that, with respect to everything that can be used in the [phallic] function (φ_x), is in the realm of the infinite."[46] According to Lacan, feminine jouissance is infinite because it cannot be contained by language, precisely because it is not contained *in* language. For Lacan, men and women relate to one another through this gap between them, which is the unattainable object of desire—the *petit objet a*—that is not a literal object or person but the experience, or fear, of castration. According to Miller, the castration complex is key to the nonexistence of the sexual relation:

> What is it that blocks the experience? What, according to Freud, does not come to pass? It is the clause which prescribes to a man how to be a man for a woman, and to a woman, how to be a woman for a man. Freud finds that this clause, which he anticipates, fails to appear, and therefore he posits the castration complex as irreducible.[47]

Unlike Freud, who positioned this moment of differentiation as an awareness of a biological reality, Lacan understood it as inextricable from the meaning implied in language. Language, in turn, is not simply a series of symbols that stand for objects or concepts in the "real" world but is a coded set of beliefs and perspectives that simultaneously reflect and reinforce our relations. The phallocentric language that Irigaray describes as "[t]heir words, the gag upon our lips"[48] strangely serves a dual purpose of alienating the feminine while suggesting an infinite realm of possibility afforded to the unnameable.

Lacan's Freudian approach to sexual difference is problematic for feminist thinking, as it reduces the feminine to a nonspeaking role in the dialectic of desire. Irigaray offers a harsh critique of *Encore*, claiming that by uttering so emphatically the impossibility of the sexual relation, psychoanalysis "remains caught up in phallocentrism, which it claims to make into a universal and eternal value."[49] She questions Lacan's claim of the inequality of the sexual positions in relation to language, and his resulting conclusion as to the nonexistence of the sexual relation, arguing that "the fact that the sexual relation is in that respect incapable of articulation is what allows him to keep on talking."[50] Her argument suggests that Lacan's claim of the "impossibility" of the sexual relation perpetuates male dominance in discourse and the ideologically imposed distance between men and women. Mockingly, she prods:

> The production of ejaculations of all sorts, often prematurely emitted, makes him miss, in the desire for identification with the lady, what her own pleasure might be all about.
> And . . . his?[51]

Here, she recognizes the inherent desire for identification that locks the masculine subject into a preassigned ideological position that makes any relation, indeed, nonexistent.

Irigaray's discourse on the "feminine" provides an entry point for an alternate narrative of sexual intimacy that retains a materialist orientation to sexual difference while suggesting ways to loosen the binaries of masculinity and femininity. Irigaray is associated with a wave of "French feminists writing in the 1970s and 1980s [... who] argued that feminist theory must both expose the ways in which women's bodies have been understood as lacking, castrated, or other and simultaneously craft an alternative tradition that takes gender difference (and other differences) as a grounding condition."[52] In regard to sexual difference being merely biological or "simply a social or cultural stereotype,"[53] Irigaray rejects either proposition. After performing clinical studies that focused on language, she concludes: "I realized it was mostly a relational difference between the two. When you are born with a female body, this body has a different relationship potential than the male one. For example: It's not the same thing to carry a child inside your body than outside. It's not the same to make love inside your body than outside."[54] Irigaray challenges the psychoanlaytic narrative of sexuality, accusing it of being patriarchal, inaccurate, and inapplicable to the female, as well as to, I contend, gender-nonconforming populations. Nevertheless, Irigaray insists upon a fundamental separation between the experience of those born into female-assigned bodies, who she claims function in a type of interiority, and those born into male-assigned bodies, whose exteriority can be found both anatomically and in the gestalt of their own subjectivity.

Irigaray offers a poetic feminist rebuttal to Lacan in the form of an intra- and *inter*subjective exchange between females and their own sexual organs, anatomically positioned for self-stimulation. In *When Our Lips Speak Together*, she writes: "When you say I love you—staying right here, close to you, close to me—you're saying I love myself."[55] For Irigaray, the female body is a site of dialogue with the self, a feminine jouissance that can only be shared among women, at the exclusion of the masculine. She attempts to overhaul this old patriarchal language with a new feminist language, but does she succeed in overcoming the impossibility of sexual rapport? According to Irigaray, "the issue is not one of elaborating a new theory of which woman would be the *subject* or the *object*, but of jamming the theoretical machinery itself, of suspending its pretension to the production of a truth and of a meaning that are excessively univocal."[56] How might such a poetic and theoretical praxis of radical intimacy operate as a disruptive element in ideology?

Lacan invites a poetic discourse into the analytic paradigm when he states, "[t]hat is the act of love. To make love, as the term dictates, is poetry. Only there is a world between poetry and the act."[57] Jong's monograph is as much about the poetry it houses as it is about its graphic anatomical depictions. Though we may define poetics as encompassing a number of mediums, manifesting in material far beyond the realm of written language, I turn our attention directly to the literary form of poetry that Jong employs in her poem in a lyrical ode to her husband's cock. According to Jong, through the poem "she expresses the realities of passion, addiction and fear that also affect her."[58] The poem's opening stanzas

> Your cock
> Smells like me, Smells like you, Inside

set the tone for a journey into an intimacy doused in body fluids, smells, and tastes that blend the masculine and feminine into an undifferentiated musk. Jong's husband's cock transforms from a symbol of phallic power to an object through which an attempted synthesis of two fluid subjectivities takes place, an intimacy sustained by its own failure and an aromatic signifier of intimate exchange. Irigaray, by contrast, resists the masculine body by renouncing its unyielding contours. She implores to her female interlocutors and partners in intimate dialogue to overturn the phallic discourse: "Speak, all the same. Between us, 'hardness' isn't necessary. We know the contours of our bodies well enough to love fluidity. Our density can do without trenchancy or rigidity. We are not drawn to dead bodies."[59] Jong's exchange with the masculine reimagines the role of such stiffness. No longer the carrier of the signification of power as described by Lacan, nor the rigid dead flesh rejected by Irigaray, the hardened male member redistributes jouissance within a nonbinary system of sexual, intimate alterity through which the limits between inside and outside are breached.

Jong's and Irigaray's poetics operate in complementary, though sometimes divergent ways. Irigaray's poetic text reads as a love letter, feminist manifesto, and celebration of love between women (perhaps an eroticized version of her concept of *speaking-among-women*). The analogy between the lips of the mouth that renders speech and the lips of the labia that define female-assigned bodies articulates Irigaray's emphasis on feminine speech as embodied and specific to the female body's material reality. Irigaray refers to phallic language as a suffocating and silencing gag and warns women that "[i]f we don't invent a language, if we don't find our body's language, it will have too few gestures to accompany our story."[60] She employs her own poetics to achieve just this in *Our Lips*, refuting the phallic order and Lacan's model of sexuality and its associated phallogocentrism. This new narrative, while allowing the pronouns to slip and identities to be obscured, is an affront to Lacan's model of the sexual relation in which the feminine exists purely as empty void and receptacle for male desire. Irigaray infiltrates this realm with poetry and reclaims the feminine from its prison, leaving the dead weight of masculinity behind. Her rhetoric breaks from the duality of the "One" and the "Other" and engages a discourse of multiplicity: "We—you/I—are neither open nor closed. We never separate simply: *a single word* cannot be pronounced, produced, uttered by our mouths. Between our lips, yours and mine, several voices, several ways of speaking resound endlessly, back and forth."[61] The inter- and *intra*-subjective slippage, characterized by dissolving of boundaries between selves, is shown through Irigaray's words to be an embodied poetics, the construction of new languages of physicality. She states:

> Erection is no business of ours: we are at home on the flatlands. We have so much space to share. Our horizon will never stop expanding; we are always open. Stretching out, never ceasing to unfold ourselves, we have so many voices to invent in order to express all of us everywhere, even in our gaps, that all the time there is will not be enough.[62]

In the previous passage, Irigaray's speech rejects the master signifier and instead positions the feminine as an infinite space of poetic unfolding. Jong deploys poetics to reconnect the masculine and feminine in intimate collaboration, and ushers us into the realm of poetry by acknowledging the failure of language within the intimate. She says, "you can't really describe falling in love, you don't know how it happens or what happens,"[63] emphasizing the irrational quality of love. She then points to her own chosen symbolic system, a semiotic of the body: "It's not about his cock. I just use his cock, and describe his cock, to help me describe what it is to be falling in love."[64] Jong's own questioning of language and other descriptive representations reminds us not to rely on her written speech for the poetry in her work. For Jong, the search for knowledge is enacted through the body of the other but not at the exclusion of his individual personhood.

Nevertheless, Irigaray's and Jong's feminist intentions, grounded in female materiality and historicity, are aligned. Irigaray argues that intimacy is the vessel that can traverse the expanse between different subjective positions. She claims that "the original culture of hospitality was a feminine culture" and that "to move from a culture to another we need to be able to discover what human intimacy is."[65] Jong's definition of love involves breaking down her own psychic architecture and dissolving the binary opposition between mind and body. She states:

> There is an invisible line ... that lies between my body and my mind. It withholds my deepest beliefs, fears, curiosities and desires. It is there to protect me. It is there to tell others where I stand, what is mine and why I am. In falling in love, I lost sight of my invisible line and I let it go. Love breaks down walls and sets you free.[66]

This poetic breach of language translates into a psychic breach within one's being, as well as between self and other. By relocating ontology to the body, and thereby destabilizing the foundations supporting the masculine, rational, ordered subject, both Jong and Irigaray perform an intimate poetic that has radical potential in the social-political field.

Jong's practice, particularly *Getting to Know My Husband's Cock*, operates as both an appropriation of psychoanalytic structures and a rejection of their phallocentric foundations. She offers a view of feminine enjoyment that speaks a unique poetic language of its own, drawn from the physical and psychical experiences of femininity and the arousal of desire through the phallus as object. At the same time, she questions the supposed separation between "masculine" and "feminine" by inserting herself into the position of power in looking, getting into rapport or solidarity with the phallus, and inviting her husband's sexual organ to signify both his and her pleasures. Lacan explains that "[t]here's no such thing as a sexual relationship because one's jouissance of the Other taken as a body is always inadequate—perverse, on the one hand, insofar as the Other is reduced to object *a*, and crazy and enigmatic, on the other."[67] Jong re-signifies the cock away from the primacy and paralysis of the phallus in the face of castration, using humor, tenderness, and collaboration to generate a multisensorial universe of love and desire. She leverages the enigma of sexual intimacy toward a courageous representation of the love relationship. As Lacan tells us, "[r]egarding one's partner, love can only actualize what, in a sort of poetic flight, in order to make myself understood, I call courage—courage with respect to this fatal destiny."[68] Jong looks destiny in the eye and leaps poetically into the promise of intimate failure.

5

Object-Oriented Intimacy

A place to rest my head
In the woods Inside a shed
Where lulls fall into 2
heart beats
Blood over me like a
bed sheet
An infinite Stain
Pleasure and pain
In every vein

—Ellen Jong[1]

Sex in the Sensorium: A Deeper Cave Within

Psychoanalysis offers a powerful framework for an investigation of intimacy and for a reading of Jong's monograph. Her emphasis on the masculine sexual anatomy coupled with her repeated references to psychoanalytic tropes invite the language of Freud, Lacan, and Kristeva, as well as Irigaray's feminist rebuttals. Throughout the first portion of this book, I have aligned Kristeva closely with her chosen field of psychoanalysis; however, in the reorientation offered by Jong's photographs, we may find an opportunity to reframe Kristeva's ideas through a different lens. Psychoanalysis emphasizes subject-formation and destitution as cyclical and competing movements in the sexual development of the individual. Kristeva's emphasis on abjection and revolt as a continual re-turn to the preverbal, and her discourse on abjection and revolt, play around the edges of the psychoanalytic canon while incorporating new poetic possibilities. In this chapter, I further interrogate Kristeva's intimate approach toward the object—an entity that plays an active role in the analytic structure and yet is continually seen as a mere trigger or counterpoint to the subject's desire. How might we start incorporating objecthood into a discourse of intimacy through a feminist lens that acknowledges the embodiment opened up by thinkers such as Irigaray, Kristeva, Jong, and others?

I begin with the ways that Kristeva undermines the ideology of her own field of psychoanalysis while opening it up to new and perhaps sparsely explored worlds that destabilize the category of subjectivity. I then introduce the writings of Timothy Morton and Frenchy Lunning, along with the object-oriented feminist pioneer Katherine Behar, to suggest that Kristeva's theories on intimacy can help usher in a new paradigm of thought around the subject-object divide— one that challenges ideology and breaks open the potentialities of the intimate beyond that which psychoanalysis allows. By reframing intimacy, sexuality, and art practice in terms of objecthood, we have an opportunity to develop new discourses around artists who work with radical intimacy. We can begin to understand their radicality as extending beyond the reorganization of ideologies and into a rearrangement of ideology itself, addressing the unique and novel concerns of the twenty-first century.

How can we understand Jong's work in context to Kristeva's discourse? Kristeva expounds on Freudian semiology, which, she argues, "left open the hypothetical suture of the 'pure signifier' that an overly philosophical reading, in a word a Kantian one, might compel."[2] In other words, Freud's treatment of language and symbols in his research on dreams not only embraced the "heterogeneity of the Freudian *sign*"[3] in metaphor and metonymy—the dream work's condensation function—but also left this very multiplicity infinitely open, infinitely changeable. This instability of language—its refusal to stay intact—is mirrored in the instability of the speaking subject as it attempts to define itself. Language and identity disintegrate, and the subject is left grasping at a dissolving membrane of meaning. According to Kristeva:

> The body's inside, in that case, shows up in order to compensate for the collapse of the border between inside and outside. It is as if the skin, a fragile container, no longer guaranteed the integrity of one's "own and clean self" but, scraped or transparent, invisible or taut, gave way before the dejection of its contents. Urine, blood, sperm, excrement then show up in order to reassure a subject that is lacking its "own and clean self."[4]

What does Jong's photograph of her husband's ejaculate on the head of his penis, flowing over the skin of her own hand, communicate about intimacy as philosophical discourse and the contribution of an abject poetic to a stance of radicality? According to Murat Aydemir, for Kristeva "semen occupies a thoroughly ambivalent place"[5] in the symbolic order, as it represents both purity and impurity. According to Kristeva, "[n]either tears nor sperm . . . although they belong to borders of the body, have any polluting value"[6] in religious ideology. Additionally, while "excrement and its equivalents (decay, infection, disease, corpse, etc.) stand for the danger to identity that comes from without"[7] and menstrual blood "stands for the danger issuing from within the identity,"[8] semen is not inscribed so clearly. According to Aydemir, "sperm may become both dirty and pure. Furthermore, Kristeva writes, it is only through and in an orgasmic *jouissance* that the abject 'as such' can be experienced."[9] How does Jong leverage the ambiguity of male ejaculation toward a feminist aesthetic of radical intimacy?

At first glance, Jong's photograph references a trope of hard-core pornographic imagery—the "cum shot," in which a man's ejaculate is the subject—and object— of the image, central to the moment of sexual release. According to Aydemir:

> The cum shot forms hard core's pinnacle convention. It depicts ejaculation in close-up, always occurring outside of the body of the sexual partner. Semen spurts, trickles, or gushes from the penis, and lands on the female or male skin of the buttocks, chest, belly, backside, or face. The cum shot nearly always forms the conclusion and culmination of the sexual encounters in the genre.[10]

Aydemir explains that the male climax scene in hard-core pornography contains key structural elements that code patriarchal masculinity. He argues: "Indeed, those conventions appear to be intrinsic to the representation of masculinity, constituting elements, rather than attendant gimmicks or empty codes."[11] A reading of Jong's photograph, however, introduces several atypical elements that destabilize the actual *real* organ in reference to its symbolic signifier— the *phallus*. Jong's hand is larger than the visible portion of the male sexual organ, implying a reversal of power and an engulfing of the "masculine" by the "feminine" and even a reference to the primal scene. An initial feminist reading could posit an inherent radicality in Jong's grasping of her husband's organ, explicitly displaying her active role as the facilitator of his pleasure. Only the head of his penis is visible, red and engorged, his spillage occurring over her skin. Her hand operates as a sort of foreskin, sheathing his shaft and encasing it in her own flesh, presenting one organ made of components from two bodies. Power is reversed and destabilized, as is subjectivity. As a substance ejected from the body, semen operates on the porous border between pure and impure. Along with the reversal of power embodied by Jong's hand, subjectivity is destabilized along with the designations that clearly differentiate the abject from assimilated language.

By borrowing the language of pornographic imagery, Jong takes advantage of inconsistencies in narrative structure that operate as constitutive elements for the construction of the male subject. According to Aydemir, the cinematic fragmentation that takes place in hard-core pornography disrupts and then reestablishes male subjectivity. The cuts and other editing motifs break the visual and narrative tether of the ejaculate to the image of the male subject, reorienting the scene toward the emission and away from the coherence of the individual. Through a return to the narrative continuity of the scene post-orgasm, the male subject is reconstituted and salvaged from the dissolution of his body and identity. Aydemir states:

> On the one hand, the cum shot can be seen as the furthest reach to the disintegration of masculine subjectivity. . . . On the other hand, the cum shot also shunts the narration back to the story level, so that its constituting elements or pieces are recuperated, redomesticated, through the character's subjective face, his name, and his agency. In that sense, the cum shot works to save male subjectivity from the pornographic lapse into a fragmented, pleasurable, amorphous, and bodily condition.[12]

Jong's image conflates the two bodies via the mechanism of her husband's orgasm, the seeping out of his internal fluids, and her corporeal participation. Her husband remains both faceless and nameless. The sparse black abyss looming in the back of the image's central objects—the penis and the hand—obscures context and renders the intimate scene a visual poem of heterogeneous signification that reflects a blur of subjectivities in the act of sexual intimacy. Irigaray asks "why sperm is never treated as an object *a*?"[13] She argues that although sperm is associated with the reproductive function, "[t]*he object of desire itself,* and for psychoanalysts*, would be the transformation of fluid to solid? Which seals . . . the triumph of rationality.*"[14] Sperm operates in an ambivalent relation to power and logos. Borrowing the visual language of pornography, Jong complicates the power relations embedded in the symbolic language of images of sexual gratification and develops a language of intimacy we see throughout the monograph.

Jong articulates her own pleasure, and her claim to the symbolic, in the potentially hegemonic context of erotic imagery. According to Sontag, "[t]o photograph is to appropriate the thing photographed. It means putting oneself into a certain relation to the world that feels like knowledge—and, therefore, like power."[15] Furthermore, she argues, photographs "help people to take possession of space in which they are insecure."[16] Jong uses photography for its access to a semblance of power, but her traversal through the ambiguities and porous borders of intimacy adds nuance to her relationship with the world. Within the context of this chapter on object-orientation, it is important to note that Jong herself constitutes an "object" in the symbolic order by virtue of her femininity. Beyond the articulation of love, Jong may be expressing a certain insecurity (as suggested by Sontag), which is founded in her marginalized gender status and drives her toward the embrace of power through photographic knowledge. Prior to this monograph, Jong had published a series of photographs called *Pees on Earth*, shot with a handheld camera aimed between the artist's legs, of her own stream of urine as she urinated in public places. The body of work "chronicles eight years of Jong in her 20's staking claim on her body and place by peeing in the world and photographing it . . . a sequence of intimate 'happening' that Jong declares brought her to an edge in order to discover her own voice."[17] Jong claims her own subjectivity, her female body marking territory and establishing a kind of mastery over her environment. By taking liberty with a gesture which is normally reserved for men—urinating in public—Jong claims power and agency while literally leaving her symbolic mark on the world. According to her website, "Jong sought out alternative public yet private places to document the most intimate moments with herself which in her own words was described as 'pushing and discovering boundaries, and reclaiming my body and place in the world.'"[18] Through this statement, as well as the linguistic play of the project's title, we understand that rather than being an act of aggression, Jong's public urination is an act of peace and intimacy with herself, and a gesture of solidarity with the world. In this body of work, in a strategy that we see extended into the body of work that is the focus of this present inquiry, Jong frames the body and its excretions as operating in excess of subjectivity, describing a relationship of intermingling and communion with the body's environment.

The ejaculation photograph reflects Jong's interest in the symbolic function of body fluids and pushes the notion of intimacy toward the abject by complicating the boundaries among bodies, as well as between the female body and public space. Here, we return to Kristeva's discourse on the borderlander, via her exploration of borderline subjectivities. If we are to understand Jong as the borderline/borderlander—the patient/artist—then we may see her gesture of milking the internal fluids out of her husband's intact body as an act which transforms the inversion of meaning that takes place in abjection into a space of intimacy. By committing her husband and his sexual organ to the status of object, and then symbolically rupturing the seal of his skin through the representation of ejaculation, Jong implies a destitution of subjectivity that exceeds intersubjective relations in a patriarchal, deeply hegemonic visual field. According to Kristeva:

> Rarely does a woman tie her desire and her sexual life to that abjection, which, coming to her from the other, anchors her interiorly in the Other. When that happens, one notes that it is through the expedient of writing that she gets there and on that account she still has quite a way to go within the Oedipal mosaic before identifying with the owner of the penis.[19]

Kristeva indicates that the woman operates so outside of phallic power that even as she uses language to address her desire for the other, she will never operate as the owner of the phallus and never possess its power in language. As Other, she will remain in the status of object of desire, the lost object, the object of mysticism and the unknown, in the interiority of otherness.

From the perspective of feminine jouissance and Irigaray's poetics, as explored in the previous chapter, this otherness is not a loss, rather, a gain in the realm of representation, a seizing of the imaginary and symbolic realms, generating the power to operate poetically and outside the bounds of dominant ideology. Irigaray wishes to discard the power of the phallus and use writing to "tie her desire and her sexual life to that abjection," in Kristeva's postulation. Both Irigaray's and Kristeva's writings aim for an embodied expression of philosophic inquiries, using language—specifically writing—to introduce an alternate framework for thinking through familiar concepts such as gender and speech. This reorientation amounts to a radical revision of intimacy as an ontological collapse, a theme that will become particularly relevant in our discussions of object-orientation. Kristeva emphasizes the embodied nature of the collapse of the sign and the ways these epistemological crises trigger the development of new languages—languages of the body and of emotion. In her examination of her husband's sexual organ as a gesture of love, sexual desire, and the pursuit of knowledge, Jong reorients our somatic experience of sexual difference. Intimacy does not replace love; however, love as a hegemonic structure gives way to intimacy as a nonhierarchical and poetic new paradigm that has been thrust not out of logical reasoning but out of the body. Can intimacy—in its conflation of inside and outside, and its challenges to subjective autonomy—operate as a new language that mirrors a new philosophical epoch?

I continue to explore Kristeva's theories on abjection as a fulcrum for the shift in philosophical positioning of subjectivity as a construct (as seen in post-

1968, poststructuralism, postmodernism) to the question of a post-subjectivity philosophical epoch that will necessitate an overturning of our understanding of love, sexuality, and—by extension—intimacy. By the end of *Powers of Horror*, we are reminded that Kristeva, herself, does not believe in discarding the subject and that abjection, rather than effecting a complete destruction of ideology, subverts it. She reminds us that the analytic relation is one based in love and criticizes analysts who "take the place of the mystic" by allowing themselves to get wrapped up in "mummifying transference."[20] These missteps, she argues, paralyze the free flow of language, and with it the poetry and the void that comprises the unconscious, and the "incompleteness of the speaking being."[21] Kristeva's argument also addresses the role of the artist in society, as she rues "our unwillingness to have a face-to-face confrontation with the abject"[22] and the consequent obsession with achievement and control that results in "art not too far removed from the level of the media."[23] For Kristeva, abjection is a necessary destination for the psyche—arrived at via the intimacy of writing, art, and analysis—but also a place from which we return, newly constituted, in a subjectivity that has perhaps shed some of its ideological rigidity and begun to embody its own freedom.

It must continually be emphasized that Kristeva's interest in radical culture holds an intense skepticism of the identity politics that was, and continues to be, a dominant force of resistance among marginalized communities. She explicitly calls out adherents of such ideological constructs as the antithesis of who she deems as the true artists that, she believes, weave the new languages of subjectivity. She states: "Leaving aside adherents of a feminism that is jealous of conserving its power—the last of the power-seeking ideologies—none will accuse of being a usurper the artist who, even if he does not know it, is an undoer of narcissism and of all imaginary identity as well, sexual included."[24] How do we reconcile Kristeva's resistance to identity politics as a new hegemony, with a desire to articulate a feminist politics through radical intimacy in art practice? Here, we may return to the concept of *revolt* and frame Kristeva's abjection not as a constant destruction but as a revolution from inside to outside, a regurgitation and rejection of values in exchange for catharsis. Kristeva turns to art to replace the catharsis missing from contemporary secular society, delineating the importance of the pure/impure ambivalence in Jong's work. According to Kristeva:

> The various means of *purifying* the abject—the various catharses—make up the history of religions, and end up with that catharsis par excellence called art,

both on the far and near side of religion. Seen from that standpoint, the artistic experience, which is rooted in the abject it utters and by the same token purifies, appears as the essential component of religiosity.[25]

Jong's photograph of her husband's ejaculate conflates the borders between herself and her other—her object—and brings to the fore our questions about feminism, sexual difference, and the effect of intimacy on hegemonic discourses. According to Irigaray, "[f]luid—like that other, inside/outside of philosophical discourse—is, by nature, unstable."[26] By presenting that which on its surface operates in the realm of the masculine—the phallus and its contents—through her own feminine gaze; by inverting the visual hierarchy of the photograph; and by employing the mechanics of fluids as a challenge to patriarchal norms, Jong participates in a reordering of the visual sphere that goes beyond an equalizing (or re-possession) of power structures. In Irigaray's words, "a reckoning with *sperm-fluid* as an obstacle to the generalization of an economy restricted to solids remains in suspension."[27] The feminine does not simply overtake the masculine. The ambivalence between masculine and feminine is revealed in poetic form, through the performance of sexual intimacy, via the gaze of the camera eye.

I now return to Kristeva's *Intimate Revolt* and Lacan's concept of *feminine jouissance* to question how psychoanalysis, despite its patriarchal roots, might continue to provide language for understanding and participating in intimacy in today's shifting ontological climate. I seek to find the roots of a radical ontology fit for the twenty-first century in an ideology so closely aligned with discourses of the modern subject. Kristeva discusses what she refers to as "the radicality of psychoanalysis"[28] for the role it plays in reshaping our relationship to our own interiority. Kristeva makes a forceful argument for the upheaval psychoanalysis brings into the philosophical tradition, through its attention to the physical body and the heterogeneity of its symptoms. She believes that by insisting on the symbiosis of speech-language and the communications of the body, psychoanalysis both rehabilitates the soul and destroys the duality between thinking and feeling, mind and body. Throughout her discourse on abjection, and the intimacy of the analytic experience, Kristeva continually returns to the breakdown of verbal language and the effervescent quality of the alternate languages that take over when logic fails. This effervescence is manifest through the body, in abjection and jouissance. We may understand Kristeva's abjection to be this speech of the body, when it fails to find language to articulate itself. We see the revolt of the bowels or mouth as the rejection of their contents in exchange for formlessness. Jong's image, however, suggests that the formlessness of orgasm can be seen not through the horrific and revolting side of abjection but through the lens of love, knowledge, and jouissance.

For Kristeva, the intimate revolt of psychoanalysis is that it is more than a medical cure; it is a spiritual cure for the secular era in which interiority is threatened by the spectacle. She diverts from the analyst's couch to the Christian world and St. Augustine's *loquela* and discusses intimacy as a world of representation—a world of images, or the imaginary realm. The *loquela*, she explains, is "an intimate word, . . . a speechless voice, at the borders of affect and hallucination, that initiates representation . . . and, later, the signs of language."[29] She states: "This internal vision (an essential element of our 'intimate') is warehoused in the memory and becomes 'vision in thought' only when recollection seizes it."[30] It is therefore the register of memory, and the verbal tool of recollection, that completes the codification of experience from the purely sensory into the singular representation of the speaking subject's unique language system. This is the goal of analysis: to articulate the desire of the subject through speech via the deconstruction of memory-images. Kristeva describes the role of the imaginary in relation to the mind-soul dichotomy:

> Neither perception nor thought, it is image, or imaginary. Between the sensory world and the universe of desensorialized, judging thought, increasingly likened to a separation from reality and identified to an extraneousness, if not a death, the domain of images (of the imaginary) represents this intimacy that will assure the life of the mind, strictly speaking, by despiritualizing it in turn, sensorializing it, corporealizing it.[31]

According to Kristeva, the intimacy of the analyst's couch pulls the purely abstract, disembodied idea down to earth, into the life of the body. There, the duality between mind and body prescribed by Cartesian philosophy is shown to be arbitrary, and the language of the body—the language of the organs and their symptoms—is given voice. Kristeva concludes that "the intimacy that Freudian theory proposes is a recasting of the soul/mind dichotomy, a recasting that encroaches on the somatic. . . . Psychoanalysis introduces the body and soul into understanding or, if you prefer, listening."[32] Through the mutual listening of mind and body, facilitated by the mutual listening of analyst and analysand, the soul appears both as representation in the form of words and images, and as jouissance.

For Kristeva, this jouissance is the key to the creative manifestation of intimacy. Here, we follow Kristeva into the internal sanctum of what she refers to as the *sensorial cave*, an alternative space hidden beneath Plato's cave of representations. From her perspective as a clinician, Kristeva evokes the malady of "autism, which bars a subject's access to language while an often complex sensorial life remains subjacent to this silence."[33] Just below Plato's cave of shadows, Kristeva argues, is another cave, a deeper and more intimate space. She explains:

> Because it is not subjected to language, it is even more profoundly and untranslatably a sensorial cave without symbols—without shadows, in Plato's sense. Within these confines, a sensorial experience (*Erlebnis*)—not informed by cognitive experience (*Erfahrung*) and often definitively resistant to it—can nevertheless find thing-presentations in which it manages to form itself. This sensorial experience, borne by thing-presentations, is an essential part of the psychical experience of every speaking subject, and word-presentations do not necessarily convey it.[34]

How do these thing-presentations find their form and how are they different from word-presentations? How does the sensorial cave differ from the Real? Kristeva offers an alternate view of the role of the artist in the symbolic order by introducing the concept of style, as it relates to the process of writing. She does this in order to show that the sensorial cave, while prelinguistic, still has the capacity to translate into our experience of the real. While autistics "live it as a psychical catastrophe" and hysterics "take jouissance" from "the gap between feeling and saying," "others try to include it in normative discourse by producing the coalescence of sensations and linguistic signs that is called style."[35] For Kristeva, the sensorial cave—that place in our psyche that will never translate into words but that will always manifest itself through the language of the body, emotions, and artistic practice—is the part of our psychic architecture that makes us uniquely singular, irreducible to structure. Here, we find the profound world of the poet, the writer, the artist.

Jong's monograph flows from page to page, traversing both images and words—word-presentations that operate as thing-presentations from the sensorial cave. For Kristeva, the realm of the artist-poet, despite its utilization of words to "represent" concepts, operates on the level of the imaginary—specifically, the prelinguistic imaginary. Kristeva, in fact, likens the sensorial cave to the photographic universe when she refers to the former as "this remote room of inexpressible sensation . . . this camera obscura"[36] that invites us to read Jong's photographic representations as thing-presentations that perform the intimate life of the psyche from deep in the sensorial cave. Kristeva's writings express her appreciation for the mind's ability to travel back in time—

to a preverbal, pre-symbolic archaic cave of the senses. Jong reproduces this psychical process through the lens of her camera, creating thing-presentations not just of her personal memories of falling in love with her husband and getting to know his body but also of the primordial memory of nondifferentiation and nonsexualization.

We see this gender ambivalence taking place in Jong's monograph, particularly as we read it as a linear narrative sequence. As previously discussed, the monograph both begins and ends with images evoking death and the corpse, but what of the professed object of the book—the cock? According to Kristeva in her discussion of abjection and defilement in religious rites, "[t]hrough language and within highly hierarchical religious institutions, man hallucinates partial 'objects'—witnesses to an archaic differentiation of the body on its way toward ego identity, which is also sexual identity."[37] How does the cock as object operate on the level of sexualization and intimacy, and as a hallucinated partial object? Jong's poem begins with the simple fragment "Your cock," written in pencil on a sheet of cheap toilet paper. As if answering the call, the very next image displays her husband's crotch, with a white lily positioned just in front of where the called-for object—the cock—would be visible. Taking the place of Jong's husband's genitals is the luminous white lily, with its pistil, stigma, and stamen— the co-present male and female organs of the flower—limply hanging out as a prosthetic penis. Behind him on the bathroom floor is a roll of toilet paper and a phallic-shaped plastic toilet paper holder. This image evokes castration, as well as an ambivalence of sexual identities. It plays an important role in terms of the radicality of Jong's work, as she presents intimacy as a conflation of masculine and feminine, calling into question the "naturalness" of sexual difference. Her husband operates as the holder of multiple sexes and the phallic object behind him a reminder of the ever-present inscription of the symbolic.

Beginning with the specter of the corpse, Jong's text descends into nondifferentiation of subject and object. We see a constantly disappearing object, an evasive sign that refuses to make itself known. Jong gazes at her husband and sees her own sexual organs mirrored in his body—and we also hear the echo of the void in his open mouth. Further along, Jong presents a fragment of her husband's body as he lays nude atop a mattress, city lights glimmering in the background, his knee bent so that his genitals remain hidden from view. He is once again the bearer of an always-escaping object, an ever-withdrawing object that seems to evade the gaze. His hand coyly covering his genitals, his pose evokes a headless Olympia. A series of images follow—a toy horse on a beach amid windswept wreckage and weeds, his backside and lashes, tropical trees blowing in the wind over a pair of bungalows—evoking the passage of time and a quiet tenderness between lovers.

Finally, in a reflection in a plate glass window, revealing Jong's husband about to penetrate Jong from behind, we encounter sexual intimacy itself as a conflation of inner and outer space, subject and object. In this highly layered image, we see the interior of a room—table and chairs, a laptop, and a vase of flowers, as well as a doorway leading into a deeper chamber of the dwelling into which we are peering—and realize that we are actually situated outdoors with the couple, the wash of blue skies and external wall of a building looming over his shoulder. Opposite this image is the second line of the poem: "Smells like me, Smells like you, Inside." Here, Jong is explicit in her convolution of inner and outer space, and her desire to present her husband's body as a fluid mixture of both of their bodies, nondifferentiated. She pushes our experience of intimacy— an experience vicariously lived through these thing-presentations—to a point of ambivalence between *me* and *you*, woman and man, subject and object, in defiance to the primal scene. Following this pronouncement of ambivalence, Jong begins to reveal the erect penis, as an adjacent moment in their lovemaking features Jong's husband standing behind her, displaying his erect organ within the decontextualized mixture of inside and outside.

Jong turns the primal scene into an obscenity by disrupting the surface of representation and introducing instead a multisensory poetics of intimacy. She also engages the object—the cock—within a sensorial field that contextualizes and constructs a narrative that circulates around its objecthood, in close and perhaps even uncomfortable proximity to the edges of the viewer's subjective visual frame. Foster asks: "Can there be an obscene representation that is not pornographic?"[38] He makes the distinction as follows: "The obscene is a paradoxical representation without a scene to stage the object so that it appears too close to the viewer. The pornographic, on the other hand, is a conventional representation that distances the object so that the viewer is safeguarded as a voyeur."[39] Jong implicates and includes the viewer as voyeur by presenting titillating representations that nevertheless break the screen of conventional representation, inviting a myriad of emotions and sensations. The following image appearing in the monograph is a shot from inside a dark chamber, looking out onto a sunny day in the countryside, as we imagine the couple is on a beach vacation. A photograph of Jong's husband on a sunlit bed follows, his cock once again hidden beneath a sheath of shadows, harsh white highlights performing the same obfuscation function as darkness, making his body's contours elusive to the eye. A subsequent shot framed from knee to navel of his reclined body and flaccid organ features a beam of light so crisp and so delicate that we see the veins and hairs lining his scrotum and the knobby texture of his penis. These details are essential for us to note as we enter the sensorial cave of Jong's consciousness, in order to grasp the scope of her contribution to a discourse of intimacy. Beyond interiority, beyond the conflation of subject and object that is presumed (or desired) to occur in the meeting of two (or more) subjectivities, intimacy in the sensorial cave is predicated on a loss of language and identity, and the shifted stance of the object.

Serving us presentations of sensual moments, and sensual objects that the words on this page can barely graze, Jong invites us into a sensorial cave constructed around her relationship with her husband and his sexual organ. If the sexual relation is nonexistent, precisely because the object of desire maintains the relation in the realm of fantasy, then Jong leverages the object to disrupt the need for a unifying relation and instead offers an intimate landscape beneath language and representation. Throughout the rest of the narrative, Jong's husband's organ grows hard, then soft, pictured as if from his point of view, and absent entirely as in a scene of cunnilingus in which Jong points the camera between her own legs to capture her husband's face buried in her genitals, eyes closed and nose muffled by his partner's neatly trimmed pubic hairs. Her hand juts out between the camera lens and his head, forcing the flash to etch harsh striped shadows across his eyes and forehead. The scene is evocative of the mutual pleasure of Jong and her husband's love, a pleasure not dependent on the organ of our attention. Environmental shots follow, evoking explosions and effervescences, and the release of sexual orgasm. We see Jong's genitals again, this time encased in delicate hair, a tattoo of a teardrop on her left inner thigh evoking both grief and arousal. The camera frame askew, her husband's hand grasps the phallic leg of a white table, and gravity seems to slip. In following pages, energetic images abound—a jumpy lens trapping urban lights in zigzag formations, Jong's husband's cock encased in a pink vibrating cock ring beneath a crookedly hung painting of an idyllic country patio scene. Finally, we are reminded of the tragedy inherent in love with the final line of the poem, scrawled on a fragile square of toilet paper—*till death do us part.*

The Intimacy of Objects

Jong's monograph challenges us to consider the possibilities for intimacy in the field of sexual difference, in which binary codes often operate as limiting factors.

How might a contemporary feminist theory and praxis take an intersectional approach to sexual difference while considering female materiality in its biological and social forms? New paradigms of thinking, as suggested by Kristeva and Irigaray, appear to be taking shape in the contemporary space of art praxis, technology, and intersectional feminism. We see one example in Behar's object-oriented feminism (OOF), "a feminist intervention into philosophical discourses—like speculative realism, particularly its subset OOO [object-oriented ontology], and new materialism—that take objects, things, stuff, and matter as primary."[40] Behar's research helps to recalibrate our position on radical intimacy from one that considers the human subject in a process of continual construction and deconstruction, to one based on objects and their relations to other objects. I explore Behar's contention that "to study objects while being an object oneself . . . allows OOF to develop three important aspects of feminist thinking," which she identifies as *politics, erotics* and *ethics*.[41] This approach proves relevant to an investigation of radical intimacy in contemporary art as Behar, who is a practicing artist herself, interrogates burgeoning philosophical fields heavily invested in contemporary art—particularly performance and participatory practices. Introducing the framework of object-oriented feminism allows us to develop a discourse on sexual intimacy that responds to the material realities of sexuality, gender, and interactivity in the twenty-first century.[42]

Behar makes the bold claim that "object-oriented thinking stands to evolve feminist and postcolonial practices to reconsider how the very processes of objectification work."[43] Does object-oriented thinking simply recodify the ideology of subjectivity, transforming it into an ideology of *objectivity*, thus nullifying the radicality of abjection as an *instability* of the subject and object positions? Does object-oriented thinking merely amount to a new ideology, or does the play of language, meaning, and material allow object-oriented feminism to lend us new language for reading Jong's relationship to the object? Behar's argument hinges on the notion that subjectivity cannot escape its humanist presuppositions, which are themselves couched in patriarchy, capitalism, and the correlationism that defines Kantian discourse and which object-oriented thinkers seek to challenge. Behar asks: "What is the transformative potential for a feminist politics that assumes no transformation, when all things are and remain objects?"[44] The result, she claims, is a deeply material political posture that "is real without being speculative"[45] and which I hypothesize may help bring the arguments in the preceding chapters to the politico-aesthetic field in a manner that emphasizes their material impact, not just their ideological aspirations. In other words, how do the works of our selected artists operate as radical interventions into politics and not solely ideology? Is instability sufficient for radicality or must a new paradigm be established to fulfill these art practices' subversive trajectory?

What does it mean to be objects in relation with other objects? Several qualities help define Behar's conception of OOF and the political agency she attributes to such repositioning. The first is "a classic tenet of feminism, the ethic of care,"[46] which OOF extends to nonhuman objects such as animals, plants, and cyborgs. This stance comprises the *politics* of OOF by challenging the power hierarchies that stabilize patriarchal, hegemonic systems. According to Behar, "[a] feminist perspective imparts political urgency to the ideas that humans and nonhuman objects are of a kind, and that the nonsubjective quality of being an object is grittily, physically realist."[47] By empathizing with our environment, other nonhuman living beings and even mechanical "objects" that display some kind of sentience, we shift our thinking to one of mindfulness and care in a world of diverse singularities. Rather than reject our status as human objects, and the "utilitarianism, instrumentalization, and objectification"[48] that accompany that ontological position, we embrace our objecthood and confront these hegemonies head-on. The desired result of such political strategies is to shed the habits of subject-oriented thinking and forge ethical relations with other objects in the world, including other human objects.

As a practicing artist, Behar celebrates the experimental nature of OOF and its praxis-oriented approach to political activism. She explains: "In any milieu, experimentation is always participatory, always both observational and interventionist. This allows for tinkering with received truths, priming us for alliances with hacked realities, investigative arrangements in living, and radical aesthetic practices in art."[49] In OOF's participatory model, hegemonic thinking is constantly dismantled through intimate exchange between objects, comprising the theory's erotics. Behar states that in contrast to "life- and self-affirming" ideologies such as Audre Lorde's eroticism, for example, "OOF's erotics are better aligned with a version of eroticism theorized by Georges Bataille, as the radical surrender of self in becoming other-than-subject."[50] Though Bataille's approach remains too subject-focused for Behar, if only due to its intention to erode subjectivity as a directional movement from subject to nonsubject, she still calls upon his deployment of absurdity and abjection as an important step toward an object-oriented stance, in which "individuals attain continuity with the object world."[51] Bataille's erotics, couched in abjection, play an important role in the development of object-oriented thinking, breaking down the distinctions between subjects and objects, thereby setting the stage for OOF's object-based ontological field.

The ethics of OOF are not limited to its liberation from the correlationism of subject-oriented humanisms. By embracing "a postmodern legacy in which truth is first and foremost radically relativized,"[52] while nevertheless remaining skeptical toward any approach being taken for a master narrative, OOF invites "an erotics of generative thinking and doing."[53] Furthermore, the theory's insistence on praxis instrumentalizes humans-as-objects' functioning as a set of tools and attributes, to be used in interventionist practices. In "a global culture that fetishizes programmability,"[54] Behar argues, taking a stance as objects comprised of sets of attributes—for example, gender, race, and nationality—allows the object to participate on the materialist level of real relations, rather than the imaginary level of ideal forms such as humanist notions of subjectivity borrowed from patriarchal, capitalist, and Eurocentric belief systems. By focusing on the individual right to self-expression, self-possession, and political agency, do subject-centered humanist positions prevent us from operating as integrated systems in an ethical framework of political relations? Does Kristeva's notion of intimacy as an ambivalence between inside and outside, subject and object, and a return to the pre-symbolic realm, help us to further push past the problematics of representation and sexual difference? Can abjection lead us into the world of object-orientation, in which objects interact transparently as the objects that they are?

In their contribution to Behar's collection, "All Objects Are Deviant: Feminism and Ecological Intimacy," leading object-oriented ontologist Timothy Morton asserts that "because of withdrawal, objects are intrinsically deviant. They are never straight. They always swerve."[55] For Morton, "all beings *withdraw*, that is, they are incapable of being (fully) accessed by another entity"[56] and are therefore always already out of reach. Just like the proximate strangeness of Lacan's extimacy, withdrawal affords objects the space to operate in the *most interior*, with its requisite eternal re-significations of language, memory, and identity. Morton leads us straight into a conversation about intimacy when they note: "*Withdrawal* is a paradoxical term, since it might be better to imagine what it consists in as an *intimacy* or *proximity* that makes a thing impossible to access because it is *too close*. Impossible to 'see' not because they [objects] are too far away but because they are too intimate."[57] Morton's notion of *withdrawal* closely mirrors my present discourse on intimacy, with its built-in contradictions and deconstructive tendencies that imbue concepts with the potential to activate a poetic and generative praxis. Morton is careful to note that "[n]onmetaphysical proximity is better thought when we replace the language of vision with a language of kinesthesis."[58] Rather than replacing a subject-centered correlationist approach with a detached third-party position that could be construed as "objective" in the scientific sense, Morton and their fellow object-oriented thinkers allow the object to occupy a point of view contingent on its own unique positionality or, in Haraway's words, a "situated knowledge." This ability, especially when understood within Behar's insistence on participatory practices, has deep implications to our discussions of radical intimacy in contemporary creative practice.

Morton's notions of withdrawal and deviance can be leveraged to address Lacan's concerns about intimacy in a symbolic order predicated on sexual difference and Irigaray's rebuttal to his phallocentric discourse. By revisiting Irigaray's argument and Jong's monograph through the lens of OOF, we can recalibrate our understanding of objecthood in the intimate field of vision. Morton helps us to expand our own field of inquiry to consider the ethics of object-based thinking in terms of ecological awareness, which Morton defines as "coexistence with beings that are sometimes terrifyingly real at least in spatiotemporal, scale terms, yet downright impossible to locate as constantly present."[59] For Morton, the withdrawal of beings from ontological presence belies their extreme impact on one another in ecological terms. To consider intimacy in the sexual field, and within a society that deems sexual difference paramount to subjectivity, leads us to a discussion of the larger ecosystem of contemporary feminist art practice.

Morton argues that, in effect, Irigaray is an early innovator of object-oriented thinking and that her works embody the radical political stance that OOF aims to insert into the OOO framework. Morton begins with a twist on Plato's Cave, arguing for a philosophy of radical immanence: "Reality is literally all over me—in the sweat from the fire's heat, in the dancing shadows. Reality is already here. Plato seems to want us to struggle away from this reality to see the truth that must reside somewhere outside it. But what is more interesting is that there is a kind of 'beyond' *within* things, not *outside* them."[60] They draw from Kant's transcendental model, noting that just as raindrops exploding against one's scalp, to Kant, are mere phenomena, while the noumena—the thing-in-itself—remains irrevocably inaccessible, all objects are intrinsically withdrawn. Considering the relational aspect of objecthood, they note: "The intimacy of a thing, the intimacy afforded to me by its haptic nudging, reminds me not of its constant presence but of its withdrawnness."[61] Here, they engage intimacy in similar terms as Kristeva, emphasizing its paradoxical proximity that invites, by virtue of its own impossibility, a persistent turning and *working-through* in Kristeva's terms. For Morton, an object's withdrawnness negates its metaphysics of presence, introducing what they refer to as *weird essentialism*: "a return to the kind of essentialism advocated by 1970s feminism, but with a weird twist,"[62] the twist being its swerve away from presence as noumena. How might this ontological redirect support a feminist praxis of radical intimacy, specifically in regard to the sexual relation?

According to Morton, Irigaray's theories embody weird essentialism in that "female physicality cannot be thought either as one or as two but as a weird touching between one and two, a loop-like self-touching denigrated as narcissism."[63] Object-oriented thinking proposes that all objects withdraw and therefore inherently deviate from straight trajectories—a theory that, in many ways, mirrors Lacan's formulation of the Real as that which cannot be symbolized. Rather than the human subject being trapped, lassoed, by the object of desire, OOO proposes that both human and nonhuman objects are lassoed by each other in a circular loop of allure and withdrawnness. Morton concludes: "Thus Irigaray's theory of woman as self-touching loop is in fact a theory of everything."[64] I suggest that Jong leverages photographic representation to articulate the fraught position of the object of desire in the sexual relation and the constant withdrawal of objects, but also to challenge the supposed impossibility with a suggestion of intimacy as the beyond of the sexual relation. According to Sontag, "[b]y furnishing this already crowded world with a duplicate one of images, photography makes us feel that the world is more available than it really is."[65] Photography creates an alternate reality, taking us beyond the inaccessibility of the world through speech and the image. Jong's monograph speaks a poetic language of withdrawal, allure, and abjection. Both her husband and his sexual organ are perpetual objects in withdrawal, never fully available to us—not through the image nor through sexuality. Rather, Jong explores the intimate gray zone between having and being, presence and absence, seeing and touching.

This notion of withdrawal can also be seen in Kristeva's writings. According to Lunning, there is allegiance between Kristeva's *abjection* and objected-oriented ontologist Graham Harman's notion of *allure*. According to Lunning:

> In the explication of both movements is the use of the metaphor as a mode of narration to explain the invisible, the real/not real, and the possibilities of the desire-disgust binary as not only the generator of the gestures of separation and attraction but also the landscape of a potential agency, as they lie at the very limits of representation.[66]

Lunning uses Harman's *allure* to re-situate Kristeva's *abjection* in relation to visual practices, specifically the aesthetic potential of dismantling of identity via the separation of objects from their "qualities" or "attributes." This move proves valuable in object-oriented feminism because it allows feminist "objects" to detach their identifying qualities from their withdrawn beings, leveraging those qualities in performative ways while maintaining self-protection. Qualities describe but do not define the feminist object and generate tension and activity that is attached to the object without necessarily compromising its unknowable internal being. From the standpoint of intimacy, both allure and abjection operate in the ambivalent boundary between inside and outside. Lunning describes Harman's allure as "a special situation in the interaction of objects [. . . that] seems to operate in the aesthetic realms."[67] According to Harman:

> What seems to happen in every form of allure is that a special form of interference occurs in the usual relation between a concealed sensual object and its visible symptoms. What we have, in other words, is strife between an object and its own qualities, which seem to be severed from that object. . . . If objects are what recede from us, qualities are simply defined as whatever *does not* recede, allowing us to bathe in them at every moment.[68]

These malleable constructions between objects and their qualities are also reminiscent of word-presentations and thing-presentations in Kristeva's sensorial cave. Where language fails, it also creates new sensual objects. As Lunning explains, "[a]llure, which provides the process for metaphor, does not take us any closer to the object—but merely translates it into object language."[69] The notion of detaching qualities from always-withdrawn objects opens up both linguistic-poetic possibilities and the possibility of agency for human and nonhuman objects. For artists, this agency proves essential to the construction of new languages, metaphors, and representations.

Lunning describes how allure operates on the level of metaphor, suggesting a kinship to Lacan's failure of the sexual relation but with an ambivalence toward gender. Severed qualities, which operate as markers of identity in a symbolic universe, maintain the objects' poetic instability, allowing them to operate in an intimate mode of failure. Lunning states: "Despite Harman's assertion of ensnarement, these objects made of severed qualities never totally consummate their attraction. Instead, they remain forever in foreplay, in flux, in desire, and sometimes, in disgust. And it is in that strange alchemical exchange that the metaphor is successfully achieved."[70] Though OOO positions itself as an ontology that Harman describes as "A New Theory of Everything,"[71] it is a story told by "human objects" about their own being in relation to other objects in the world. Object-oriented feminism operates beyond the ontology of its patriarchal counterpart, offering a new way of considering Irigaray's and Kristeva's feminist responses to Lacan, as part of a contemporary feminist theory. Lunning emphasizes the relationship between Harman's concept of allure as facilitator of metaphor and Kristeva's literary theory: "Such a metaphoric play is found in much of Kristeva's work on abjection . . . as a gesture of a violent repulsing thrusting aside of 'otherness'—the otherness that is the 'subject/object.' . . . Abjection entails a denial of an aspect of self, a denial that appears desirable within a regime that expects it."[72] Abjection refuses identity in a culture that prizes subjectivity, leaving an object in a state of constant refusal of attributes and therefore in constant metamorphosis. Lunning describes Kristeva's abjection: "It is a state in which meaning breaks down, in which we are left trying to locate the boundaries of self and other, subject and object. It is before language, before words can comfort with their defining and naming functions, and thus removing the dread of the drifting amorphous state between abjection and language."[73] This amorphous state, the space of drifting and immateriality, defines Kristeva's approach to intimacy as an ambivalence, a shimmering state of nondefinition. Here is where the artists of this project operate—not in the complete expulsion associated with abjection but in the intimacy between abjection and language.

Jong frames her husband's sexual organ as both the object of desire and as a detachable, displaceable attribute of the masculine subject/object. She appropriates the castration complex as a structure for resistance to patriarchy, using repetition to de-signify the phallus and its power through the bodily organ that represents it. By doing so in the intimate context of her sexual and love relationship with her husband, Jong performs an ideological and poetic act predicated on the blurring of boundaries between subject and object of desire. Lunning concludes with the following call to action for artists and cultural producers working with objects: "[M]etaphor provides a transformation in identity of subject/objects, and ultimately, in the culture—itself a metaphor for the vast hive of eternally transforming severed qualities—the active agent-objects of cultural production."[74] Artists responding to this invitation leverage identity and materiality and otherwise marginalizing attributes, such as the tropes of femininity, and appropriate the objects that hold power in order to displace the power systems inherent in these object systems. According to Lunning, the ability of metaphor to continually transform these subject/objects "is the key to the revolutionary and paradoxical agency created in the allure of the severed qualities, soldered together through metaphor, to form new objects and, ultimately, the hyperobject theater of transforming cultures."[75] Through Jong's deliberate act of objectification, her husband's sexual organ becomes an active agent-object that symbolizes mutual jouissance and the sensorial cave below language through which intimacy articulates itself. Its withdrawal and reemergence—and its persistent unavailability—express the inherent frustration of intimacy, as well as its wealth of jouissance.

The Object Revolts

Jong's work advances our discussion of radical intimacy, as she complicates the symbolic organization of the love relationship through the appropriation and restaging of the phallus as object of desire. Her contemporary feminist praxis operates politically and ideologically, as well as poetically in intimate revolt, in and through the gendered social landscape. Jong's practice may fulfill Kristeva's call for a culture of revolt that resists spectacle in favor of interiority and love as a journey inwards. In an interview with her own husband, Philippe Sollers, Kristeva advocates "proposing an alternative to that aggressive, efficient and yet constricted mentality encouraged in us by hyperconnection."[76] She elaborates:

> To rethink *inner experience* from this angle is not simply an epistemological challenge . . . with all the revolutions going on, it's the love experience that matters. We could do with a lover's discourse able to take the measure of the intimate by locating it in that interaction we call experience, able to constitute it as creativity, starting over, and renewal.[77]

If we are to accept Kristeva's theories on intimacy, then we enrich our understanding of Jong's monograph as a contribution to a culture of revolt and appreciate its capacity to withdraw female subjectivity into a poetics of objecthood.

How might a discourse of love and objecthood impact the ideological apparatus on a broader scale? Kristeva reminds us of the contribution of the "great rebels" to which her text is devoted "—Aragon, Sartre, Barthes—who revived the privileged place of the imaginary, from the intimate to the political, in order to make their revolt heard."[78] Jong's view of intimacy, presented through the medium of her husband's sexual organ, is an act of revolt for its restoration of the prelinguistic, nondifferentiated poetics of the speaking being in the sensorial cave. Through the journey Jong weaves, in the creative space beyond autistic paralysis, we traverse the pleasure and pain of love, sex, and elusive meaning, and are invited to continually rethink Lacan's views on the sexual relation. We see the ways that Jong, Irigaray, and Kristeva unravel the structures imposed by sexual difference, as well as the broader notions of subjectivity and desire. We also witness a radical reorientation of our attachment to subjectivity as a defining trait of human ontology and the impact of its replacement by an object-oriented frame. A tremendous amount of work in the field of feminist art and practice has been done on the level of the subject, including its destabilization in embodiment, poetic language, and relationality. In order to make their revolt heard, however, artists working with radical intimacy must make the traversal from the intimate to the political, as well as embed the one in the other. In the final chapters of the book, I explore the political stakes of art practices that employ radical intimacy as a tool, including the practice of feminist object-orientation, and suggest the ways that a non-subject-based mode of thinking may represent the next phase of radical philosophy, visualized in the works of contemporary artists.

Part IV

The Politics of Subjects and Objects

6

Postcolonial Intimacy

And this is the hope on offer: to be objects, generously and generatively, together; to recognize how fraught that position is, always for all parties, as power articulates itself through each and every arrangement of objects; and from this recognition about objecthood, which is to say self-recognition in objecthood, to cultivate a praxis of care.

—*Katherine Behar*[1]

Exposing the Object

Using the language of radical intimacy, abjection, and revolt, Chapters 6 and 7 examine the political implications of complicating subject-object relations and the potential political power of assuming objecthood. Through experimental praxes, artists and theorists question subjectivity, desire, and the body. In these final chapters, I conclude my present research on radical intimacy with a reflection on its operations in the current aesthetic and political climate.

In Althusser's ideological model, a society's laws and cultural institutions are mutually complicit in constructing subjects that reify and mandate their own (and others') subjectivity to ideology. These two superstructures—legal-political and ideological—rest upon the economic base; therefore, law, culture, and capital are mutually dependent. Althusser argues that ideology's "concrete forms are realized in the Ideological State Apparatuses . . . inserted into practices governed by the rituals of the ISAs,"[2] which include its cultural and political institutions. Furthermore, "the state apparatus secures by repression . . . the political conditions for the action of the Ideological State Apparatuses," conditions "which are in the last resort relations of exploitation."[3] In Althusser's model, the legal-political and ideological apparatuses work symbiotically to construct and maintain subjects through rituals and practices endemic to those institutions.

Contemporary artists employing radical intimacy participate in the subversion of the ISA from within one of its internal components—the institution of art, its production and dissemination. The artists in this book destabilize the subject-object divide, acting as important mediators of intimate revolt as it operates poetically and politically to disrupt and reorient hegemonic thinking.

This chapter maintains its framing through object-oriented feminism, in mutual consideration with Kristeva's abjection and revolt. While suggesting that OOF reorients the subject-object divide to disorient and question the hegemony of ideology, I also heed Oliver's warning that, "taken to its extreme, the deconstruction of the subject threatens the politics of radical democracy and an ethics of difference, both of which require the possibility of finding some means of communication across differences."[4] I continue to examine the nuances of OOF's object-oriented discourse to avoid using objecthood as a mere semantic substitution for subjectivity and to explore the possibility that occupying a performative stance of solidarity with objects offers political agency through radical intimacy. I suggest that object-oriented feminism presents a viable political challenge to subjectivity, without necessarily compromising individual or artistic freedom, and thereby fosters interconnectedness and communication through radical intimacy. Behar cautions that, "[o]n the one hand, the separateness of objects recalls . . . political affiliation of individuals mobilizing around an issue without being reduced to group identity. But on the other, withdrawn objects suggest an end to affiliation as such, and with it the neoliberal imperative to network individuals into populations."[5] According to Behar, "[t]his ambiguity should give us pause."[6] OOF's contribution helps us consider Kristeva's concerns about the current state of intimate revolt in the arts, by providing examples of contemporary experimental praxis that participate in continual, radical questioning through the intimate. I begin with an exploration of Barbara DeGenevieve's *The Panhandler Project*, a series of photographs and a video that the artist produced in order to challenge assumptions about objectification and exploitation of marginalized people. I then introduce the series *New Natives* and accompanying video *Hula Kahiko Kane*, a body of work by Joseph Maida to problematize the notion of the object in a hegemonic medium and examine how intimacy complicates the subject-object divide implicated in objectification. In the next and final chapter, I will introduce the works of Lorraine O'Grady, whose essay "Olympia's Maid: Reclaiming Black Female Subjectivity" and associated artwork *The Clearing* help us to circle back to the question of subjectivity and its importance for marginalized communities. Finally, I look deeper at the challenges that Behar's object-oriented feminism poses to the correlationism of subject-oriented discourses and OOF's contribution as both theory and practice-based artistic activism. I conclude the final chapter (and the book) with a suggestion that intimacy—specifically *radical intimacy* in artistic practice—destabilizes the subject-object binary and forces us to continually question our own status as subjects, which necessarily subverts the politics of subjectivity and the institution of art.

This book explores intimacy as an instability between inner and outer space, and an inherently paradoxical concept that requires boundaries and edges to be continually breached in order to articulate itself. These chapters work to understand how the cultural landscape of our century promotes, and yet simultaneously complicates intimacy, as power continues to reveal its symbiosis with the ideological fabric of our societies and the artistic forms that we use to describe that reality. Furthermore, this final section positions object-oriented feminism as a useful performative paradigm for exploring the tension between subject-formation and objectification in representational practices.

Power and Possession: Barbara DeGenevieve's *The Panhandler Project*

In her introduction to OOF, Behar presents *The Panhandler Project*, a photographic series by Barbara DeGenevieve, for which the artist paid homeless African American men to pose nude in a hotel room. Explicit in DeGenevieve's discourse is her own questioning of her status as "a white female university professor"[7] and the power dynamics implicit in the work that deliberately invite concerns about exploitation and objectification. DeGenevieve offers the following statement on the project:

> It is routine to denounce this project as an instance of exploitation and objectification of a cultural group to which I don't belong. I am interested in challenging these accusations as a predictable response to an unexamined political correctness, which in fact, removes any agency these men have in making the decision to work with me ... I believe that the ethical and social dilemmas that this project presents to the viewer involve long overdue conversations about the volatile issues that arise with regard to race, class, and the sexualization of bodies of men, who are rarely if ever seen as sexual objects.[8]

Behar goes into little detail about the project but asserts that it "reflects a critical question for object-oriented feminism: is it time to abandon subject-oriented terms like control, consent, and coercion if our aim is object-oriented self-possession?"[9] We must continue questioning whether the mere action of asserting humans' ontological status as objects is sufficient to be termed "radical thought" and whether this intention is actualized in meaningful, ethical, and politically effective ways. Is the praxis component of OOF significant enough as radical activity to render radical intimacies and their artistic manifestations crucial actors in a culture of political revolt? At the time of the project, DeGenevieve was a professor of photography at the School of the Art Institute of Chicago, a prestigious art academy. She photographed five men who she met on the streets of Chicago and who agreed to pose nude for her in exchange for $100 in cash, meals, and a night's rest at the hotel. The resulting documentation includes the photographic portraits, as well as a 28-minute video comprised of footage of each portrait session, shot by DeGenevieve's various assistants who also serve as occasional interlopers into the dynamic between photographer and model. Even more than the still photographs, the video provides valuable information about the exchanges of power between DeGenevieve and each man, her attempts to steer the sessions in directions she deems desirable for her project, and the underlying ideological frameworks that undergird the entire scene. DeGenevieve insists that her project addresses a simple question of exploitation: Should we understand these men as having been exploited and objectified due to the fact that they are homeless? She contends that we should not. A deeper look at the video, however, brings to light a far more complex backdrop of historical, institutional, and, ultimately, ideological abuses of the men's agency and identity. The social and political contexts of the project come wrapped in the skein of the intimate, with its ambivalent shifting of edges, conflation of identity and environment, and the complicity of enjoyment.

The video begins with Gordon K. Wooten, whose portrait *Gordon #6* presents as demure, inviting, and seductive, almost feminized. In the photograph, Wooten lays on his right side, left leg curled up toward his chest, his left arm draped across his body to lightly hold his left foot. The gold-striped sheets and warm lamp glow in the background lend the scene a homey, yet luxurious, feel, and his melancholic expression appears forlorn as he presses his face into the bed and gazes into the camera. The contortions of his body conceal his genitals, allowing his sexuality to communicate through the perfect synthesis of seduction, vulnerability, and the visual tropes of the intimate. Overall, the portrait feels soft and emotionally layered, almost an affront to the notion of cool exploitation that DeGenevieve claims to debunk. A very different reality is revealed in the behind-the-scenes footage depicted in the video, which is peppered with almost-constant laughter and the perpetuation of deeply embedded race dynamics. In one prominent example, the video opens with Wooten toweling off after a shower, happily singing "Singin' in the Rain." He exclaims: "Ooh that feel good! . . . And they use so many towels! Ooh, these rich people! I've got to become rich!" In the foreground sits a partially emptied bottle of Palo Viejo Puerto Rican rum, a glass of the liquor, and a pack of menthol cigarettes. This opening fragment emphasizes the disparity between Gordon's material reality and DeGenevieve's economic power. It also nods uncomfortably toward the painful history of minstrel shows, which cemented the caricature of the "happy Negro" into white consciousness. In *Scenes of Subjection*, an exposition of slavery-themed melodrama and the tradition of minstrelsy, Saidiya Hartman argues:

> The affiliation of performance and blackness can be attributed to the spectacularization of black pain and racist conceptions of Negro nature as carefree, infantile, hedonistic, and indifferent to suffering and to an interested misreading of the interdependence of labor and song common among the enslaved. The constitution of blackness as an abject and degraded condition and the fascination with the other's enjoyment went hand in hand.[10]

Wooten's performance reads as both a genuine expression of joy after the rare clean shower and, by virtue of DeGenevieve's choice to highlight this moment and open her video with it, a repetition of a historical ritual that continues to assuage the conscience of a white supremacist culture.

DeGenevieve's chosen languaging around the project reveals its direct implications to our discussion on abjection and objecthood. The work was presented in a 2006 exhibition at Gallery 400 at the University of Illinois in Chicago, entitled *Objectifying the Abject: Exploitation, Political (In)Correctness and Ethical Dilemmas*. The artist explicitly labels the men's abjection as the object of the inquiry, celebrates (and challenges) the political incorrectness of the project, and acknowledges the ethical gray area traversed by its economy. Seemingly in alignment with Kristeva's incredulity of identity politics, according to catalogue essayist Michael Weinstein, DeGenevieve "advances beyond the debates that have become rigidly frozen, opening up new possibilities for relations among social groups and for experimentation with social identity."[11] Implicit throughout is that the men's abjection is taken for granted—it is the foundational assumption of the project. How is abjection being qualified in this scenario? Implied is that the men's downtrodden social and economic status places them at the lowest rungs of society; however, abjection, as elaborated by Kristeva, is a rejection and reorientation of these very social strata, as emblemized in identity. The abjection itself makes the project possible, because the ambiguity of categorization is at the center of DeGenevieve's contention that the men are empowered in their agency. Weinstein claims that DeGenevieve "restages in contemporary terms an imaginary associated with racist discourse in which the civilized and vulnerable white woman is imperiled by the figure of the lustful, feral black male" and that she actually "puts that imaginary to rest once and for all."[12] Besides the absurdity of the notion that one white artist can put these nefarious and historically ingrained imaginaries to rest, the assertion that play and enjoyment somehow neutralize these racist narratives ignores the much more potent forces that abjection and jouissance bring to light. Without abjection, and without the perceived social dominance of one body over another, enjoyment cannot be had. This project is not about equalization; it is in fact completely dependent on power differentials as well as the destabilization of identities that these differentials effect. By performing political "incorrectness" in the ethical gray zone, I suggest that DeGenevieve amplifies the object status of the men, rather than creating a space for agency and human compassion.

Wooten continues to perform for both the still and video cameras as DeGenevieve directs him on the bed. At one point, he yells "cheese!" while holding his fingers in peace gestures and diverts the shoot toward his own ends. When DeGenevieve implores him to put the drink down for a photo, he insists, "I want that one for myself" and succeeds in having her capture him comically protruding his tongue into the glass of liquor, a photo that makes it into DeGenevieve's video in a segment at the end of each sitter's sequence that shows outtakes from the shoot. Wooten knows what DeGenevieve wants—a seductive and serious intimacy worthy of art gallery walls, or, in her words, "serious, sexy, maybe romantic... if you can pull that off"[13]—and continuously undermines that very same energy between each frame. He capitulates, performs, and gives her what she paid for but not without inserting his own levity. Is Wooten's seemingly joyful participation the response that DeGenevieve wants us to see in order to support her rejection of accusations of exploitation? Or might we once again draw a parallel to the painful histories of the performance of blackness for white audiences? Hartman explains: "On the minstrel stage, the comic inversions, bawdy humor, and lampooning of class hierarchies nonetheless operated within the confines of the tolerable, particularly since this transgression of order occurred by reproducing the abject status of blackness."[14] Does DeGenevieve's project actually reveal agency and participation on the part of the homeless men, thereby successfully refuting claims of exploitation? Or is it just another manifestation of an attempt to alleviate white guilt via the red herring of consent and the appearance of pleasure?

DeGenevieve claims that all of the men, when asked whether they were being exploited, answered "no."[15] The video provides several examples of such exchanges, which complicate our reading of the project as well as DeGenevieve's argument about its merits as social critique. At the start of Leon "Twin Dog" Pitcher's shoot, the conversation reveals that another man who Pitcher had accompanied to the hotel had decided at the last minute not to participate, leaving Pitcher to take his place. Pitcher indicates that he is "grateful" that this happened because he would have asked DeGenevieve if he could participate regardless. He states: "I already knew I was gonna make the proposition to *you*." He spends the shoot flirting with DeGenevieve and noting his perception of her desires and arousal. He appears confident and in charge, as well as an eager participant in the process.

Similarly, during Wooten's shoot, DeGenevieve and her off-screen assistant try to explain the academic context of the project as Wooten argues that "homeless people are no different than anybody else" and therefore should not be singled out as being vulnerable to exploitation. DeGenevieve fervently agrees yet insists that the project is necessary to "overturn" the academic discourse about exploitation of vulnerable populations. She claims, "just because you're homeless, there's gonna be somebody who says I'm exploiting you, because I've asked you to take your clothes off . . . that is the ultimate in the art world, of exploitation." Wooten's response is to throw the towel off with a big grin and exclaim, "Shit, if I made 50,000 a year I'd take my clothes off!" Wooten seems intent on proving that he is there by choice, that he wants to participate in the exchange regardless of his economic position, and that he is absolutely not being exploited. In a later cut, however, he emphatically emotes: "You are so gullible! All humans on this earth are gullible. There is nothing on this earth that any human out here won't do." She asks him if he is gullible, and he cautiously admits that he is, momentarily opening up a dialogue that reveals a personal vulnerability. DeGenevieve responds playfully, "Well, you're really gullible because you thought I was gonna give you a hundred bucks for doing this." The mood in the room thickens for a moment and Wooten responds: "No, I'm not real gullible cause if I don't get a hundred bucks you gonna die!" He then laughs and says that he's kidding, and the room once again erupts with laughter. The confrontation reveals the underlying tension between the homeless men's real economic need and DeGenevieve's power to offer and then withdraw their earned pay, as well as a perverse pleasure she seems to take from wielding that power both financially and psychologically. It also underlines the threat of violence that sits beneath the surface of the entire project—violence that may appear to be one-sided, from the men toward the white photographer, but is actually interwoven into the fabric of the intimacy they share, itself founded on power differentials.

By peddling in the pleasures of sexual intimacy, DeGenevieve seems to want to prove that her project is enjoyable for all involved. Inescapable, however, are the blatant fact of sexual labor and the abject conditions of the men's lives outside the hotel room, both of which create a mixture of pleasure and pain inherent to the jouissance at play in the scenes. The model that most explicitly embodies sexual reciprocity is Michael Stewart. In the first portion of his shoot, he has an erection, which clearly excites DeGenevieve as she comments lasciviously on his "hot" pose and asks for the "sexiest" look he can give her. She later orders pornographic movies for Stewart, to assist him in achieving the erection desired for the next portrait. As he sits quietly watching the television and sporting the requisite symbol of arousal, DeGenevieve makes jokes and mimics the sexual sounds emitting from the screen. The scene is noteworthy for her apparent discomfort and simultaneous excitement when faced with the material reality of sexuality, signified in Stewart's arousal. Through it all, Stewart appears relaxed and compliant, fully occupying his position as the producer of sexual labor while also seeming to take genuine pleasure from the situation. We are left wondering the extent to which his complicity is a performance enacted to please his client, how much it reflects his own sexual enjoyment, and the ways that these two poles intersect and support one another. I suggest that DeGenevieve's motivations are also ambivalent, likely not even fully visible to her, and are variously academic and artistic, as well as sexual in nature. We realize that this ambivalence exists in each man's shoot in a different form and that the enactment of sexual objectification and exploitation are actually inseparable from the apparent sexual enjoyment of the participants.

DeGenevieve's video is an essential companion to the photographic portraits, providing a platform for each model to comment on the scenario and continuously complicating our understanding of who is in charge, whether exploitation is taking place, and the extent to which the homeless men are being objectified. What emerges from the narrative, however, is not a simple binary response to the question of exploitation and objectification but a complex picture of the layers of objectification that have formed each person's sense of themselves and the situation. In each shoot, we witness the interchange of three individuals—DeGenevieve, her assistant, and the homeless man—each of whom occupy a historically marginalized position. Each person performs their position and their status as human object, as described in OOF, calling attention to their ideological makeup while simultaneously working to overturn it. In one exchange with the model Lester "Dee" Sanders, a soft-spoken man of a larger stature than the other men, DeGenevieve's young assistant jumps into the frame for an outtake. The assistant, identified as V. Rodriguez in the credits, wears low-slung jeans, a sports jersey, an athletic cap and sneakers, and adopts a mock fighting stance while gleefully bouncing up and down on the bed over Sanders, who lays nude in a dramatic defensive pose as if he were being beaten. While I do not presume to know Rodriguez's self-identified sexual, racial, or gender identity, they present as transmasculine and white (or at the very least non-Black), and they are considerably smaller than Sanders. The pair's performance of white violence upon a Black body disturbingly echoes the military and police brutality that has become more visible in the media in recent years while also emphasizing Rodriguez's own position as a marginalized person vulnerable to assault, and their potential desire to undermine that fear by asserting domination in a physically safe environment. The scene frighteningly brings to light the complicity of all participants in re-creating images of such violence, thereby normalizing and perpetuating it via laughter and fun.

In the video, the men do get an opportunity to turn the tables on DeGenevieve, alluding to the question of the extent to which DeGenevieve wishes to complicate her own stated intent. The men participate in challenging the artist's claim that consent equals agency, while also asserting their own power in the scenario. Their personhood comes through in their words, actions, and physical gestures. They shift the energy from sexy to humorous and back again, remain stoic while she cracks awkward sexual jokes, verbally challenge the assumptions and premises undergirding her project, and reveal their own desire to be seen as sexual objects. Perhaps more revealingly, the unfolding of each shoot unveils how DeGenevieve herself behaves in ways that mirror the problematic histories of white domination over bodies of color. At one point as DeGenevieve directs Wooten's pose, she physically adjusts his leg, slaps his buttocks and says, "Oh, you're ashy" before proceeding to rub lotion on his backside. The exchange follows an earlier moment when Wooten had explicitly asked if he was ashy before the start of the shoot, prompting lighthearted jokes and laughter. The subsequent scene shows DeGenevieve becoming more confident in taking control over Wooten's body, commenting on racially specific attributes, and allowing herself the right to touch and groom him to her liking. After looking on impassively for a moment, Wooten breaks the tension by exclaiming, "I don't like her nerve! 'You ashy'" and all participants laugh. The camera then cuts to

Wooten saying, "everybody's a joke, but that's what makes life loveable," to which DeGenevieve responds by ordering him to freeze mid-gesture so she can snap a photo. The scene becomes stilted and frozen, offering a moment to reflect on the contrived nature of each expression and the erasure in the final formal photograph of Wooten's possible feelings of violation—as well as the potential of his ambivalent enjoyment—in being touched.

In her short exploration of *The Panhandler Project*, Behar indicates that "OOF's fundamental tension between objectification and self-possession is brought to the surface"[16] in DeGenevieve's work. Notable in both Behar's exemplification of the project in her introduction to OOF and my own reading of the project is that the question of exploitation and objectification is an oversimplification. According to Behar: "OOF emphasizes ontology as a political arrangement, realism as an arena for self-possession and relation, and objecthood as a situational orientation, so as to apprehend and alter objects' intersectional prospects for self-determination, solidarity, and resistance. The internal resistant quality of objects may deserve our closest attention."[17] From this perspective, *The Panhandler Project* and, particularly, the video operate as an arena for complicating the intersectional relations among human objects who occupy varying degrees of power and privilege. While DeGenevieve appears to aspire to solidarity with the homeless men in order to demonstrate the lack of objectification taking place in her project, it is the men's "internal resistant quality" in their occupation of the objectified position that makes the stronger statement. By participating in this way, they shine light on the deeper patterns of exploitation that necessarily come to the surface through the radicality of intimacy, implicating DeGenevieve in much broader ways than the simple ethical questions presented by this particular project's arrangement of labor.

Photography in the Hegemonic Field: Joseph Maida's *New Natives*

My questions about objectification and exploitation in a postcolonial, hegemonic field lead me to an examination of Maida's work, who I suggest utilizes radical intimacy to complicate the very notion of objectification, situating his practice in an ambiguous ideological and political space. I introduce Maida's work to examine the ideological mechanisms at play in his project *New Natives*, and the aesthetic and ethical implications of shifting to an object-oriented model of inquiry. By doing so, I continue to expand our discussion on radical intimacy to consider the dangers of objectifying marginalized bodies—specifically, the depiction of human beings as objects of sexual desire, in a gray zone of individual agency—and the potential of assuming agency, and intimacy, through objecthood. I suggest that object-oriented feminism gives us access to a nuanced vocabulary of intimacy, with which to reframe moments of objectification as critical inquiries into the ideological mechanisms of representation and the processes of subjectification that construct modern societies. By complicating subject-object relations through intimate practice, the artists discussed in this book participate in a radical reordering of subjectivity and ideology. How do we deal with the act of looking, and the engagement of "subjects" that operate as such in their self-conception, while occupying unequal power positions in the visual field? In other words, when one "subject" is invariably doomed to being objectified due to the power dynamics at play, is there a danger to claiming objecthood a priori? Behar responds to such counterarguments by stating that "speculative realism's nonanthropocentric conception of the world as a pluralist population of objects . . . provides a welcome respite from theories of subjecthood that many feminist philosophers point out are fundamentally dependent on the logic of phallocentrism"[18] as is articulated, for example, in Irigaray's critique of Lacan. For Behar and her fellow object-oriented feminists, the real and most usable form of radicality does not stop at the complication of subject and object but proceeds to claim universal objecthood as an interventionist strategy. Though Behar and her fellow authors offer numerous examples from the aesthetic field, some of which I will cite, I will refocus these arguments onto the works in which I am most invested in this book—those offering an intimate revolt in the lineage of Kristeva.

Maida is a New York City-based contemporary American artist working primarily in photography, video, and research-based practices. *Hula Kahiko Kane* is a 1-minute, 24-second video that accompanies Maida's project *New Natives*, for which he photographed young Hawaiian men who aspire to become models and whom he found via social media. An exhibition at Daniel Cooney Gallery in New York City in 2013 presented *Hula Kahiko Kane* alongside the still portraits from *New Natives*.[19] The photographs in *New Natives* were shot on a large-format camera near the city of Honolulu but away from mainstream tourist destinations, with the locations selected by the models themselves. The men are dressed in a combination of "Western" and "traditional" attire, also self-selected. Maida puts significant attention on the men's ethnic heritage, citing their own self-identifications—almost always plural—in each image title. Examples include *Nick (Hawaiian, Chinese, Portuguese, Irish, Norwegian, German)*, 2013, and *Remy (Japanese, Black, White, Cherokee)*, 2012. While the range of the men's gender expressions is as varied as their heritage, Maida chooses not to reveal or explicitly name their sexual identities. The tension between words and images, as well as slippages in epistemological and ontological meaning, is striking in this work and extends to the video of my interest.

Maida has long been interested in the relationship between the United States, East Asia, and the Pacific Rim. Prior to his work in Hawaii, from 2007 to 2012, Maida produced a series in Japan entitled *Dream Factory*, which proposed to explore "the promises and shortcomings of postwar Japan as it reflects and interprets the American Dream."[20] Maida then shifted the locus of his practice to Hawaii, a liminal space between "East" and "West," "America" and "Japan," with the aspiring models representing the complexities of postwar identity in constructions of masculinity. He partially credits the 2008 election of Barack Obama—in the words of Elizabeth Avedon, "the first non-white, non-mainland [in fact, Hawaiian-born] elected President of the United States"[21]— as inspiration for *New Natives*. This anecdote elucidates the engagement of the artist with contemporary global politics and its ideologies. Furthermore, it distills the relevance of this project to a discussion on the nature of intimacy in a contemporary postcolonial globalized society in which subjectivities and politics are interpellated by social media, image-sharing, and the complexities of identity in the twenty-first century.

Maida's discourse around *New Natives*, and the optics of the work itself, suggests a cultural hybridity at play. Both the title and the relationship between Maida and the models indicate a hierarchy that positions Maida (and his camera) as the colonizer and the model as the object of desire and intrigue. In an interview with Matthew Leifheit in *ArtFCity*, Maida states, "I'm interested in the relativity of exoticism, because if you're from Hawaii, the landscape is not exotic. New York is exotic."[22] This statement points to a desire on Maida's part to destabilize the power imbalance inherent in the work and to question the very notion of "otherness" and cultural hegemony that it implies. If Maida's work is meant to highlight complexities and upend our thinking about categories, to what extent is he successful? Furthermore, where might the work lead us in terms of considering intimacy—and beauty—in the twenty-first century, when conversations about identity, political power, and the right of representation dominate the discourses pertaining to our arts institutions?

On the project's surface, Maida appears to succumb to the pleasures of the colonial gaze, finding beauty and eroticism in the bodies of the underrepresented. This is evidenced by the *Huffington Post*'s headline "8 Scantily Clad Reasons to

Rethink Your Understanding of Masculinity" followed up with a nod to "all you readers who requested sensuous images of macho men."[23] Maida himself, however, insists that he is actually "resisting" the notion of beauty in this work by emphasizing its subjective nature and hegemonic undertones. In response to Leifheit's question "Do you find these men beautiful?," Maida states:

> What I'm fascinated with in these subjects is that they have aspirations to be models, to be recognized for how they look and many of the cues that they receive come from a mainstream [American] approach to masculinity. These guys don't fit that bill. They can't. They're not built in a way that can look like that. And the idea that they would aspire to be something that doesn't fit into a traditional or conventional idea of beauty is really interesting to me.[24]

Maida's cool distance as he discusses *New Natives* effects a separation between himself as a subject of desire and the men seeking affirmation and approval from the Western gaze. A harsher critic may argue that Maida takes advantage of the men's aspirations—hopes and dreams stoked by a powerful American ideological machine—to gain access to a privileged view of the exotic Other for the purposes of erotic and aesthetic titillation. In response to Leifheit's question about "fetishizing otherness" in the lineage of painters such as Gaugin, Maida replies: "Well, the big difference is that now the local people are aware of those depictions of themselves, and for better or for worse are informed by those things . . . Hawaii is not this remote place in the middle of the ocean that has no contact."[25] It appears, however, that despite Maida's thoughtful conceptualism, the project still teeters on the edge of exploitation, if only at the hands of mainstream media—a dangerous proposition in the current era, particularly for an artist with Maida's professional and academic pedigree.[26]

How do we reconcile these concerns with a genuine respect for Maida as an artist and thinker? I suggest that the video *Hula Kahiko Kane* opens up a new space of intimacy not readily available in the still images from *New Natives* and allows Maida's work to be read outside of—and alongside—rigid notions of cultural appropriation, exploitation, and beauty. This shifted critical framework invites a different kind of questioning on the relationship between Maida and his subjects that does not ignore the problems of representation evident on the work's surface, but actually leverages those unavoidable concerns toward an expanded discourse on intimacy between postcolonial subjects. According to Pratt and Rosner, "[t]he intimate directs us to an ethical stance toward the world—namely, an approach that neither simplifies nor stereotypes but is attentive to specific histories and geographies."[27] My hope is that such conversations produce new options for sensitively addressing issues of freedom, responsibility, and artistic representation in polarized, hegemonic societies. My research suggests that intimacy plays an integral role in this process and Maida's work an important reference point. Intimacy seems built-in to the structure of Maida's project. As an openly gay photographer with several other bodies of work exploring sexuality and desire among men—including a series of intimate portraits of his partner Isaac[28]—Maida's practice carries with it the ideological implications and complications of sexual desire between photographer and model. His Instagram-based still-life series *Things "R" Queer* deconstructs what he refers to as "food porn" and assigns queerness to such reordered arrangements of mouth-watering artificiality and seductive visual fantasy.[29] His work continuously highlights performance and visual codes as signifiers for sexuality, desire, and identity—codes that he claims to question.

Maida's questioning and the instability that it engenders are eloquently and provocatively explored in *Hula Kahiko Kane*. The video documents the performance of a "sacred, pre-Western hula by one of Hawaii's premiere male dancers."[30] Rather than scoring the dance with the chants and drumbeats that typically accompany such performances, Maida overlays the accelerated beat of his own heart as the rhythm of the video. Unlike the still portraits from *New Natives*, in which he operates as a silent and invisible watcher—the unseen half of a pair—Maida infuses the video with his own excitement. We cannot describe the nature of this excitement—whether it signifies sexual arousal, fear, intrigue, identification with the dancer's physical catharsis, or other state of apotheosis—but we can note the ways in which it recodes the video, and the dance, into a space of intimacy.

If we are to understand intimacy as an instability of borders, a paradox and self-defeating prophesy that nevertheless is poetically and aesthetically generative in terms of creating and re-creating new possibilities, then we glimpse an opening for Maida's work to be discussed in this context. He is invited on a private excursion and presumably given access to the men's interior, ideologically coded psychical space. This interior sanctum is marked by their plural identities and their sexual expressions, the latter of which remain uncoded by symbolic language in *New Natives*. The inclusion of *Hula Kahiko Kane* into the project more directly invites us into a discourse of intimacy by virtue of two important characteristics of his practice. First, Maida reveals *his own* interior expression—physical, emotional, and spiritual—in relation to the dancer's performance; and second, he is granted access to a sacred ritual that suggests an access point to Kristeva's project of "reconnecting the semiotic and the symbolic, [by which] art can achieve a transformation of meaning and subjectivity."[31] Maida uses the heartbeat to signify the multitude of interpretations and understandings that he intends for his work to provoke. His artist's statement asserts: "A primal signifier of life, fear, and excitement, the accelerated pulse invites interpretations that are as layered as the dance itself."[32] Here, we also see the intimate materiality of the bodily organ as it exceeds subjectivity, responding to and articulating the ambiguity of borders between himself and the object of his gaze. Maida's excitement can be interpreted in a variety of ways, but the implication of sexual arousal as it relates to the concept of "primal" or primordial nature should at least be considered. By unsealing his own interiority—specifically the marginalized subjectivity and unstable borders of queerness, in combination with the arousal of the postcolonial gaze—Maida exposes his position as excited observer shaped by the ideological fabric of hegemony and the weight of sexual desire in the visual field. The ambiguity of the eroticism between Maida and his subjects, and the slippage of subjective positions among them (as suggested by the decentered, re-signified heartbeat), is part of the poetic slippage of the work and suggests an instability in identity and categorization.

Such complexities are mirrored in the technology of photography itself, as is articulated by Christopher Pinney in *Photography's Other Histories*. According to Pinney, "[a] greater sense of the fragility and instability of the relationship between images and their contexts might allow the exploration of why certain images prove capable of recoding while others are more resistant, and many others are completely intractable."[33] Through his interrogations of masculinity, beauty, and identity, Maida strives to recode these ideologies, but are his images capable of the revolt he suggests? Here, I invoke Kristeva to segue back to my continued discussion of radical intimacy and its revolutionary potential in the political-aesthetic field. Kristeva defines the intimate as a questioning of prescribed meanings and a toppling of the hierarchy of societal values, an operation that takes place through discourse. The mode of questioning and challenging implied in Maida's discourse calls forth Kristeva's notion of "revolt" which she offers as an alternative to what she considers to be an inadequate culture of subversion in aesthetics and politics. Kristeva insists that in addition to exploring economic and psychical contradictions, a culture of revolt can be aesthetic, poetic—*beautiful*—lest it devolve into a mere spectacle of politics mired in categorization. According to Kristeva:

> To speak of revolt does not call to mind integration, inclusion, an unchanging social idyll but underscores that economic, psychological, and spiritual

contradictions exist and also that these contradictions are permanent: they are not solvable. When one recognizes that the contradictions of thought and society are not soluble, then revolt—with its risks—appears as a continuous necessity for keeping alive the psyche, thought and the social link itself.[34]

How, then, might an aesthetic culture of revolt operate through the mediation of intimacy? In her essay on abjection, Kristeva discusses rites that "shift the *border* . . . that separates the body's territory from the signifying chain; [that] illustrate the boundary between semiotic authority and symbolic law."[35] Though Maida's work does not directly engage abjection, defilement, or the explicit, physical excesses of the body, the movements generated by the dancer's body and the heartbeat generated by the watcher's body illustrate and subsequently destabilize the border between subject and object, observer and observed. On the surface, we ingest the dance in an exoticized ritual of performance and consumption; however, the insertion of the audio track not only establishes a communal spectacle in which artist and viewers collectively form an audience but also disrupts the dialectic of the intersubjective gaze by inviting an observation of Maida himself as he reveals himself to us.

By removing himself from the position of detached observer, Maida's use of the heartbeat adds a layer of participation and vulnerability through which the autonomous, subjective observer articulates solidarity with the object of desire. Here, I note that Behar advocates human solidarity with nonhuman, including nonliving objects, complicating our understanding of object-orientation between humans. She states: "Feminist politics might also arise from outward orientation, from looking to the abounding realm of inanimate, inert, nonhuman objects. In this case, the call for solidarity should be to rally around objects, not subjects."[36] Behar nevertheless contends that OOF's internalization of the external, object world amounts to a radical shift in feminist ontological and political positioning. Relating to the Hawaiian men as fellow human beings with desires and fantasies perhaps analogous to his own, Maida nevertheless exposes their status as objects of the postcolonial gaze and simultaneously as ideologically formed subjects in the lineage of what is, according to Behar, "[p]rimarily a white, male, hetero, abled, rational heir to Enlightenment humanism."[37] Similarly to DeGenevieve's project, Maida's work questions the ontological categories of subject and object in order to vulnerably and openly examine the hegemonic, ideological constructions of subjectivity and to demonstrate the potential for radical intimacy to disrupt the rigidity of these constructs. Both DeGenevieve and Maida perform this questioning while making visible and apparent their own complicity and desire.

In their projects, we are faced with the discomfort and instability of not being able to situate the precise contours of power or the edges of control.

Neither my nor Kristeva's projects ask for a complete annihilation of epistemological and ontological positions (including the subject), rather they call for practices through which an interplay of words, bodies, and relations upend a priori categories and generate new bodies of knowledge and a radicalized symbolic order. This discussion therefore necessarily involves a consideration of "queerness" as it relates to Maida's work specifically and more broadly as a theoretical framework for constructing strategies of difference and negotiating power and intimacy in the twenty-first century. José Esteban Muñoz describes queerness as a rejection of political categorization: "Queerness is a longing that propels us onward . . . that thing that lets us feel that this world is not enough, that indeed something is missing. Often we can glimpse the worlds proposed and promised by queerness in the realm of the aesthetic."[38] How does this promised world relate to the notion of fantasy, which, according to Maida, is "a huge part of the work?"[39] Maida states: "Identity is often a projection of how you want to be perceived—it's a fantasy. And when I go down and meet with these male models, it's an opportunity for them to project a fantasy."[40] By applying a psychoanalytic framework to this discussion of fantasy, fantasy itself may be understood to be a projection onto reality, facilitated by the circulation of the *object a*—the object of desire. To be more exact, according to Lacan, "the object *a*—which is not to be situated in anything analogous to the intentionality of a noesis, which is not the intentionality of desire—is to be conceived of as the cause of desire . . . the object lies *behind* desire."[41] In the still photographs, Maida claims to give space to the models to project their own fantasy/identity, which is partially unconscious. As author and artist, however, he projects *his* own fantasy back through the camera lens, which is itself a response to their projections. The projection of fantasy that emits from the object-cause of desire, back into the subject's gaze, becomes the object-cause of the subject's desire, and we find ourselves co-desiring along with Maida and the camera eye.

Maida's discourse, however, continually implies a slippage from a mutually participatory experience toward his own exertion of control and desire in the exchange. *He* creates an opportunity for the models to express *their* fantasies; *he* "offers up a private performance of a sacred, pre-Western hula."[42] It is only via the soundscape of *Hula Kahiko Kane*, I argue, that Maida inserts himself into the projection of sexuality, masculinity, and performance in a way that introduces a discourse of intimacy, reciprocity, and the instability of borders, as explored by Kristeva in her discussions of revolt. This helps to recalibrate our discussions around his work and situate *New Natives* as an attempt to work through intimacy and vulnerability in an inherently hegemonic space, disrupting the subject-object divide and operating against ideology. My research thus far indicates that this "repetition, working-through, working-out internal to the free association in transference"[43] is an essential component of intimacy. Furthermore, deploying intimacy toward radical ends requires engaging the unconscious in new modes of thinking, which can be understood as working through the semiotic realm of the primary processes, in order to rework the symbolic realm of language into a signifying process. According to Beardsworth, these pre-Symbolic processes, when funneled through analytic speech and recollection, "articulate drive facilitations and their stases into a combinatorial system that amounts to a space but not a place: the semiotic *chora*. Subject and object positions are missing from the *chora*."[44] The displacement and condensation that take place in *Hula Kahiko Kane* re-signify the clearing by the beach as a non-space that blurs the edges of meaning and identity, and marks a shift toward the materiality of body, object, and environment.

Kristeva celebrates what she considers to be radical art because it "revolt[s] against identity: the identity of sex and meaning, of ideas and politics, of being and the other" and "raises the question of another structuring of subjectivity."[45] In analysis, this operation takes place through discourse, in which subjects engage unconscious memory and desire in the retelling of their own narrative and in the process displacing categories. This process can also occur in art and perhaps most radically through radically intimate art practice. Beardsworth describes Kristeva's early view that "[a]rt's confinement to a subjective enclosure amounts to an attachment of the most unstable moments of the signifying process, drive re-jection, to the unity of the subject."[46] In other words, art mirrors the early analytic attachment to the ego just as "psychoanalysis is irredeemably captured by the structure it discovers—narcissism—because of the need of identification in the transference-relation."[47] In the transferential relationship between photographer and model, rather than universalizing humanity by erasing difference, Maida front-loads difference by highlighting the models' cultural and ethnic heritage as signifiers of their identity—an identity also defined by plurality, fantasy, and slippage. He seems to attempt to label while at the same time destabilize the very labels that he (and the models) employs through the somatic and semiotic responses of his own body.

As a radically intimate practice, we may question what role Maida's work plays in the contemporary imagination and its challenge to ideologies of sex, gender, and identity. An opportunity may then arise to usher in the possibility of a more nuanced discourse about intimacy in a hegemonic field than the strict binary that the subject-object divide allows. We must continually circle back to the following recurring question: Is instability sufficient for radicality? At stake in this discussion are the social bond and the ability to collaborate and commune within the social body. If Maida himself can be understood as the analytic subject in this particular formulation, then his partnerships with the Hawaiian men and the representations he constructs in intimate collaboration with them are itself an analytic process that positions Maida as the subject in need of the forgiveness that Kristeva claims is inherent to the analytic process—forgiveness for the shame that inevitably accompanies the Western gaze, whether or not it is sanctioned by the bounds of normativity.[48] If the work can be considered to be "intimate"—and I suggest that *Hula Kahiko Kane* comes closest of Maida's work to explicitly exhibiting the vulnerability and interiority I believe to be essential to intimacy—then is he contributing to an aesthetic culture of revolt, as called for by Kristeva herself? If so, then it is our duty in our artistic, scholarly, and institutional practices to hone a more nuanced discourse around works such as Maida's, as well as DeGenevieve's, that place postcolonial subjects in close, intimate contact via the hegemonic lens of representation.

7

Subjectivity Reclaimed, Reoriented

Lorraine O'Grady: Reclaiming Subjectivity

Much of what we witness in the realm of visual representation involves artists in positions of power—racial, sexual, and economic—turning their gaze and their intellectual curiosity toward those who may be seen as vulnerable to exploitation. How might artists from underrepresented and historically silenced communities leverage the visual realm to explore their experiences as marginalized subjects and objects of the hegemonic gaze? In this final chapter, I introduce the art and writing of Lorraine O'Grady, whose diptych *The Clearing* from her body of work *Body Is the Ground of My Experience* presents a controversial view of Black female sexuality and, by extension, Black female *subjectivity*, as interwoven with the legacy of slavery. O'Grady emphasizes the importance of reclaiming subjectivity, particularly for individuals and communities whose subjectivities have been historically suppressed. This particular piece and accompanying writings, however, evoke questions about the role of the object, as elaborated upon by Behar in object-oriented feminism, and the power that may be located in performatively occupying this role as a political strategy. Regarding her work's political impact, O'Grady states: "no one is going to go out and man the barricades after seeing a piece by me. . . . My work is too complex for that kind of response. . . . The most I really expect my work can accomplish politically is a small contribution to the task of creating a climate of questioning and refusal."[1] I will explore O'Grady's work from two seemingly opposed perspectives— on the one hand, the construction of Black female subjectivity through the trauma of slavery and the importance of Black women reclaiming the right to express their own subjectivity; and on the other, my argument that O'Grady ventures into object-oriented feminism as a powerful performative praxis. By doing so, I demonstrate that the radicality of intimacy overturns ideology's binary thinking by destabilizing subjectivity, calling into question a founding principle of modernism while offering pathways to social and political power for marginalized populations.

Of all of O'Grady's works, the art and writing I will discuss in this chapter are perhaps the most explicitly sexual and confront intimacy from the ambivalent and historically charged position of the oft-objectified bodies of Black women. Alongside this artwork, O'Grady's essay "Olympia's Maid: Reclaiming Black Female Subjectivity" discusses Black women's status as invisible objects in Western art and philosophy, and the author's primary concern, which is "the reclamation of the body as a site of black female subjectivity."[2] O'Grady provides an important complement (and challenge) to object-orientation, claiming that "[t]o name ourselves rather than be named we must first see ourselves."[3] O'Grady ties the notion of *seeing* and *naming* one's self directly to subjectivity and its historical exclusion of Black women. Behar, by contrast, advocates for reclaiming the position of object, which could be seen as a subjective act due to its implication of self-identification, in some ways mirroring O'Grady's insistence on the importance of self-recognition as an act of affirmation. Seeing one's self, and subsequently naming one's self, if understood through the psychoanalytic structure of the mirror and the Althusserian notion of ideological interpellation, is the very location of subject-formation, even if the subject being formed is, in Lacanian theory, a misrecognition. How might these two feminist positions support one another despite their apparent contradictions?

The question of Black subjectivity cuts to the heart of how Black people are seen and see themselves, and, crucially, the kinds of positions of resistance Black communities may adopt in the pursuit of true and lasting emancipation. Supporting as well as complicating O'Grady's discourse using contemporary Black psychoanalytic scholarship, I introduce Sheldon George's proposition that African Americans should strive "to become the agency that makes the traumatic Real of slavery speak, to displace the trauma from its location within the register of the Real through an investigation and articulation of this trauma's determinative relation to personal subjectivity."[4] George advocates for the discarding of race as a determinative factor in Black people's experience of their identities, in order to shed the historically weighty shackles of slavery from their sense of self. He envisions this happening in part through the articulations of trauma in art, music, and literature, a position aligned with Kristeva's. O'Grady argues that to see one's self does not mean capitulating to the illusory mirror of the colonial gaze but to acknowledge that one's subjectivity is imagined via one's reflection in a hegemonic world, and recast this problematized subjectivity in one's own hybrid, diasporic language. Radical intimacy, however, leverages the slippage of inside and outside to disrupt and distort ideology and, by extension, subjectivity. O'Grady explains: "[W]hen you are the object of irrational contradictions, then you are in a position of having to struggle in contradictory ways."[5] I suggest that O'Grady's engagement of the sexually intimate—the contradictions and drives that complicate subjectivity, language, and desire—is both a poetic and political form of radical intimacy that challenges subjectivity at its ideological limits.

How does O'Grady's radical artistic gesture reclaim subjectivity while simultaneously destabilizing it? Object-oriented feminism proposes that women and people of color have always understood themselves to be positioned as objects in relation to the Cartesian/Kantian thinking subject, which remains dominant in Western ontologies, and therefore should find power and agency in their role as objects. If we are objects, asks OOF, referring to women, people of color, and other marginalized groups, then how can we operate as objects, to embody and theorize from the position in which we have been imprisoned by patriarchal interpellation? According to philosopher and poet Fred Moten, "[t]he history of blackness is testament to the fact that objects can and do resist,"[6] deepening the conversation about the risks and opportunities that object-orientation offers to marginalized communities. By operating as objects, and actively taking on this stance, OOF claims greater political and ideological agency for marginalized people. According to Behar, "[o]bject-oriented feminism's intervention is to approach all objects from the inside-out position of being an object, too."[7] From this vantage point, using the tools of objecthood, artists in particular can critique and change humans' relationship to objects, living and nonliving, from within—a position that in itself begins to consider the political agency of intimacy, the "most interior."

By assuming a stance of solidarity with objects such as plants, environmental elements, artificial intelligence systems, and even artworks themselves, Behar contends that artists may contribute to the production of an ethical ecological model of interconnectedness while maintaining the protection of their inherent withdrawnness. Her inclusion of the element of withdrawal is both an acknowledgment of the ultimate unknowability of any "thing-in-itself" and a protective barrier for vulnerable and potentially overexposed populations. Behar herself asks "whether, when deployed, [OOF] lives up to its promises?"[8] Specifically, she wonders if OOF and other contemporary philosophical movements can "truly banish philosophy's thinking humanist subject? Can they manage, finally, to put philosophers into contact, and philosophy into action, with and within the world? In other words, do these ideas 'work' in an artistic sense?"[9] Finally, she reveals OOF's method: "Can philosophy hold its own as performance art?"[10] Rather than aligning exclusively with the object position proposed by OOF, I contend that the contradictions and vulnerabilities that arise, even in object-oriented feminist praxis itself, activate the questioning and eternal return of Kristeva's revolt and Baudrillard's radical thought.

George and Behar offer important frameworks for thinking through subjectivity and objecthood in creative practice, specifically for populations that have been relegated to social strata that have material consequences toward their physical and psychical well-being. Politically, subjectivity has been a powerful tool for emancipation, but what are its limits when it is tethered to damaging historical constructs? O'Grady clearly argues for traversing through empowered, informed subject-formation before attempting the postmodern game of deconstruction of subjectivity. By being forced to see themselves as always already subordinate to the other, specifically the white other, Black women are robbed of opportunities to articulate their own inner experience. O'Grady instead argues for an art practice that looks directly into the mirror of Black women's subjectivity, as constructed through white patriarchal ideologies, in order to fully see—and presumably come to understand—one's being in the world. She says, "[c]ritiquing *them* does not show who *you* are: it cannot turn you from an object into a subject of history."[11] At first read, it seems that O'Grady's view is quite the opposite of Behar's; however, both Behar and O'Grady seek a feminist art practice that acknowledges and works from the perspective of positionality—whether it be from the position of subjectivity (seeing and reclaiming one's ideological formation in a hegemonic field) or object-orientation (seeing one's own objectification as an equalizing and empowering force in an ecology of objects). As I will explore in the following section, Behar's and O'Grady's approaches are nevertheless aligned as experimental, materialist, and *intimate* feminist praxes that complicate and politicize the distinctions between subject and object, between interiority and the extimacy of ideology.

In order to understand O'Grady's contribution to a discourse of intimacy, particularly as I continue to explore the intimate as a place where the boundaries between inside and outside, subject and object, "legal" and abject, become questionable, I turn to her practice as a visual artist. O'Grady's theoretical intentions may be best expressed by her image *The Clearing*, which she later renamed *The Clearing: or, Cortés and La Malinche, Thomas Jefferson and Sally Hemings, N. and Me* (Figure 4). This renaming was performed in part due to the artist's desire to be more explicit about the personal nature of the image and her own participation in an interracial relationship as following a historical lineage

Figure 4 Lorraine O'Grady, *The Clearing: or Cortés and La Malinche, Thomas Jefferson and Sally Hemings, N. and Me*, 1991/2019, archival pigment print on Hahnemühle Baryta pure cotton photo rag paper in 2 parts, 40 x 50 in each (101.6 x 127 cm each) 40 7/8 x 50 7/8 x 1 3/4 in framed each (129.2 x 103.8 x 4.4 cm framed each). Courtesy Alexander Gray Associates, New York. © Lorraine O'Grady/Artists Rights Society (ARS), New York.

of intimacy deeply rooted in exploitation. The diptych "explores the artist's own interracial relationship through the evocation of notorious interracial pairings in American history. O'Grady attempts to provide a voice for the black women involved in these relationships with famous, powerful white men."[12] *The Clearing* is a black-and-white diptych photo-montage portraying a sexual scene between a white man and a Black woman. Both photographs are of the same grassy clearing among a thicket of trees. The image on the left, subtitled *The Clearing: Green Love*,[13] depicts a nude couple embraced in the missionary position—a Black woman on her back with her knees spread and a white man perched atop her, seemingly locked mid-coitus. They float in the sky above the clearing, while a boy and girl frolic with a ball in the grass below, running toward a pile of clothing that presumably belongs to the ecstatic couple. According to Williams and Willis, "[t]he seemingly mixed-race children both stumble on their history and embody the future as they run heedlessly toward the pile of rumpled garments."[14] In the right panel, subtitled *The Clearing: Black-and-White Love*,[15] the couple reclines in the grass alone, the white man wearing tattered chain mail and bearing a skull instead of a formed head and face. Leaning on one arm, turned toward the woman in the grass, he gropes the female's breast—she who lies rigid and stoic on her back beneath him, staring up into the sky.

According to O'Grady, the piece was "less about sex than it was about culture,"[16] specifically the ways that Black female subjectivity is constructed in relation and in subordination to white masculinity and its desire. According to O'Grady, *The Clearing* "is an autobiographic, 'both/and' (not 'before/after') piece. It represents the simultaneous extremes of ecstasy and exploitation in a troubled and still under-theorized, historic relationship."[17] O'Grady's point was to imagine herself, and fellow Black women, not through the white colonial gaze but from her own situated perspective as she gazes at her own reflection. According to Williams and Willis, "O'Grady claims both victimization and agency for the black female, alluding to the complexity and danger of both laying blame and attributing stereotypes."[18] Regarding the layered nature of the image, and the colonized subjectivity it describes, O'Grady states: "First we must acknowledge the complexity, and then we must surrender to it."[19] According to O'Grady's accounts, the piece was not well-received and has been continuously fragmented and decontextualized in order to de-emphasize its potent message. As described on her website, "O'Grady had not anticipated the intensely negative response, especially from white male viewers, to The Clearing, a diptych showing black and white bodies in what director John Waters calls 'the last taboo.' One white male Harvard professor told her it was difficult to look at because it showed 'how erotic domination is.'"[20] The discourse that has been repeatedly censored is twofold: first, the image posits that Black female subjectivity (and sexuality) cannot be considered independently of its formation as a "lingering structure of invisibility"[21] that participates in and supports white, male subjectivity; and second, it presents the controversial stance that this structure of invisibility does not foreclose sexual intimacy between subjects who hold unequal power in relation to one another. According to Williams and Willis, "[t]he innocence of child's play is ominously juxtaposed with an image of sexual predation and one of mutual abandonment and pleasure."[22] The children do not yet realize their ideological origins, perhaps like all subjects. As ideological questioning, the diptych speaks of the unconscious undercurrent of ambivalence between pleasure and pain to which we continually return in our discourse on radical intimacy.

An illuminating moment in the history of the piece sheds light on its operations as a radical work employing sexuality as a tool. Invited to participate in an exhibition about women's sexuality at David Zwirner Gallery in New York City, O'Grady first realized how difficult her particular rendition of Black female sexuality would be. According to O'Grady, "the hidden agenda of the [Zwirner] show was to express in visual art this moment of sexual exuberance on the part particularly of white women. OK, this was the moment when white women were like really exploring and dynamically reinventing themselves sexually."[23] Behar joins in pointing out the continued exclusion of Black women from many discourses, including her own contemporaneous project. She concedes: "We must recognize that even this volume, OOF's first effort, contains too little material on the specific concerns of people of color."[24] Far from being a site of freedom for O'Grady, she found her artwork censored and sanitized of content that runs counter to the myth of idealized sexual emancipation, fueled by a largely white contingency of activists. To her dismay, the curator chose to only display the left side of the piece, in O'Grady's view "[b]ecause this show was about . . . sexuality as an uncomplicated, positive blessing. Not sexuality as a complicated life issue or even sexuality as an issue far more complicated for women of color than for white women, none of the modulations of sexuality were to be present in the show."[25] The idealism around feminine sexuality expressed in this exhibition contrasts with the ambivalence of radical intimacy, manifest in O'Grady's piece.

The interrogation of interracial relationships in *The Clearing* speaks to the complexities of individual couple-hood—negotiating the slippage of subject/object, self/other—within a personal dynamic of desire, pleasure, and jouissance. As recalled by O'Grady, a white male curator rejected the piece from another exhibition, telling her, "'That's not what sexuality is, or at least that's not what it's supposed to be,'" to which O'Grady responds, "But well, that's what it is."[26] For O'Grady, sexual intimacy is an interplay of desire shared between singular individuals and the social and historical structures that determine the power relationships between them. O'Grady herself uses the term "intimacy" to describe interracial relationships that she traces back to slaveholding times. She asserts:

> I don't think most people want to think about the compromising, difficult parts of sexuality even among normally married couples, you know. But they certainly don't want to hear about that difficulty in interracial relationships, or certainly they don't want to have the historical nature of this relationship exposed *en plein air*. . . . It's very very very difficult for people to be living in the kind of intimacy that obtained on the Southern plantation without desire going in totally unexpected or unpredictable ways.[27]

Here, O'Grady makes clear that what is so radical about her assertions, and her piece, is that she takes ownership of a subjectivity built on oppression and the sexual desire that fuels deeply hegemonic sexual relations. She embodies George's suggestion that "the African American subject who is attached to race, who is in effect a subject dominated by a trauma that dictates both speech and identity, must begin to possess the trauma, becoming, like the blues artist, a more conscious agent of its utterances and expressions."[28] O'Grady possesses the trauma while also continuing to allow it to possess her, as an extimate and deeply internal expression of her being. An interesting moment takes place midway through an interview with Andil Gosine, when O'Grady describes the sexual act as somehow prior to, or separate from, the social discourse of power: "[T]he amazing thing is that when we're actually involved in the sexual act, we're not thinking socially, or we're not feeling socially. We're feeling totally individually. But then we're called to account. Once the orgasm is finished, then we're called to account and, then, things, life get very much more complicated."[29] In this statement, she seems to indicate that desire and sexual pleasure can exceed, or even momentarily suspend, racist ideologies, before they are reconsidered through the lens of hegemony.

The Clearing itself mirrors this arc of thinking, spanning from the pure bliss of ecstatic intermingling, during which differences between lovers are erased to create beautifully harmonic children, while simultaneously acknowledging the post-orgasmic "reality" of cold institutionalized oppression and death. The only clue to the impending awakening of the lovers to their ideological conditions—positioned by O'Grady as occurring chronologically in tandem with their bliss—is the gun on the clothes pile in the left-hand image. According to O'Grady:

> The skull-headed figure wears tattered chain mail because this relationship, in tandem with imperial and slave culture's "cult of true (i.e. white) womanhood," may have rung the death knell of "*amour courtois.*" . . . The relationship was symbolically the matrix of the process of colonialization and historically the end of an "age of innocence."[30]

O'Grady presents the interracial relationship, steeped in exploitation and cruelty, as an ideologically ambivalent intimate engagement that mirrors white patriarchal society's insistence on maintaining a hegemonic boundary between itself and communities of color through colonization, enslavement, and systemic oppression. Furthermore, O'Grady combats the invisibility of Black women in the realm of intimacy by unveiling and symbolizing the unconscious currents of desire that complicate subjectivity in a culture of persistent abuse and exploitation.

Detailing into O'Grady's discourse, it becomes clear that her ambivalent message is rooted in her own memories and psychical representations. In the aforementioned interview, O'Grady gets more personally revealing. Discussing her own dreams, memories, and sexual experiences, she states:

> A lot of the work in *BodyGround* was based in dream imagery . . . I was at a point where my dream life was as real to me as my day life. . . . When I think about it, *The Clearing* comes from my intellectualization, but also from events in my life, and. . . it really wasn't until we were talking about this that I began to realize,

[Oh My God . . . my son] was conceived in a clearing. . . . That was a moment when I was actually, sexually in a clearing, and I remember every bit of it.[31]

Here, O'Grady reveals the "real" intimacy driving the production of this piece— the intimacy in the past (with the father of her child, as well as with her child as the physical part of her body that grew and then was expelled from this same body) *and* with the intimacy of memory itself. O'Grady's son is born into his ideology, as subject of the Oedipal structures that underlie the Western psyche, through these acts of intimacy. The past comes back to haunt the present, and *The Clearing* gives us a glimpse not just of the social and cultural structures O'Grady seeks to reveal with her image but also of the internal workings of sexual intimacy itself—as a radical space that challenges hegemonies, as much as it operates as ideological reflection. Through dream imagery and a confrontation with trauma, O'Grady reactivates pre-Symbolic desires while generating new symbols and a reconfigured imaginary realm to reflect contemporary subjectivity bound to ideology. In parallel, in his analyses of African American literature, George notes that "[t]rauma here reveals itself as that which forces upon the subject not only a confrontation with the void of the Real but also a resuturing of subjectivity through a rewriting of identity."[32] This rewriting of identity that O'Grady performs as an act of reclaiming subjectivity also serves to destabilize the invisible and contingent subjectivity that has been assigned to Black women by white patriarchy.

Are we to agree with O'Grady in her insistence that "self-expression is not a stage that can be bypassed. It is a discrete moment that must precede or occur simultaneously with the deconstructive act?"[33] For O'Grady, seeing one's self in one's imagined subjectivity is mandatory, and postmodernist theories that too readily deconstruct the subject ignore the political importance of subject-formation. O'Grady's work and discourse suggest that sexual intimacy is not far from ideological interpellation, which it also interrupts and complicates. We may posit the Althusserian-derived notion that in seeing each other in the intimate realm, we assign identity (and subjectivity) to each other and to ourselves, while the unconscious drives and desires distort and disrupt these very identities. In sexuality, we may assign and perform gender roles and historic power relations, and (in a psychoanalytic model) roles derived from the Oedipal. If self-expression as a gesture of reclaiming subjectivity is a stage that cannot be bypassed, and O'Grady chooses to portray Black female subjectivity through the lens of interracial, highly hegemonic relations, then any radicality located in the work operates as a resistance against the hegemonic ideologies being played out in the performance of sexuality. Here, we could begin reading O'Grady's work in a similar manner as we did Ledare's, noting where the very act of seeing her self (and, by extension, Black women categorically) as subject of white patriarchy, colonialism, racism, and the Oedipal complex is a radical act. O'Grady argues: "For if the female body in the West is obverse and reverse, it will not be seen in its integrity—neither side will know itself—until the not-white body has mirrored herself fully."[34] Here she sides with psychoanalysis in ceding that femininity in the West is seen as the "other side" of masculinity or the object to masculinity's subject. Sexual difference, however, is only one measure of difference in a hegemonic field, and bodies of color introduce numerous, ever-shifting reflections into the imaginary realm—the visual field of ideology. Marginalized positions must be mirrored, in order for society at large to know itself; and this, we may surmise, is how O'Grady sees her role as artist-activist.

A Complicated Subjectivity

This book draws largely from psychoanalytic and poststructuralist sources—prime targets of O'Grady's critique. Does reading her work through these theoretical lenses constitute a fair analysis of her intentions and, by extension, the underlying structures of intimacy in the image in question? O'Grady herself both resists and invites psychoanalytic readings when she states: "We need to send this field back to basics. The issue is not whether the unconscious is universal, or whether it has the meanings psychoanalysis attributes to it (it is, and it does), but rather that, in addition, it contains contradictory meanings, as well as some that are unforeseen by its current theory."[35] O'Grady thus seems to want to rehabilitate psychoanalysis and use its modernist dispositions in pursuit of the story of Black female subjectivity while maintaining a highly critical distance from its roots in European Enlightenment-era thought. This gesture results in an alternate imaginary and symbolic realm that reflects Black female subjectivity in languages previously unspoken in dominant Western discourses but with roots in the realities of ideological formation in a postcolonial society. O'Grady believes that the act of claiming the imaginary—which for Kristeva includes creativity as well as the symbolic—is a subjective act, therefore, subjectivity itself is the only way to resist. She inquires: "When, I ask, do we start to see images of the black female body by black women made as acts of auto-expression, the discrete stage that must immediately precede or occur simultaneously with acts of auto-critique? When, in other words, does the present begin?"[36] Here, she introduces the lens of modernism and the notion of self-critique—a function of the symbolic—to question Black women's participation in the modernist moment and insert Black female subjectivity into discourses and practices of self-recognition.

O'Grady's work seeks to represent and symbolize Black female subjectivity, but the ambivalence of the intimacy depicted in *The Clearing*, as well as O'Grady's discourse surrounding the piece, nevertheless reveals an investment in destabilizing subjectivity and reorienting subjectivity through the intimate. For Kristeva, abjection operates not as a destruction but as an archaeological uncovering—and poetic rearranging—of subjectivity, the drive, and speech. According to Kristeva, "it is the 'poetic' unsettlement of analytic utterance that testifies to its closeness to, cohabitation with, and 'knowledge' of abjection."[37] How can we attempt to understand O'Grady's gesture of radical intimacy within a psychoanalytic framework while respecting her critique of the institution for "its seeming binarial *rigidity*" and "narrow base in sexuality?"[38] O'Grady argues that psychoanalysis' focus on sexuality and sexual difference operates via a Eurocentric mode of thinking that ignores the complex intricacies of Black subjectivity. She argues, "I suspect most African Americans who are not in the academy would laugh at the idea that their subjective lives were organized around the sex drive and would feel that 'sexuality,' a conceptual category that includes thinking about it as well as doing it, is something black people just don't have time for."[39] Far from ascribing a kind of asexuality to African Americans, she clarifies, "[n]ot that sex isn't important to these folks; it's just one center among many."[40] Here, we may begin to understand O'Grady's view of sexuality as departing from Freudian theory's emphasis on the Oedipal and instead emphasizing the decentralization of subjectivity.

O'Grady's description of the architecture of Black sexuality combines an ancestral relationship to the African continent and its philosophical traditions, with the impact of centuries of oppression and servitude. In this way, she underlines the social and political formations through which power differentials have constructed sexual intimacy in African American subjects. She also directly connects this subjectivity to Black art practices and discourses, which she suggests have been able to transcend the binary tendencies of the psychoanalytic model. She states:

> Black artists and theorists frequently refer to African Americans as "the first postmoderns." They have in mind a now agreed understanding that our inheritance from the motherland of pragmatic, "both: and" philosophic systems,

combined with the historic discontinuities of our experience as black slaves in a white world, have caused us to construct subjectivities able to negotiate between "centers" that, at the least, are double.[41]

Though she allows that "[t]he space spirituality occupies in the African American unconscious is important to speculate upon," she nevertheless emphasizes that "[s]ubjectivity for me will always be a social and not merely a spiritual quest."[42] O'Grady's social sphere is one that is not limited by rigid structures of sexual difference and the Oedipal but one that investigates a complex set of constellations that include the power structures that have worked to omit Black female subjectivity from the visual field of sexuality. O'Grady states: "There is a gulf between Western and non-Western quotidian perceptions of sexual valence, and the question of how psychic differences come into effect when 'cultural differences' are accompanied by real differences in power."[43] O'Grady wishes for artists to be the ones to approach theory in their practice while they "remain alive to what may escape the net of theoretical description."[44] She incorporates psychoanalysis while questioning its structural hegemony and participates in our discourse on radical intimacy by exposing the slippages and unconscious drives that underlie categories, identities, and desire.

    O'Grady predicts the demise of psychoanalysis, yet she wishes to leverage its tools toward the inclusion of Black female subjectivity in a discourse of subjectivity. She states: "Psychoanalysis, after anthropology, will surely be the next great Western discipline to unravel, but I wouldn't want it to destruct completely. We don't have to reinvent that wheel. But to use it in our auto-expression and auto-critique, we will have to dislodge it from its narrow base in sexuality."[45] Western feminisms, she claims, by focusing on the articulation and expression of white femininity, essentially erase the unique, multifaceted, decentralized formations of Black female subjectivity as it is ideologically constructed in relation to masculinity and whiteness. She seems to suggest that focusing on sexuality as a dominant psychical structure that determines the social and political structure is a privileged position that has to contend only with the male-female dichotomy and not the complex intersection of race, class, and postcolonial history—which is part of what makes *The Clearing* so impactful. In her desire to represent Black female subjectivity, which "revolves about a series of variable 'centers,'"[46] she homes in on the act of sexual intimacy itself, as it relates to both the social whole and her own personal history. Through this lens, sexual intimacy becomes a broader and more nuanced configuration than the sexuality posited by traditional psychoanalytic theory.

In *The Clearing*, the left-hand side of the diptych features the interracial couple embraced in the sexual missionary position, with the man on top, woman's legs spread. Besides the obvious reference to colonialism in the choice of this apt-named sexual position, the embrace seems idyllic and happy. On its surface, the diptych presents the binary opposition of ecstasy and abjection; however, according to Kristeva, "'ecstasy' is another word for 'abjection.' Have we sufficiently considered this similarity?"[47] The ambivalent border between pleasure and pain, shame and passion, punctuates the intimate exchange and particularly O'Grady's discourse on the intimacy between postcolonial subjects in hegemonic relation to one another.

A detailed investigation of each image reveals additional subtleties that emphasize the emotional complexities of the scenes. In the left image, the woman's head is angled back, as she reveals the vulnerable crook of her neck, and an ambiguous half-smile plays on her lips. Her hands claw into her lover's back, as the architecture of their two bodies reveals tension, aggression, and ambivalence. Her face impenetrable and her eyes closed, her jaw pushes against his cheek. His eyes angle down toward her, but his eyelids appear closed. They are each encased in their own imaginary universe, while their bodies perform the desire between them and the eroticism of their drives. In the right-hand tile of the diptych, she lays beside him on the grass, rigid and immobile under the weight of his hand on her breast, and, according to O'Grady, "looking off into the distance with a very bored expression."[48] Her head slightly tilted, and her gaze directed toward the sky, her eyes angle toward the right side of her field of vision. As she lays prone on the ground, she appears to be remembering and, perhaps, escaping. She seems neither dead nor fulfilled but contemplating her own subjectivity, perhaps yearning toward a memory tethered to their lovemaking in the sky? The implication of an act of recollection in the presence of the observer and the third element (speech) results in a poetic reconfiguration of language and memory that Kristeva attributes to the abject. Furthermore, Kristeva reminds us that abjection is the side of the coin obverse to language and the law, both opposed and invisible to its other half, and yet inextricable from it.

Kristeva offers a way to consider the relationship between language as written speech and the imaginary manifestations of the unconscious through the sublimation of fear into metaphor, as takes place in poetic writing. By following her argument, we may re-situate O'Grady's work in terms of fear of the unnameable and the pre-symbolic object relation brought into the realm of speech and the law. Kristeva describes the phobic (as exemplified by Freud's Little Hans) as "a subject in want of metaphoricalness,"[49] incapable of transforming the images of the unconscious into language that would operate as a "cure" for the neurosis. Curiously, she compares the role of the artist and writer with that of the analyst, whose job it is "to give back a memory, hence a language, to the unnamable and namable states of fear, while emphasizing the former, which make up what is most unapproachable in the unconscious."[50] If the role of analysis, writing, and art is "not as the only treatment but as the only 'know-how' where phobia is concerned,"[51] then how does O'Grady's piece operate on an epistemological, linguistic level? How does she employ abjection, and the radicality of intimacy, to explore the taboo sexual relation and its role in subject-formation?

Another way of interpreting the ambiguous emotional state of the woman in *The Clearing* is that she is rendered paralyzed in the second frame of the diptych. She lies rigid, her eyes tilted upwards in an awkward way, suggesting an inability to turn her head. The power her partner exerts upon her prone body renders her immovable and mute. The aggressive drives she displays in the first panel have been subsumed beneath the weight of oppression, and the narrative of history binds the two subjectivities together inextricably. What O'Grady refers to as "boredom" takes on a timbre of emotional detachment and withdrawal. She neither acquiesces nor resists—does she display paralysis in the face of fear and trauma or the ambivalence of abjection through which subjectivity itself becomes unstable? Perhaps both/and. Kristeva describes "fear—a terrifying, abject reference. We encounter this discourse in our dreams, or when death brushes us by, depriving us of the assurance mechanical use of speech ordinarily gives us, the assurance of being ourselves, that is, untouchable, unchangeable, immortal."[52] The figure in the diptych is touched; she is changed; she confronts death. Deprived of the assurance of speech, the intimacy that silences her also forces a collision with the abject.

Here, O'Grady's semiotics become interwoven with her politics and manifest in her fantasy construction in its visual form. Kristeva asserts that "phobia does not disappear but slides beneath language."[53] Despite written speech being only a small portion of *The Clearing* (in the form of its title and its iterations—not insignificant), the symbolic *as law* manifests as overarching specter of meaning and control, personified by the male figure in the fantasy. O'Grady's desire, as depicted in her fantasy construction as well as in her personal identification with the act of intimacy, expresses what Kristeva describes as Freud's "infantile, perverse, polymorphous sexuality, always already a carrier of desire and death."[54] This inseparability of desire and aggression in the interlacing of the drives is the epitome of intimate ambivalence. Kristeva argues that "*want* and *aggressivity* are chronologically separable but logically coextensive . . . [they] are adapted to one another. To speak of want alone is to repudiate aggressivity in obsessional fashion; to speak of aggressivity alone, forgetting want, amounts to making transference paranoidal."[55] Here, Kristeva makes use of Freud's duality of *eros* and *thanatos*—the covalent drives toward unity and destruction—however, she also strongly implies that when we speak of violence without fully considering the nature of desire, we merely end up threatened by the images we construct to replace the lost object. In making transference—in Lacanian theory, *love*—paranoidal, language is once again discarded in favor of images and "[t]he fantasy of incorporation by means of which I attempt to escape fear (I incorporate a portion of my mother's body, her breast, and thus I hold on to her) threatens me none the less, for a symbolic, paternal prohibition already dwells in me on account of my learning to speak at the same time."[56] Here, desire and prohibition are intertwined and symbiotic, threatening the subject engaged in the intimate relation.

In converting images from the unconscious into words, as takes place in both writing and analysis, fear is transformed into intimacy. O'Grady presents us with both the visual form of the imaginary realm—the locale where misrecognition first takes place and through which the split subject continues to reflect itself—and the symbolic realm of language and knowledge. She provides an added insight on the breadth of the piece, which she claims "is saying something interesting and complex about relationships. Not just about this particular relationship, but about all sexual relationships."[57] She suggests that intimacy be understood as a complex interplay of language—as described through Lacanian semiotics, which extend the Freudian Oedipal model beyond that of biological sexual difference and into the structure of language itself—via the unconscious. Kristeva's exploration of *phobic hallucination*, by which she means that "an *object* that is a *hallucination* is being made up,"[58] provides another opportunity to explore the construction of new languages that takes place in abjection—through the failure of the object relation as evidenced by the inability to ever consume the object of desire. Kristeva describes speech as an expression of desire/want and aggressivity: "Through the mouth that I fill with words instead of my mother whom I miss from now on more than ever, I elaborate that want, and the aggressivity that accompanies it, by *saying*."[59] This meaning, by being unreachable, is constantly being ejected from the realm of meaning and therefore abjected. For Kristeva, in line with her allegiance to the analytic process, it is only via the integration of the symbolic into the fractured psyche that allows for psychic healing. It is here that the imaginary realm can be reentered, through the abject and its expressions.

O'Grady describes the role of Black subjectivity as the reverse side of the coin from the side of white subjectivity—isolated from, and invisible to, the obverse and yet essential to defining whiteness. She echoes theorists such as Hortence Spillers and Michele Wallace in lamenting the "disempowerment of not-white women"[60] in contemporary art practices and discourses and at the same time calls for "a cooperative effort between white women and women and men of color," which she emphasizes is "predicated on sensitivity to differences among ourselves."[61] A complete shedding of subjectivity, according to O'Grady, "will not be easy. So long unmirrored in our true selves, we may have forgotten how we look."[62] O'Grady's work performs a key function of activist art practice that is supportive of both her and Behar's projects—which is to see the self clearly, through one's own eyes, and to rearticulate that vision in the form of artistic representation. O'Grady warns, however, that "the greatest barrier I/we face in winning back the questioning subject position is the West's continuing tradition of binary, 'either: or' logic, a philosophic system that defines the body in opposition to the mind."[63] The subject-object divide operates as a limiting binary in Western thought and is complicated by the radical intimacy at work in *The Clearing*. O'Grady argues that "the method of reclaiming subjectivity precisely mirrors modernism's description of the artistic process . . . it needs an act of will to project the inside onto the outside long enough to see and take possession of it."[64] The instability and paradoxical relation between the agency implied in subjectivity and the hegemonic superstructure that supports it operate in the ambivalence of intimacy, where meanings collapse and new discourses emerge. O'Grady argues that "the postmodern concept of *fragmentation*, which evokes the mirror of Western illusion shattered into inert shards, is less generative than the more 'primitive' and active *multiplicity*. . . . This *multi* produces tension, as in the continuous equilibration of a *multiplicity of centers*."[65] This approach mirrors object-oriented feminism's practice of engaging multiplicity over fragmentation and a plurality of focal points as opposed to a singular, shattered reflection.

By lending her own intimate history to her exposition of the ideological position of Black female subjectivity, O'Grady personalizes and shares in collective memory from the perspective of her own objectification. She implicates herself by representing a taboo sexual intimacy that is often excluded from discourse. I will suggest in the following section that such marginalization of subject-formation can be reimagined through the radically intimate reconfiguration of object-orientation.

OOF as a Politics of Intimate Revolt

The artists explored in these final two chapters—O'Grady, DeGenevieve, and Maida—collectively produce representations that acknowledge and engage their own personal, *intimate* relationship with the hegemonic structures of race and their associated drives and desires. By revealing their own desire—desire signifying the lack that participates in meaning in subjectivity—they reveal the ideological formations that are ejected from and unformulated in our symbolic realm (our shared languages), and whose foreclosure indicates, and perpetuates, the invisibility of marginalized subjectivities. Their gestures of self-analysis and reflection result in highly vulnerable ambivalences in representation and produce images that are perhaps at odds with the identities that they are expected to embody. These artists expose the psychically complex interplay of power, desire, and oppression in postcolonial relationships, making them vulnerable to attack and criticism. How might radical intimacy, as it operates in experimental praxes, contribute to new languages that allow for these ambiguities to emerge and express themselves? I contend that one such new language is object-oriented feminism, variously explored in the chapters of this book. I suggest that this radical reordering of the modernist creed of subjectivity aligns with the intentions of radically intimate artists such as O'Grady, despite the dominance of the discourse of the subject in her writings. Finally, as I conclude this project on radical intimacy in contemporary art practice, I argue that the destabilization offered by the intimacy of object-orientation serves a political end as it destabilizes institutional structures from within.

O'Grady's professed project is largely ontological—an articulation of subjectivity—however, her methods are performative, even when she herself is not performing. By producing and exhibiting her work she not only seeks to express the qualities and textures of being a Black female, but she also aims for a broader reclamation of Black female subjectivity and a shift in stance, both internally in the individual and in broader society, regarding how Black women's ontologies are articulated and understood. O'Grady produces change by questioning established binaries and complicating perceived ideologies. Though O'Grady's artistic discourse aligns with humanist frameworks, she employs tenets of object-oriented feminism, an explicitly non-humanist model. OOF's emphasis on politics, erotics, and ethics—broadly, engagement with histories of oppression, humor, and ethical positions that eschew truth claims—are manifest in O'Grady's projects. Furthermore, OOF's interest in the power of withdrawal—

the inherent inaccessibility of objects—supports a discourse of intimacy and the strange exteriority of the extimate. Object-orientation maintains that objects remain withdrawn not only to external entities but also to themselves, providing an opportunity for feminists to both acknowledge the workings of the unconscious and deploy strategies of resistance that protect individuals from becoming overly visible. My investigation of O'Grady's strategies both allows us to understand her contributions from the perspective of a discourse on subjectivity, supported by psychoanalytic components even as she challenges their Eurocentric assumptions, and suggests a transition into thinking through objecthood. By doing so, we may not only reframe O'Grady's practice in the terms offered by a promising new theory and praxis but also open the door to object-orientation as an intimate and political orientation ripe for further exploration.

OOF's potentialities for political engagement through art practice are perhaps best visualized in the work of its founder, Katherine Behar. In addition to her contributions as a theorist and educator, Behar herself is a practicing artist and developed OOF out of a desire to establish a feminist praxis that is both materialist and political. According to Behar's website, "[h]er artwork spans interactive installation, performance, public art, video, and writing to explore issues of gender and labor in contemporary digital culture. She is known for projects that mix low and high technologies to create hybrid forms that are by turns humorous and sensuous."[66] Examples include videos in which the artist, cloaked in a bloated foam suit evoking the physicality of obesity, performs as "big data" to question "how computer culture favors hoarding, overproduction, and excess";[67] or one in which two Amazon Alexas "entertain each other in a cryptographic guessing game"[68] which momentarily promises to mimic a human exchange before very quickly devolving into incoherence. Her work is contemporary, challenges assumptions about the relationship between humans and technology, and contributes to both practice- and theory-based discourses of radical intimacy.

Behar's position in the academy[69] as a scholar *and* practitioner allows her to operate disruptively from within the ISA, strategically appropriating its codes and structures to destabilize its politics. She states: "Many artists, myself included, approach art practice as applied philosophy. My initial interest in object-oriented ontology stems from my intuition that these ideas serve artists' interests well. Its main tenets coincide nicely with many of the aesthetic pretensions and practical intentions of contemporary studio practices."[70] These pretensions and intentions may include the materialism of OOO—relating to objects as active agents in their environment, as well as Behar's emphasis on the performativity of objects. She states: "OOF's methodological stakes in praxis introduce object theory to forms of feminist and social justice activism that also interrogate and seek to transform the very power relations objectification describes."[71] Framing Kristeva's *revolt* in the terms offered to us by object-oriented feminism allows us to further articulate the role of radical intimacy in contemporary art practice, political discourses, and acts of resistance. As a theoretical *and* experimental praxis, OOF paradoxically enacts the radical return of the subject in process as it continually questions its own ideological origins. By challenging the subject-object binary, OOF introduces an intimacy to ontology that is missing from its patriarchal origins in OOO and creates opportunities for new feminist discourses and praxes.

OOF, unlike its male-dominated counterpart, is not strictly speaking *ontological* but is rather *political*, in that it is a strategy for reclaiming agency in the symbolic order. Behar explains, "object-oriented feminism professes no innocence, but offers a prescriptive activist practice, rejecting the noninterventionist, descriptive stance of ontologists—which remains too redolent of the aloof distancing of orientalism."[72] This strategy employs objecthood as a political tool for questioning hegemonic structures of power and oppression. According to Behar:

> Orienting feminism toward objects means attuning it to the object world. While at first such a move may seem to risk abandoning the concerns of real human subjects (i.e., women), the object world is precisely a world of exploitation, of things ready-at-hand. . . . This world of tools, there for the using, is the world to which women, people of color, and the poor have been assigned under patriarchy, colonialism, and capitalism throughout history.[73]

Furthermore, Behar explains: "Perceiving continuity with other objects in the world, not as subjects but as subject to subjects' dominion, allows us to rework assumptions about feminist political priorities and the what and who of feminist ethics. Object-oriented feminism does not abandon feminist attention to interiority."[74] Rather, Behar argues, OOF uses interiority—and the shifting borders between inside and outside of both intimacy and ideology, which function in tandem—to shed light on "external" (though internalized) ideological structures. In parallel, Kristeva argues that "anxiety, repulsion, nothingness are essential aspects of freedom. That's what revolt is. When one abolishes revolt that is linked to anxiety and rejection, there is no reason to change. You store things up and keep storing. It's a banker's idea, not an idea of a rebel."[75] In this regard, understanding both revolt and object-orientation as strategies of interruption via repetition and regurgitation, OOF consumes and internalizes objecthood, and reproduces it in the form of poetic (and comedic/erotic) acts and representations.

OOF's intentions are to be an interventionist, activist practice, rather than merely a speculative stance. According to Behar, OOF has a "penchant for experimentation over speculation. Where an ontologist might speculate, describing the world, 'This is the way things are,' object-oriented feminists and feminist new materialists engage in the world using experimental praxis, 'This is a way of being with things.' Or more simply, 'This is a way of being things.'"[76] This book addresses art practices that directly involve humans and human activity, while OOF often turns its attention toward the explicitly inanimate; however, Behar and her fellow authors place significant attention on human artists and their appropriation of object-like qualities in their explorations of objectification. By doing so, they draw parallels and foster solidarity between the human and nonhuman world, as well as shed light on the institutionalized disempowerment of human "objects." Perhaps most potently, these newfound connections reveal strategies for political action.

Performativity has been a unifying thread throughout the various artists and works explored in this book, and according to Behar, objects have performative qualities. She states: "Experience shows that while objects are not substance, their performance does have material consistency."[77] In her exposition of the erotics of OOF, Behar describes an affinity toward Bataille's theories of erotism, which were also highly influential to Kristeva's theories on abjection. Behar summarizes Bataille's contribution as "the radical surrender of self in becoming other-than-subject" through which "individuals attain continuity with the object world."[78] She describes the importance of humor and the absurd to the erotic strategies of OOF, arguing that "[l]ike laughter, fomenting erotic fusion with an object, as a means of becoming object, is a creative, generative act."[79] She makes these points not to render the work at hand a joke but to acknowledge the apparent absurdity of OOF as a model for empowerment and to argue for its deliberate use of irony and humor as a political tool, for, she argues, "[e]rotic nonsense breaks down ideology's common sense."[80] Radical intimacy introduces erotic non-sense to break down ideology via the ambivalence between subject and object, and the political instability that this ambivalence implies. OOF offers an opportunity to employ the tenets of radical intimacy in a theoretical praxis which helps us reframe works of contemporary art in a discourse of the politics of intimacy.

Despite my concerns about objectification in the field of representation, I suggest that the very notions of "objectification" and "exploitation" can both be complicated by, and harnessed in service to, my investigation of radical intimacy. Without disavowing the importance of reclaiming subjectivity when one's subjectivity—and, therefore, one's very personhood in modern society—has been historically excluded and debased, I accept Behar's invitation to "undertake an important political function"[81] that she believes can only be adopted via the flipping of orientation from subject to object. Specifically, she argues: "Redirecting feminism from a paradigm of personal visibility toward what Elizabeth Grosz calls the impersonal politics of imperceptibility, object-oriented feminism shifts its operational agencies from a 'politics of recognition,' of *standing out*, to a politics of immersion, of *being with*."[82] I suggest that the power of DeGenevieve's, Maida's, and O'Grady's work be found not only in the assertion of personal—and to some extent, collective—subjectivity but in the steps the works take *beyond subjectivity*, exposing the ideological mechanisms of objectification from the "inside out" position of the object.

OOF is a performative stance and a political proposition that operates as intimate revolt by confronting the extimate quality of ideology and, by extension, subjectivity, with the alternative gesture of objecthood. Behar assures us that in OOF, "there is neither an interest in resolving difference nor an investment in arriving at an ontologically 'correct' master theory."[83] As previously discussed, Kristeva also questions the paradigm of "the political" as she is generally wary of once-transgressive ideas becoming new hegemonic ideologies. She argues that "[p]eople have reduced, castrated and mutilated the concept of revolt by turning it only into politics."[84] Kristeva offers intimacy as a source to which to turn for a deeper catharsis of ideological formulas, which themselves threaten the sovereignty of the individual. She explains her position on revolt:

> The history of the last two centuries has gotten us used to understanding "revolt" in the political sense of a "revolution" that confronts a Norm and transgresses it by a Promise of paradise. You know what happens afterwards. We have to get back to the intimate well-springs of revolt—in the deep sense of self-questioning and questioning tradition as well, sexual differences, projects for life and death, new modalities of civil society and so on. It's about re-rooting the self that takes us nearer to revolt in the Augustinian sense—*se quarere*, i.e. put yourself on the line to reciprocally stimulate memory, thought and will.[85]

How might the intimate reveal itself in its political workings, without devolving to a promise of paradise? As Kristeva argues, "Freud's insight means an invitation to revolt (anamnesis, desire, love and hatred) all the better to reveal oneself (to create and re-create the self)."[86] The artists in this project expose and symbolize the unconscious stirrings of such revolt in sexual intimacy, and upon the omnipresence of culture (i.e., the symbolic), which takes over even in the throes of sexual jouissance. By reanimating revolt in the intimate realm, artists may impact the political machine and its infiltrations into private life and the life of the psyche.

In the spirit of intimate revolt, the artists in this book use the imaginary realm to take us beyond signifying representation into the poetic world of speech as eternal discourse. Despite her celebration of visual artists alongside writers throughout her decades of scholarship, Kristeva refuses to surrender the primacy of written language to the visual realm, as a staging ground for revolt. She warns: "Be aware that the image can become an [sic] honey trap for the kind of rebellion I'm trying to rehabilitate as a form of scrutiny. . . . There is nothing better than words, above all words to deepen and sustain debate. If the image isn't subservient to the word, it just reduces meaning into stereotypes."[87] Kristeva specifically warns of the danger of attuning ourselves to the media and its narcissistic misrecognitions without the slippages and creativity of the symbolic and semiotic. Though the image always threatens to become a "honey trap," discourse and the eternal return to interiority usher a true culture of revolt. Kristeva claims to want to "rehabilitate" the concept of revolt in its "astronomical meaning, the eternal return,"[88] as a looping back into the most private interiority of the self, via recollection in speech. Through the narrative retelling of personal history via analytic speech, subjects revisit their traumas and persistent psychical conflicts. Kristeva states: "It is the conflicts that are eternal because there is pleasure in conflict. The individual, in this return to him or herself, experiences division, conflict, pleasure and jouissance in this fragmentation."[89] By emphasizing the role of pleasure and the failures and ambiguities of jouissance in the psychic apparatus of subject-formation, Kristeva continually invites us back into the realm of sexual intimacy, for it is there that the greatest ambivalence emerges that invites us to question the very foundations of our subjectivity.

By participating in a culture of deep questioning and interiority in the conflict between subject and object, OOF establishes a position of radical intimacy, in solidarity with the object world. Behar concedes:

> For while the intention to slough off the humanist trappings of subjecthood is worthy as a gesture toward feminist camaraderie with nonhumans, in practice it is likely to remain aspirational; and while, for those not already accustomed

to it, human objecthood (which is not to say subjecthood) can be illuminating, rarely will it prove liberating. Certainly examples of objectification's benefiting the objectified are few and far between.[90]

How might we reconcile Behar's prediction of object-orientation's ethical and political failures with her own insistence that its stance is essential for solidarity and political agency? Behar acknowledges the inherent wrongness of OOF—its "flat indifference to correctness"; however, she argues, "being wrong in this way is radical, political work. It means setting aside truth and correctness in favor of being artificial and botched, all to make room for an erotics of generative thinking and doing."[91] This wrongness may reveal itself in DeGenevieve's cool objectification of homeless men of color and her open discourse about her intentions. It is perhaps evident in Maida's racing heartbeat as he desires the exoticized Other or in O'Grady's bringing to light the exploitation insolubly woven into the fabric of Black female sexuality. Here I return to my initial introduction of the intimate as that which seeks being most inside. Intimacy is inherent contradiction, the most extimate conflict, just as OOF strives toward "being beyond untrue, in an erotic sense, in excess of singular truth."[92] OOF's wrongness, and Behar's willingness to posit a theory for its potential impact rather than for its factual accuracy, allows it to operate in the borders of truth and subjectivity, along with intimacy in revolt.

Ideology into Intimacy

Intimacy coexists with and complicates ideology, speaking its own language that extends far beyond the hail of the law and our own complicity in the response to that law. Intimacy operates in the *extimate*—the deep exteriority within us, which includes the unconscious in its radical otherness but encompasses and activates far more than the unconscious. Intimacy adopts the stances and significations of ideology to construct its own poetic language. Ushering the possibility of revolt—the retrospective, retroactive return to this radical exteriority within—radical intimacy subverts the constructs that keep us bound to our conception of our own selves and the environment that surrounds us.

The artists featured in this final section of the book explore subjectivity, objecthood, and the intimate strife between them, operating on the level of abjection, poetry, and the semiotics of intimacy, producing the rifts in meaning essential to revolt. While exposing the co-presence of ideology and desire, and their workings upon one another, DeGenevieve and Maida allow for the disruption of the somatic body to destabilize these very relations of subject and object. Via memory-traces of sexual intimacy in the representational realm, and the unveiling of the ideological (subjective) formation worked through via this intimacy, O'Grady employs Behar's *being-with* as a praxis of care. By *being with* fellow women of color in their constructed subjectivities, by asking viewers to *be with* her as a singular individual representing the construction of her own unconscious, we enter into an intimacy beyond the sexual that nevertheless relies on desire. The artists in these chapters operate in a state of radical play with the notion of objecthood, objectification, and marginalization in the Ideological State Apparatus, which includes culture, political parties, the family, religious institutions, and the educational system. They participate in the eternal questioning of institutions in which they are active, contributing members, operating as the extimate other within the ISA. By complicating the terms with which to identify right/wrong, true/false, subject/object—and the nuanced terms "objectification" and "solidarity"—they demonstrate the potential of radical intimacy to disrupt ideological thinking and, by extension, political ideologies, their institutions, and the rituals within these institutions.

The need to establish a more nuanced vocabulary around the politics of radicality and intimacy in contemporary art is not merely theoretical but points directly to our sites of art production, dissemination, and critique. The art world has been wracked with ideological controversy in the last several years, controversies grounded in questions of representation, ethics, and narrative authority, as well as institutional responsibility. In one pivotal example of the 2017 Whitney Biennial of American Art, the art world has been divided around the question of who gets to represent whom and which stories must be told from first-person positions. On one side, we have Hannah Black pressing the Whitney to remove and destroy Dana Schutz's painting of Emmet Till's open casket because "white free speech and white creative freedom have been founded on the constraint of others, and are not natural rights."[93] On the other, we have Coco Fusco arguing that "the argument that any attempt by a white cultural producer to engage with racism via the expression of black pain is inherently unacceptable forecloses the effort to achieve interracial cooperation, mutual understanding, or universal anti-racist consciousness."[94] On a vernacular level, members of the art community have expressed sadness at the possibility that artists can only ethically represent those that share their identities, but this argument falls apart as soon as one acknowledges the power dynamics inherent in all forms of representation and the dangers that this poses to individuals and groups seeking to reclaim their subjectivity. How do we—artists, philosophers, educators, curators, and scholars—responsibly and sensitively engage discourses that are inextricably mired in legitimate concerns about exploitation and silencing of marginalized communities? We must better understand our intentions as artists and thinkers, as well as our relation to objects—including, and particular to this investigation, human "objects." We may leverage the language of intimacy to aid us in having these conversations and better understanding ourselves and our intentions when making, exhibiting, and critiquing work.

Coda

Being is Heard in the Intimate

Radical Intimacy

Intimacy is a poetic function deployed in the spirit of activism. It disrupts ideological thinking and both expresses and facilitates radical thought through the conflation of inner and outer space, subjectivity and objecthood. It is a form of play and metamorphosis in line with radical thinking and feminist praxis, a subversive element within this constellation. In the passage through abjection, Kristeva argues, the subject-in-formation rejects itself and commits a subversive act. She states: "'Abjection' or the abject is what is neither subject, nor object but unceasingly returns, disgusts, rejects, fascinates. It is near but not able to be assimilated."[1] What is the relationship between abjection and revolt? According to Kristeva, "[t]he permanence of contradiction, the temporariness of reconciliation, the bringing to the fore of everything that puts the very possibility of unitary meaning to the test (such as the drive, the unnamable feminine, destructivity, psychosis, etc.): these are what the culture of revolt explores."[2] Revolt, it seems, puts abjection to work in the working-through of ideology and subjectivity in intimate and artistic praxis. Kristeva invites artists to participate in this culture of revolt by manifesting intimate psychical life through aesthetic and poetic acts. By flipping the ideological balance away from subjectivity, and toward a discourse of objecthood, artists in praxis *with objects* and *as objects* work around the edges of ideology—not *outside of* but as the radical other *within* ideology.

Kristeva remains skeptical about the contemporary state of visual art, blaming the failure of the faculty of representation and the lack of intimacy in contemporary communications. If intimacy is under threat, suggests Kristeva, then so is revolt—the ability to turn inwards and uncover one's deep and singular truths. Faced with the inability to represent, she seems to suggest, our imaginary realm becomes no longer ours and we foreclose our own chance of freedom. Intimacy is inherently impossible, and yet the striving toward intimacy comprises the very working of intimacy as it destabilizes our very subjectivity, the ideology of our modern sense of self. According to Kristeva, however, intimacy is key in our search for continual renewal. She demurs, "[w]e are no doubt permanent subjects of a language that holds us in its power. But we are subjects *in process*, ceaselessly losing our identity, destabilized by fluctuations in our relations to the other, to whom we nevertheless remain bound by a kind of homeostasis."[3] In our ambivalent and sometimes difficult intimate engagements, we experience the slippages necessary for reconstruction of the eternally subversive self.

Artists, curators, and theorists have a compelling stake in Kristeva's investigations due to the direct challenge she poses to the viability of art practice as a culture of revolt. Kristeva's notion of intimacy engages the perpetual reorientation of meanings and values. We may thus draw a direct arc from her theory of intimacy to Baudrillard's radical thought. Baudrillard likens radical thought to the radical use of language in poetry: "because of its very form, it leads to the spiritual and mental imagination of sounds and rhythm, to the dispersal of meaning in the event of language, just as muscular functions are dispersed in dance, and just as the reproductive function is dispersed in erotic games."[4] Baudrillard marks even radical thought as a contradictory and self-defeating entity, in line with the paradoxical nature of intimacy, and highlights its inherent eroticism—a poetic function that disperses meaning and, therefore, ideology. Baudrillard establishes the poetic language function of radical thought as a playful, rhythmic dispersal of ideology. Kristeva argues for the special role played by writing and psychoanalysis, of accessing, through questioning, "this border region of the speaking being that is psychosis."[5] Writing, in particular, "attains non-sense too by unfolding meaning to the point of sensations and drives, finding its pulse in a realm that is no longer symbolic but semiotic."[6] By merging the poetic with the somatic, Kristeva and Baudrillard locate language for suggesting the workings of radical sexual intimacy in contemporary art.

Art, the Object, and Beauty

The art practices discussed within this book challenge us not to look away but to allow ourselves—from our own subjection to language—to be abjected along with them as they shimmer on the edge between abjection and the law. These examples of creative practice operate at the intersection of radical intimacy and politics, considering the political as the "apparatus, and its practice, or practices"[7] of the politico-legal layer of the ISA. Radical intimacy works through the drive and jouissance, both of which participate in sexual desire, and in the dance of meaning and non-meaning engaged in art practice. Lacan is clear in articulating that "the drive—the Freudian drive—has nothing to do with instinct. . . . Libido is not sexual instinct."[8] Instead, the drive is always a pull, a "constant force" toward the articulation of meaning. The impossibility of satisfaction generates jouissance in the drive to signify and surplus-jouissance in the failure to signify. According to Žižek, "*jouissance* is the basis upon which symbolization works, the basis emptied, disembodied, structured by the symbolization, but this process produces at the same time a residue, a leftover, which is the surplus-enjoyment."[9] More than a displacement and quieting of the libido, sublimation in the Freudian sense generates articulations of the psyche in the form of artistic representations, but the language generated is a language of loss and destitution. According to Kristeva, the death drive produces in the ego "its own aptitude to imagine, to signify, to speak, to think: the ego invests *signifiance* when it deeroticizes and utilizes the death drive internal to its narcissism."[10] Radical intimacy works through the death drive without deeroticizing it. Radically intimate practice allows for the erotic to emerge as a drive toward subjective destitution and infinite enjoyment in the playful, destabilizing, terrifying loss of borders. In the aesthetic play of radical intimacy, beauty is inextricable from death, the threat of loss of the other and loss of self.

We may understand radical sensibility to be the employment of the body in materialist practices that challenge the mind-body-soul divisions. What role does the object play in contemporary art and how might radical intimacy destabilize the relationship between object, artist, and audience? The transcendental subject creates a hierarchy among beings in the universe, with Man at the top of the ontological food chain. For women, people of color, those living in poverty, immigrants, and other marginalized people, the hierarchy that places them in the role of object assigns them a lower rung of the ladder of subjectivity. By aligning radical intimacy in contemporary art with the breakdown of subjectivity and the emergence of the object as a site of agency, I have explored the ways that shaking the foundations of subject-object relations—not merely by complicating the borders between them but by using performance and intentional stance-setting to investigate the nature of objects from within—invites the material *and* human objects of contemporary art to participate in a radical challenge to ideological thinking. OOF's stated aim of "reorienting from feminist subjects to feminist objects"[11] shines light on the workings of objectification in contemporary practice. According to Morton: "An object is deviation—*objects in general turn* . . . [m]ovement is part of being a thing, period, such that a thing deviates from itself, just to exist. Preventing a thing from deviating is called destroying it."[12] With subjectivity itself threatened, assuming the radicalized ontological stance of the abjected, rejected other—the object excluded from the world of meaning— these agents in the form of human objects, artist-objects, occupy a deviant space between language and abjection, and there they build culture and discourse from the position of their own exclusion. By witnessing object-orientation at play in the artist-philosopher's toolkit, through the vector of radical intimacy, we find a new language for understanding the anarchic agency at the core of radically intimate artistic practice.

Radicality in Contemporary Art

My inquiry on radical intimacy extends beyond the borders of sexuality, to include a broader framework of ecological, social, and political concerns. From an Althusserian perspective, politics may be considered as part of the material practices and rituals that establish the law and perpetuate our subjectivity to that law. These practices become institutionalized in the ISA, and of particular interest to this inquiry is art and its institutions. During the writing of this book, relevant questions about radicality have surfaced in the discourse of the New York City art world, particularly controversies relating to representation and institutional ethics. According to Andrea Fraser, "[f]rom 1969 on, a conception of the 'institution of art' begins to emerge that includes not just the museum, nor even only the sites of production, distribution, and reception of art, but the entire field of art as a social universe."[13] With this backdrop for contemporary institutional critique, the 2017 Whitney Biennial of American Art was mired in controversy regarding the limitations of empathy, and the right to self-representation in an inherently hegemonic space, while the 2019 iteration was steeped in condemnations of institutional leadership and its responsibility toward human rights.[14] As previously cited, the earlier debate erupted in response to Dana Schutz's painting *Open Casket* and Hannah Black's open letter calling for the removal and destruction of the artwork.[15] The 2019 biennial—perhaps reeling from this episode—was heavily focused on social justice, but nevertheless was castigated by some critics for being more politically correct than politically impactful. According to veteran art critic Linda Yablonsky in *The Art Newspaper*, the exhibition was "missing a radical spirit,"[16] and Paddy Johnson's review in the *Observer* claims that "[o]verwhelmingly, artists articulate a desire for a more equal and just society, though usually from a stakeless and safe vantage point."[17] According to

Yablonsky's review, published shortly after the show's opening, "for an exhibition that aligns with the politics of resistance, it doesn't ruffle many feathers.... Some artists in the show identify as activists, but there are no revolutionaries among them."[18] Complaining of "jargony wall labels"[19] and the lack of abstract paintings in the exhibition, Deborah Solomon of WNYC quips that "this is a show that favors sociology over poetry."[20] These varied concerns collectively illuminate the difficulties faced by art that claims political and social agency, and compel us to meet our own expectations of revolutionary art practices with thoughtful and nuanced discourses about strategies of revolt in contemporary art.

According to museum scholar and critic Seph Rodney, these criticisms raise bigger questions for contemporary art—questions that Yablonsky has sidestepped in making her argument against the biennial's artists. Rodney cites Yablonsky's review as "by far the most dismissive and scornful of all the pieces I've read" and accuses her of making "[a] damning judgment that allows no response."[21] Ultimately, Rodney argues, Yablonsky's point fails because she has failed to define her own terms: "she never explains what she means by 'radical' or 'radicality.' It's a buzzword, and a shorthand way of signifying her supposedly astute, bona fide perspective. But ... it's not clear what these terms, in her usage, actually refer to."[22] Offering his own critique of radicality, Rodney asks "whether [Yablonsky] appreciates that radicality in the arts has always already been aestheticized. The term 'radicality' is fetishized as a stand in for social change that cannot be undone or rolled back later." Rodney challenges Yablonsky without necessarily claiming that the artists participate in "real" social change. Instead, he highlights the ways that radicality itself has become—and perhaps always already was—a commodity. Yablonksy asks: "Ultimately, it returns us to the question of what we want from art and its institutions. Pleasure? Confrontation? Agency? Sensory stimulation? Historical reckoning?"[23] With this question also arises the question of what we want from intimacy and its subversions. Reminding us of the intimate operations of ideology, Fraser argues, "just as art cannot exist outside the field of art, we cannot exist outside the field of art, at least not as artists, critics, curators, etc. ... It is because the institution is inside of us, and we can't get outside of ourselves."[24] What if we were able to get outside of ourselves by accessing the radical otherness and discomfiting interiority of the intimate? When we question ourselves, we question institutionalized structures and ideologies, embedded deep within us. What role can radical intimacy play in the aesthetic and political fields for the next generation and the future of humanity?

Kristeva reminds us that "it is not only the biological but being itself that is heard in the intimate,"[25] suggesting that if we listen to our own intimacy, we can reconstruct our own ontology. Intimacy is not merely a biological relation or a dialogical conversation. Intimacy's radicality emerges as a poetic intervention that operates on ideological, political, and institutional levels. In an era facing multiple existential threats to the human race—climate change with its deadly biological conditions and accompanying mass migrations; technological advancements in artificial intelligence that subvert the agency of human subjects; and the diminishing dominance of human touch posed by the rise of the virtual (to name just a few)—we must consider strategies of salvaging access to that which is most inside us and yet remains radically out of reach. According to Morton, "[a]rt can help us, because it's a place in our culture that deals with intensity, shame, abjection, and loss. It also deals with reality and un-reality, being and seeming."[26] Ideology and intimacy mirror each other in their extimate structure—inside and outside fluctuating in an ambivalence that threatens the collapse of divisions between inner and outer space, subject and object, self and not-self. We are reminded of our complicity in the surrender of individual agency for institutionalized subjectivity, just as we remain aware of our power as subjects-in-process, to revolt through a continual return to our own interiority. This internal sanctum will undoubtedly evolve with our species, our environment, and the technologies that we introduce as intimate mechanisms in our increasingly automated and virtualized existence. Kristeva reminds us of the singularity of intimate life and the need to work through that heterogeneity in collaboration with others. If the intimate fulfills Kristeva's desire for a return to the interiority of the soul, then radical intimacy is a radical return, a revolutionary play of otherness within our interior lives, within ideology, extending outwards into a collective culture of revolt.

Notes

Introduction

1 Julia Kristeva, *Revolt, She Said: An Interview by Philippe Petit* (Los Angeles: Semiotext(e), 2002), 100.
2 Julia Kristeva, *Intimate Revolt: The Powers and Limits of Psychoanalysis* (New York: Columbia University Press, 2002), 43.
3 Ibid.
4 Ibid., 44.
5 Ibid., 267.
6 Sigmund Freud and Peter Gay, "Civilization and Its Discontents," in *The Freud Reader*, 1st ed. (New York: W. W. Norton & Company, 1989), 723.
7 Ibid., 724.
8 Jacques Lacan, *The Four Fundamental Concepts of Psychoanalysis: The Seminar of Jacques Lacan Book XI*, ed. Jacques-Alain Miller, trans. Alan Sheridan (New York: W. W. Norton & Company, 1998), 164.
9 Ibid., 163–4.
10 Ibid., 166.
11 Ibid., 165–6.
12 Kristeva, *Revolt, She Said*, 30.
13 In her more recent scholarship, Kristeva has expressed her belief that gender is produced creatively in our intimate relationships. I therefore refuse to hold her hostage to her own past essentialist viewpoints on gender and invite a rereading of her work through her own evolution as a scholar and feminist.
14 Judith Butler, *Gender Trouble* (New York: Routledge, 2007), 109.
15 Ibid., 110.
16 Kristeva, *Revolt, She Said*, 32.
17 Ibid.
18 Hermoine Hoby, "The Reinventions of Genesis Breyer P-Orridge," *The New Yorker*, June 29, 2016, www.newyorker.com/culture/culture-desk/the-reinventions-of-genesis-breyer-p-orridge. A key artist in this book, Genesis P-Orridge has been accused of such pathological behavior. Their moniker "wrecker of civilisation" was adopted after being named as such by the British government and having

their home raided by Scotland Yard. According to an article in *The New Yorker*, "[i]n 1976—following an exhibition entitled 'Prostitution' at London's Institute of Contemporary Arts—the Conservative M.P. Nicholas Fairbairn described P-Orridge and h/er associates as 'wreckers of civilization.' In the early nineties, a time of widespread moral panic, P-Orridge was labelled a satanist and accused of child abuse."

19 Kristeva, *Revolt, She Said*, 31.
20 Ibid., 33–4.
21 Julia Kristeva, "The Psychic Life: A Life in Time, Psychoanalysis and Culture," *Journal of French and Francophone Philosophy* 26, no. 2 (2018): 83. https://doi.org/10.5195/jffp.2018.860.
22 Kristeva, *Intimate Revolt*, 237.
23 Freud and Gay, "Civilization and Its Discontents," 733.
24 Kristeva, *Intimate Revolt*, 13.
25 Julia Kristeva, *The Sense and Non-Sense of Revolt: The Powers and Limits of Psychoanalysis*, trans. Jeanine Herman (New York: Columbia University Press, 2000), 7.
26 Rooksana Hossenally, "Anish Kapoor on His Controversial New Exhibition at the Chateau De Versailles," *Forbes*, June 10, 2015, www.forbes.com/sites/rooksanahossenally/2015/06/10/interview-anish-kapoor-talks-about-his-new-controversial-show-at-the-chateau-de-versailles-france/#2a4ea204151a. Kapoor's exhibition was labeled "controversial" because of the innuendos of some of his sculptural forms, including the claim that his sculpture *Dirty Corner* was meant to evoke Marie Antoinette's vagina. According to Kapoor, "Louis XIV was very controversial and sexual, and all these things are there. The gardens are like a covering, nature is seen as perfect object, well it's not a perfect object. What's underneath the surface is something darker, more complex, more dangerous. I wanted to look at the question of eternity and decay."
27 Anish Kapoor and Julia Kristeva, "Blood and Light," in *Anish Kapoor: Versailles* (Paris: RMN-Grand Palais, 2015), 38, http://www.kristeva.fr/.
28 Ibid.
29 Christopher Lauer's book *Intimacy: A Dialectical Study* helped frame my own research on intimacy beyond dialectical thought, yet in constant dialogue with the complexities of recognition as illuminated in psychoanalysis.
30 Jacques-Alain Miller, "Extimity," ed. Elisabeth Doisneau, trans. Françoise Massardier-Kenney, *The Symptom* 9, *Lacanian Ink* (Fall 2008), www.lacan.com/symptom/extimity.html.
31 Ibid.
32 Louis Althusser, *On the Reproduction of Capitalism: Ideology and Ideological State Apparatuses*, trans. G. M. Goshgarian and Ben Brewster (London: Verso, 2014), 181.

33 Ibid., 191.
34 Ibid., 201.
35 Kristeva, *Intimate Revolt*, 7.
36 Jean Baudrillard, "Radical Thought," *Parallax: Cultural Studies and Philosophy* 1, no. 1 (1995): 56, doi:10.1080/13534649509361992.
37 Ibid., 54.
38 Ibid., 55.
39 Ibid., 55–6.
40 Althusser, *Reproduction of Capitalism*, 258.
41 Ibid., 259.
42 Jean Baudrillard, *Forget Foucault*, trans. Nicole Dufresne (Los Angeles: Semiotext(e), 2007), 74.
43 Ibid., 77.
44 Ibid.
45 Ibid.
46 Kristeva, *Sense and Non-Sense*, 10.
47 Baudrillard, *Forget Foucault*, 79–80.
48 Kristeva, *Intimate Revolt*, 5.
49 Ibid., 13.

Chapter 1

1 Leigh Ledare interviewed by David Joselit, "An Interview," *Leigh Ledare: et al.* (Milan: Mousse Publishing, 2012), 99.
2 Althusser, *Reproduction of Capitalism*, 206.
3 Chris Kraus and Leigh Ledare, "Pretend You're Actually Alive (Leigh Ledare)," interview by Chris Kraus, *Social Practices* (South Pasadena: Semiotext(e), 2018), 246. Originally printed in *BOMB* 132 (2015).
4 Sean O'Hagan, "Oedipal Exposure: Leigh Ledare's Photographs of His Mother Having Sex," *The Guardian*, October 9, 2013, http://www.theguardian.com/artanddesign/2013/oct/09/leigh-ledare-photographs-mother-having-sex.
5 Leigh Ledare, "In the Studio: Leigh Ledare," interview by Steel Stillman, *ARTnews*, December 1, 2017, https://www.artnews.com/art-in-america/features/leigh-ledare-63320.
6 Ibid.
7 Kraus, *Social Practices*, 252.
8 Ledare and Joselit, "Interview," 93.
9 Ledare, "In the Studio."
10 Ledare and Joselit, "Interview," 93.

11 Ibid.
12 Althusser, *Reproduction of Capitalism*, 260.
13 Ibid.
14 Ledare, "In the Studio."
15 Ibid.
16 Lacan, *Four Fundamental Concepts*, 257.
17 Ned Lukacher, *Primal Scenes: Literature, Philosophy, Psychoanalysis* (Ithaca: Cornell University Press, 1986), 24.
18 Ledare, "In the Studio."
19 Lacan, *Four Fundamental Concepts*, 205.
20 Slavoj Žižek, "Introduction: The Spectre of Ideology," in *Mapping Ideology*, ed. Slavoj Žižek (London: Verso, 1994), 12.
21 Althusser, *Reproduction of Capitalism*, 265.
22 Ledare and Joselit, "Interview," 99.
23 Stillman, "In the Studio."
24 Reiner Schürmann, *Broken Hegemonies*, trans. Reginald Lilly (Bloomington: Indiana University Press, 2003), 27.
25 Ibid., 27–8.
26 "Double Bind." Leigh Ledare, https://leighledare.com/Double-Bind (accessed July 26, 2022.). After the completion of *Pretend*, Ledare embarked on a project with Meghan, his ex-wife, to whom he had been married for five years and then divorced for five years. The project, entitled *Double Bind*, was completed in 2010 and consists of photographs taken by both Ledare and Meghan's new husband, Adam Fedderley, who is also a photographer, on private weekends with Meghan at a remote cabin. According to Ledare's website, "Ledare intervened into an existing relationship triangle to foreground and examine social processes of habitual enactment—such as what it means 'to be a husband or wife.' Through a contractually scripted series of events, the project explored emotional and material terms of exchange, thresholds of public and private fantasy, gender normativity, and symbolic boundaries of relationships."
27 Schürmann, *Broken Hegemonies*, 27–8.
28 Julia Kristeva, *Powers of Horror: An Essay on Abjection*, trans. Leon S. Roudiez (New York: Columbia University Press, 1982), 85.
29 Ibid., 85–6.
30 Lacan, *Four Fundamental Concepts*, 106.
31 Althusser, *Reproduction of Capital*, 190.
32 Lacan, *Four Fundamental Concepts*, 204.
33 Žižek, "The Spectre of Ideology," 21.
34 Sophocles, *Oedipus the King*, trans. David Grene (Chicago: University of Chicago Press, 2010), 68.

35 Ledare and Joselit, "Interview," 132.
36 Liz Kotz, "Aesthetics of 'Intimacy,'" in *The Passionate Camera: Photography and Bodies of Desire*, ed. Deborah Bright (London: Routledge, 1998), 207–8.
37 Ibid., 208.
38 Slavoj Žižek, *The Sublime Object of Ideology* (London: Verso, 2008), 42–3.
39 Ibid., 45.
40 Ibid., 184.
41 Ibid., 39.
42 Ibid., 142.
43 Ibid., 43.
44 Ibid., 44.
45 Ibid., 69.
46 Butler, *Gender Trouble*, 199–200.
47 Ibid., 191.
48 Ibid., 202–3.
49 Ibid., 104.
50 Ibid., xxxi.
51 Donna Haraway, *Simians, Cyborgs, and Women: The Reinvention of Nature* (New York: Routledge, 1991), 191.
52 Kristeva, *Powers of Horror*, 110.
53 Haraway, *Simians, Cyborgs, and Women*, 188.
54 Ibid., 196.
55 Ledare and Joselit, "Interview," 112.
56 Katherine Behar, "Facing Necrophilia, or 'Botox Ethics,'" in *Object-Oriented Feminism*, ed. Katherine Behar (Minneapolis: University of Minnesota Press, 2016), 127.
57 Ibid.
58 Žižek, *Sublime Object*, 73.
59 Ibid.
60 Ibid.
61 Ibid., 263.
62 Butler, *Gender Trouble*, 3.
63 Baudrillard, *Forget Foucault*, 73.

Chapter 2

1 Charlotte Meredith, "Oedipal Art? Man Takes Photos of His Own Mother Having Sex." *HuffPost UK*, October 10, 2013, www.huffingtonpost.co.uk/2013/10/10/oedipal-art-man-mum-sex-pictures_n_4075627.html.

2. This interview, *Leigh Ledare by Chris Kraus*, was commissioned by and first published in *BOMB* No. 132, Summer 2015. © Bomb Magazine, New Art Publications, and its Contributors. All rights reserved. The BOMB Digital Archive can be viewed at www.bombmagazine.org.
3. Kristeva, *Powers of Horror*, 208.
4. Ibid., 209.
5. Ibid., 208.
6. Ibid.
7. Žižek, *Sublime Object*, xxvii.
8. Ibid., xxvii–xxviii.
9. Ledare and Joselit, "Interview," 132.
10. Thomas Micchelli, "Leigh Ledare: You Are Nothing to Me. You Are Like Air," *The Brooklyn Rail*, October 5, 2008, https://brooklynrail.org/2008/10/artseen/leigh-ledare-you-are-nothing-to-me-you-are-like-air.
11. "Personal Commissions," Leigh Ledare, https://leighledare.com/Personal-Commissions (accessed March 5, 2021).
12. O'Hagan, "Oedipal Exposure."
13. Matt Blake, "Is This Really Art? Artist Photographs His MOTHER Having Sex with Young Men as Part of Controversial Exhibition," *Daily Mail*, October 11, 2013, http://www.dailymail.co.uk/news/article-2454175/Is-really-art-Artist-photographs-MOTHER-having-sex-young-men-controversial-exhibition.html.
14. Frankie Mathieson, "Does Photographing Your Mother Having Sex Really Qualify as Art?" *Refinery29*, October 11, 2013, http://www.refinery29.com/2013/10/55129/leigh-ledare-mother-having-sex-photo.
15. Greg Fallis, "Leigh Ledare," Sunday Salon, UTATA, March 16, 2012, http://www.utata.org/sundaysalon/leigh-ledare (accessed June 10, 2017).
16. Micchelli, "Leigh Ledare."
17. Christy Lange, "Leigh Ledare," *Frieze*, May 5, 2009, https://www.frieze.com/article/leigh-ledare.
18. Kristeva, *Powers of Horror*, 209.
19. Roland Barthes, *Camera Lucida*, trans. Richard Howard (New York: Hill and Wang, 1980), 25.
20. Ibid., 27.
21. Leigh Ledare, *Pretend You're Actually Alive* (New York: PPP Editions, 2008).
22. Kristeva, *Powers of Horror*, 83.
23. Nicolás Guagnini, "Pretend You're Actually Dead," in *Leigh Ledare: et al.*, ed. Elena Filipovic (Bruxelles: Mousse/Wiels, 2012), 62.
24. Ibid., 64.
25. Kristeva, *Powers of Horror*, 155.
26. Ibid., 88.

27 Ledare, *Pretend*.
28 Guagnini, "Pretend You're Actually Dead," 60.
29 Kristeva, *Powers of Horror*, 74.
30 Ledare, *Pretend*.
31 Ibid.
32 Ibid.
33 Ledare, *Pretend*. I use the {} to indicate additional text that is handwritten over top of the typewritten text in editing.
34 Ledare, *Pretend*.
35 Ibid.
36 Ibid.
37 Ibid.
38 Guagnini, "Pretend You're Actually Dead," 60.
39 Ledare, *Pretend*.
40 Žižek, *Sublime Object*, 134.
41 Ledare, *Pretend*.
42 Ibid.
43 Ibid.
44 Lange, "Leigh Ledare."
45 Leigh Ledare and Steel Stillman, "Leigh Ledare and Steel Stillman," presentation, SVA Theatre by BFA Photography and Video and *Dear Dave*, magazine, October 5, 2017.
46 Ibid.
47 Ibid.
48 David Velasco, "Leigh Ledare: ROTH," *Artforum International* (September 2008), 463, *Gale Academic OneFile*. https://link.gale.com/apps/doc/A185040867/AONE?u=nysl_me_sova&sid=AONE&xid=c4c840c5.
49 Kristeva, *Powers of Horror*, 72.
50 Ibid.
51 Micchelli, "Leigh Ledare."
52 Ledare and Stillman. According to Ledare, his "grandfather used psychological concepts to explain relationships in our family, because he had worked with the German psychologist Kurt Lewin, a pioneer in understanding group dynamics," resulting in Ledare using the Tavistok method to produce conferences which he filmed for *The Task*.
53 Ibid.
54 Kristeva, *Powers of Horror*, 141.
55 Ibid., 2.
56 Ibid., 88–9.
57 Ibid., 9.

58 Hal Foster, "Obscene, Abject, Traumatic," *October* 78 (1996): 113, doi:10.2307/778908.
59 Kristeva, *Powers of Horror*, 15.
60 Ibid., 85.
61 Ibid., 99.
62 O'Hagan, "Oedipal Exposure."
63 Kristeva, *Powers of Horror*, 14.
64 Jacques Lacan, *The Seminar of Jacques Lacan: Book VII, The Ethics of Psychoanalysis, 1959-1960*, ed. Jacques-Alain Miller, trans. Dennis Porter (New York: W. W. Norton & Company, Inc., 1997), 106.
65 Kristeva, *Powers of Horror*, 5.
66 Julia Kristeva, *Melanie Klein*, trans. Ross Guberman (New York: Columbia University Press, 2010), 73.
67 Ibid.
68 Kristeva, *Powers of Horror*, 72.
69 Ibid., 3.
70 Ibid., 4.
71 Ibid., 3.
72 Ibid.
73 Ibid., 45.
74 Ibid., 61.
75 Ibid.
76 Ibid., 55.
77 Ibid.
78 Ibid., 53.
79 Lacan, *Four Fundamental Concepts*, 200.
80 Ledare, *Pretend*.
81 Lacan, *Four Fundamental Concepts*, 174.
82 Kristeva, *Intimate Revolt*, 26.
83 Ibid.
84 Ledare, *Pretend*.
85 Jacques-Alain Miller, "The Wolfman I," trans. Asunción Lopez, *Lacanian Ink* 35 (Spring 2010): 43.
86 Kristeva, *Powers of Horror*, 88.
87 Ibid., 141.

Chapter 3

1 Simon Ford, *Wreckers of Civilisation: The Story of COUM Transmissions & Throbbing Gristle* (London: Black Dog, 1999), 6.30.

2 Neil Mulholland, "Dynamic Perversity," in *The Cultural Devolution: Art in Britain in the Late Twentieth Century* (Aldershot and Hangs: Ashgate, 2003), 56.
3 Genesis P-Orridge qtd. Ford, *Wreckers of Civilisation*, 6.31.
4 Scott G. qtd. Ford, *Wreckers of Civilisation*, 6.31 (this is a quote from Vile (1977)).
5 Ford, *Wreckers of Civilisation*, 6.32.
6 Kristeva, *Sense and Non-Sense*, 7.
7 P-Orridge qtd. Ford, *Wreckers of Civilisation*, 6.32.
8 Kristeva, *Sense and Non-Sense*, 10.
9 Kristeva, *Intimate Revolt*, 51
10 Kristeva, *Sense and Non-Sense*, 7.
11 Ibid.
12 Brian Massumi, *Semblance and Event: Activist Philosophy and the Occurrent Arts* (Cambridge, MA: The MIT Press, 2013), 74.
13 Genesis Breyer P-Orridge. "Genesis BREYER P-ORRIDGE Art." *Genesis BREYER P-ORRIDGE Art* (accessed November 23, 2015).
14 Ford, *Wreckers of Civilisation*, 1.4.
15 *The Ballad of Genesis and Lady Jaye*, directed by Marie Losier, featuring Genesis P-Orridge and Lady Jaye Breyer P-Orridge, 2011.
16 Ibid.
17 Ford, *Wreckers of Civilisation*, 1.15.
18 Ibid., 1.21.
19 Genesis P-Orridge, *Nonbinary* (New York: Abrams Press, 2021), 117.
20 Ford, *Wreckers of Civilisation*, 3.17.
21 Ibid., 2.11.
22 Ibid.
23 Ibid., 5.16–5.17.
24 Ibid., 11.12.
25 Siona Wilson, "Chapter 3: Prostitution and the Problem of Feminist Art—The Emergent Queer Aesthetic of COUM Transmissions," in *Art Labor, Sex Politics: Feminist Effects in 1970s British Art and Performance* (Minneapolis: University of Minnesota Press, 2015), 99. Wilson explains the origins of Tutti's name: "Likewise, read as a reference to high art—Mozart's opera *Cosi Fan Tutte*—the anglicized misspelling of the title as Cosey Fanni Tutti includes a sexual pun ('fanny' is British English slang for a woman's genitals). The opera is about sexual infidelity, and the loose translation of the title of Lorenzo da Ponte's libretto for the opera as 'women are like that' is widely recognized as an everyday form of sexism that finds its contemporary low-art equivalent in Tutti's graffiti-style signature rendition of her first name. She puts a dot in the middle of the roundly drawn 'C' and the 'O,' turning these letters into a graffiti-style image of women's breasts."
26 Douglas Osto, *Altered States: Buddhism and Psychedelic Spirituality in America* (New York: Columbia University Press, 2019), 38. In the 1960s in San Francisco,

Ken Kesey and the Merry Pranksters "threw massive LSD parties they called Acid Tests, joining forces with a band called the Warlocks (soon to become the Grateful Dead) to create venues in which trippers would be bombarded by lights, music and colors of all varieties."

27 Ford, *Wreckers of Civilisation*, 1.17.

28 Genesis P-Orridge and Richard Metzger, "Annihilating Reality: An Interview with Genesis P-Orridge," in *Painful but Fabulous: The Lives & Art of Genesis P-Orridge* (New York: Soft Skull Press, 2003), 41.

29 Ford, *Wreckers of Civilisation*, 6.30. According to Ford, "[t]he tour itself opened in mid-November 1976 with *Cease to Exist no. 1* at the Marianne Deson Gallery in Chicago. COUM performed two more parts of the series, *Cease to Exist nos. 2 & 3*, over the next couple of days at the Name Gallery, also in Chicago. COUM's next stop, on 23 November was Los Angeles and the Institute of Contemporary Arts (LAICA), where they performed Cease to Exist no. 4. The next day they travelled to Santa Monica and at the IDEA Gallery concluded the series with Cease to Exist no. 5."

30 Ibid. This quote begins with the qualifier "According to P-Orridge . . ." P-Orridge's performances were not well-documented, therefore, I understand these recollections to be subject to the instability of memory and desire.

31 Ford, *Wreckers of Civilisation*, 6.30.

32 Losier, P-Orridge, and Breyer P-Orridge. In the 2010 film *The Ballad of Genesis and Lady Jaye*, P-Orridge performs in mock Nazi costuming, yelling: "We have an absolute right to be whoever we want to be! I am so sick and tired of being told what I'm supposed to look like! This is not my body! This is not my name! This is not my personality! Someone said, 'You're supposed to look like this [throws rock] I want you to be the same as the one that went before. I am not! I refuse to be the same!"; P-Orridge qtd. Ford, *Wreckers of Civilisation*, 7.18–9. Despite their frequent and controversial use of Nazi imagery, P-Orridge maintains distance from Nazi ideology, claiming that images such as photographs of Auschwitz represent "one of the ultimate symbols of human stupidity. And I like to remind myself how stupid people are and how dangerous people are because they're stupid. . . . Humanity as a whole is stupid to allow anything like that to begin to occur."

33 Florian Zappe, "'When Order Is Lost, Time Spits' the Abject Unpopular Art of Genesis (Breyer) P-Orridge," in *Unpopular Culture*, ed. Martin Lüthe and Sascha Pöhlmann (Amsterdam University Press, 2016), 135.

34 Wilson, "Emergent Queer Aesthetic," 100.

35 Ford, *Wreckers of Civilisation*, 4.11.

36 Ibid., 5.10.

37 Ibid.

38 Cosey Fanni Tutti, *Art Sex Music* (London: Faber & Faber, 2017), 61.
39 Ford, *Wreckers of Civilisation*, 5.16.
40 P-Orridge qtd. Ford, *Wreckers of Civilisation*, 5.16.
41 Tutti, *Art Sex Music*. P-Orridge's research in sexuality continues throughout their life, through practices that aim to deconstruct societal norms and reconstruct uniquely singular beings out of a poetics of abjection and a discourse of intimacy; however, their work and life have not gone unchallenged. In her 2017 memoir *Art Sex Music*, Tutti details her relationship with P-Orridge, including claims of their rage, physical violence, controlling behavior, and dubious business dealings. Tutti's recollections imply that COUM performances were highly constructed in nature, and that the actions were often staged for the intent purpose of shocking the audience and also to create documentation that would operate as representation of the event. She describes a domestic life with P-Orridge in which she was naïve and victimized, drawn into P-Orridge's web.
42 Kristeva, *Sense and Non-Sense*, 88.
43 Ibid., 89.
44 Ibid.
45 Ibid., 90.
46 Ibid.
47 Ibid.
48 Holly Connolly, "Genesis P-Orridge on Activating a Dead Twin's Spirit," *Dazed*, October 20, 2017, www.dazeddigital.com/film-tv/article/37819/1/uncovering-a-dead-twin-obsessed-cult-with-genesis-p-orridge. P-Orridge's discourse draws from a variety of traditional and occult practices throughout the globe. According to Connolly, "[h]/er interest in reincarnation and the mother story of humanity has led h/er to Tibet, Kathmandu and most recently Ouidah, Benin, West Africa."
49 Tim Kinsella, Genesis P-Orridge, and Robert Ryan, "Undifferentiated Light: A Conversation with Genesis P-Orridge," in *The Inborn Absolute: The Artwork of Robert Ryan*, ed. Robert Ryan (Chicago: Featherproof Books and Mandible Projects, 2016), 133.
50 Ibid., 141.
51 Ford, *Wreckers of Civilisation*, 11.11-3.
52 Genesis Breyer P-Orridge, *Thee Psychick Bible*, "Acknowledgemeants" (Port Townsend: Feral House, 2006.
53 Ibid.
54 Kristeva, *Powers of Horror*, 210.
55 P-Orridge qtd Bengala, "The Intuitive Lure of Flesh: Genesis P-Orridge's Erotic Mailart," in *Painful but Fabulous: The Lives & Art of Genesis P-Orridge* (New York: Soft Skull Press, 2003), 116.

56 Breyer P-Orridge, *Psychick Bible*, 14.
57 Ibid., 46–7.
58 Ibid., 210.
59 Ibid., 41.
60 Ibid.
61 Ibid., 33.
62 Coyote 37 qtd. Breyer P-Orridge, *Psychick Bible*, 75.
63 Ibid.
64 Brother Words, "Even Further: The Metaphysics of Sigils," in *Thee Psychick Bible*, ed. Genesis Breyer P-Orridge (Port Townsend: Feral House, 2006), 392.
65 Brother Words, "Even Further," 390. This same essay is printed in *Painful But Fabulous: The Lives & Art of Genesis P-Orridge*, that cites Words's name as Paul Cecil.
66 Ibid., 393.
67 Ibid.
68 Ibid., 390.
69 Breyer P-Orridge, *Psychick Bible*, 257.
70 Words, "Even Further," 389.
71 Ibid.
72 Ibid., 390.
73 P-Orridge qtd. Bengala, "The Intuitive Lure of Flesh," 115–16.
74 Kristeva, *Powers of Horror*, 93.
75 P-Orridge qtd. Bengala, "The Intuitive Lure of Flesh," 116.
76 Kristeva, *Revolt, She Said*, 34.
77 Massumi, *Semblance and Event*, 6.
78 Ibid., 12.
79 Ibid., 2.
80 Ibid., 13.
81 Words, "Even Further," 394.
82 Massumi, *Semblance and Event*, 121–2.
83 Ibid., 124–5.
84 Ibid., 75.
85 Ibid., 159.
86 Ibid., 150.
87 D. J. Pangburn, "Worship at Genesis Breyer P-Orridge's Cut-Up Altar," *Vice*, April 15, 2016, www.vice.com/en_us/article/4xqm4d/worship-at-genesis-breyer-p-orridges-cut-up-altar.
88 Massumi, *Semblance and Event*, 14.
89 Ibid., 16.
90 Ibid., 59.
91 Ibid.

92 Jacques Lacan, *The Seminar of Jacques Lacan: Book I, Freud's Papers on Technique, 1953-1964* (New York: W. W. Norton & Company, Inc., 1991), 51.
93 Massumi, *Semblance and Event*, 12.
94 Ibid., 21.
95 Ibid., 6.
96 Ibid., 14.
97 Kristeva, *Sense and Non-Sense*, 18.
98 Massumi, *Semblance and Event*, 2–3.
99 Kristeva, *Powers of Horror*, 57–8.
100 Lacan, *Book I*, 275.
101 Holly Connolly. "Genesis P-Orridge on Activating a Dead Twin's Spirit," *Dazed*, October 20, 2017, www.dazeddigital.com/film-tv/article/37819/1/uncovering-a-dead-twin-obsessed-cult-with-genesis-p-orridge.
102 Breyer P-Orridge, *Psychick Bible*, title page.
103 Marie Losier, Steve Holmgren, Martin Marquet, Genesis P-Orridge and Lady Jaye Breyer P-Orridge, *The Ballad of Genesis and Lady Jaye* (Paris: Epicentre Films, 2011); Genesis P-Orridge, *Nonbinary* (New York: Abrams Press, 2021); Breyer P-Orridge, *Psychick Bible*.
104 Jacqueline Rose, *Sexuality in the Field of Vision* (London: Verso, 2005), 226.
105 Ibid., 227–8; Haraway, *Simians, Cyborgs, and Women*. As an example of feminist theory that positions the personal as political and identity as a construction, Haraway's *A Cyborg Manifesto* suggests "a way out of the maze of dualisms in which we have explained our bodies and our tools to ourselves" (181). Haraway describes the cyborg as a "monstrous and illegitimate" (154) entity constructed as a hybrid of human and nonhuman parts that challenges dominant ideologies and systems of oppression. The feminist approach here invites a dismantling of all systems and hierarchies, not just those of sexual difference in the process of building a new way of being.
106 Losier et al., *The Ballad of Genesis and Lady Jaye*.
107 Breyer P-Orridge, *Psychick Bible*, 445.
108 Ibid., 532.
109 Ibid., 445.
110 Losier et al., *The Ballad of Genesis and Lady Jaye*.
111 Breyer P-Orridge, *Psychick Bible*, 531.
112 Ibid., 532.
113 Connolly, "Genesis P-Orridge."
114 Ibid.
115 Miller, "Extimity."
116 Breyer P-Orridge, *Psychick Bible*, 533.
117 Dionysos Andronis and Aldo Lee, directors. *The Pandrogeny Manifesto*.

118 Ibid.
119 Ibid.
120 Sayej, "We Skyped."
121 Kristeva, *Sense and Non-Sense*, 1.
122 Ibid., 11.
123 Ibid.
124 Ibid.
125 Ibid.
126 Ibid.
127 Ibid.
128 Ibid., 7.
129 Ibid., 9.
130 Ibid.
131 Kristeva, *Powers of Horror*, 125.
132 Kristeva, *Revolt, She Said*, 34.

Chapter 4

1 Luce Irigaray, trans. Carolyn Burke, "When Our Lips Speak Together," *Signs: Journal of Women in Culture and Society*, vol. 6, no. 1 (1980): 69–79. Published by The University of Chicago Press. © 1980 The University of Chicago. Reprinted with permission from The University of Chicago Press.
2 Jean Baudrillard, *Seduction*, trans. Brian Singer (New York: St. Martin's Press, 1990), 37.
3 Ibid., 38.
4 Jacqueline Rose, "Introduction II," in *Feminine Sexuality: Jacques Lacan and the école freudienne*, eds. Juliet Mitchell and Jacqueline Rose, trans. Jacqueline Rose (New York: W. W. Norton & Company, 1985), 49.
5 Juliet Mitchell and Jacqueline Rose, Introduction to "God and the *Jouissance* of The Woman. A Love Letter" by Jacques Lacan, in *Feminine Sexuality: Jacques Lacan and the école freudienne*, eds. Juliet Mitchell and Jacqueline Rose, trans. Jacqueline Rose (New York: W. W. Norton & Company, 1985), 137.
6 Ibid.
7 Kristeva, *Sense and Non-Sense*, 87.
8 "Contemporary Artist Mixed Media—Ellen Jong," Ellen Jong, last updated 2020, https://ellenjong.com/.
9 Jacques Lacan, *Encore: The Seminar of Jacques Lacan, Book XX, On Feminine Sexuality, The Limits of Love and Knowledge, 1972-1973*, ed. Jacques-Alain Miller, trans. Bruce Fink (New York: W. W. Norton & Company, 1999), 2. As to allay the suspicion that he may be speaking about something other than literal sex, Lacan

introduces his discourse by stating, "I am first of all going to assume that you are in bed, a bed employed to its fullest, there being two of you in it," affirming his commitment with "I won't leave this bed today."

10 Ibid., 3.
11 Ibid., 7n26 (translator's note).
12 Jacques-Alain Miller, "Another Lacan," trans. Ralph Chipman, *The Symptom, Lacanian Ink* 10 (Spring 2009), https://www.lacan.com/symptom10a/another-lacan.html.
13 Ibid.
14 Ibid.
15 Lacan, *Encore*, 7.
16 Ibid., 112.
17 Ibid., 5.
18 Jacques Lacan, "God and the *Jouissance* of The Woman. A Love Letter," in *Feminine Sexuality: Jacques Lacan and the école freudienne,* eds. Juliet Mitchell and Jacqueline Rose, trans. Jacqueline Rose (New York: W. W. Norton & Company, 1985), 143.
19 Lacan, *Encore*, 7.
20 Baudrillard, *Seduction*, 8.
21 Mitchell and Rose *Feminine Sexuality*, 137–8.
22 Jong, "Mixed Media."
23 Ibid.
24 Ibid.
25 Ellen Jong, *Getting to Know My Husband's Cock*, 2nd ed. (Ellen Jong, 2011).
26 "The Social Sex Revolution," *MakeLoveNotPorn* (2019), www.makelovenotporn.com/.
27 Ibid.
28 Susan Sontag, "In Plato's Cave," in *On Photography* (New York: Picador, 2001), 14.
29 Ibid., 15.
30 Katherine Behar, "An Introduction to OOF," in *Object-Oriented Feminism*, ed. Katherine Behar (Minneapolis: University of Minnesota Press, 2016), 7.
31 Juliet Mitchell, "Introduction I," in *Feminine Sexuality: Jacques Lacan and the école freudienne*, eds. Juliet Mitchell and Jacqueline Rose, trans. Jacqueline Rose (New York: W. W. Norton & Company, 1985), 6.
32 Ibid., 7.
33 Jong, "Mixed Media."
34 Ellen Jong, "@peenessenvy_af." Artist (@peenessenvy_af) instagram photos and videos, https://www.instagram.com/peenessenvy_af/ (accessed August 15, 2022).
35 Ellen Jong and Annie Sprinkle, *Pees on Earth* (New York: PowerHouse Books, 2006).
36 Ibid.
37 Miller, "Another Lacan."

38 Jong, *Husband's Cock*.
39 Lacan, *The Ethics of Psychoanalysis*, 209.
40 Vince Aletti, "Galleries—Downtown: Ellen Jong," *The New Yorker*, July 9, 2012.
41 Ibid.
42 Kristeva, *Powers of Horror*, 29.
43 Susan Sontag, *Regarding the Pain of Others* (New York: Farrar, Straus and Giroux, 2017), 76.
44 Lacan, *Encore*, 22n24.
45 Lacan, *Four Fundamental Concepts*, 17.
46 Lacan, *Encore*, 103.
47 Miller, "Another Lacan."
48 Irigaray, *This Sex Which Is Not One*, trans. Catherine Porter and Carolyn Burke (Ithaca: Cornell University Press, 1985), 212.
49 Ibid., 103.
50 Ibid., 91.
51 Ibid.
52 Pratt and Rosner, "The Global and the Intimate," 10.
53 Luce Irigaray. "Of Relations and Rights—Interview with Luce Irigaray." *YouTube*, GBTIMES, March 12, 2013, www.youtube.com/watch?v=ODD8-wayDhM.
54 Ibid.
55 Irigaray, *This Sex*, 206.
56 Ibid., 78.
57 Lacan, "*Jouissance* of the Woman," 143.
58 Jong, "Mixed Media."
59 Irigaray, *This Sex*, 215.
60 Ibid., 214.
61 Ibid., 209.
62 Ibid., 213.
63 Jong, "Mixed Media."
64 Ibid.
65 Irigaray, "Relations and Rights."
66 Jong, "Mixed Media."
67 Lacan, *Encore*, 144.
68 Ibid.

Chapter 5

1 Jong, *Husband's Cock*, n.p.
2 Kristeva, *Powers of Horror*, 52.

3   Ibid., 51.
4   Ibid., 53.
5   Murat Aydemir, *Images of Bliss: Ejaculation, Masculinity, Meaning* (Minneapolis: University of Minnesota Press, 2007), 122.
6   Kristeva, *Powers of Horror*, 71.
7   Ibid.
8   Ibid.
9   Aydemir, *Images of Bliss*, 122.
10 Ibid., 93.
11 Ibid.
12 Ibid., 97.
13 Irigaray, *This Sex*, 113.
14 Ibid.
15 Sontag, "In Plato's Cave," 4.
16 Ibid., 9.
17 Jong, "Mixed Media."
18 Ibid.
19 Kristeva, *Powers of Horror*, 54.
20 Ibid., 209.
21 Ibid.
22 Ibid.
23 Ibid.
24 Ibid., 208.
25 Ibid., 17.
26 Irigaray, *This Sex*, 112.
27 Ibid., 113.
28 Kristeva, *Intimate Revolt*, 44.
29 Ibid., 47.
30 Ibid., 46.
31 Ibid.
32 Ibid., 50.
33 Ibid., 53.
34 Ibid., 53–4.
35 Ibid., 54.
36 Ibid., 56.
37 Kristeva, *Powers of Horror*, 73.
38 Foster, "Obscene, Abject, Traumatic," 114n11.
39 Ibid.
40 Behar, "An Introduction to OOF," 3.
41 Ibid.

42 The question may be posed of how this new object-orientation differs (or not) from the object relations theory of early British psychoanalysis, specifically the work of Melanie Klein which heavily influenced Kristeva's theories on the maternal. First, Klein still remains grounded in a subject's relation to the object—whether it be the object of love and desire, the good object or the bad object, with this relation being a central component of the subject's formation. While the mother, for example, is seen as an object during infancy, eventually the child grows to see the mother as a whole and complete person and transfers his/her/their desire onto other objects in the world. Object-orientation argues, conversely, that "the world consists exclusively of objects and treats humans as objects like any other, rather than privileged subjects" (Behar, "Introduction to OOF," 1). OOF could therefore perhaps could be argued as honoring the primordial object relation of Klein/Kristeva's pre-symbolic phase; however, instead of arcing toward an intersubjective relation, it follows the path of development of consciousness toward an inter-objective relation. Second, while Klein's work had primarily therapeutic implications, object-oriented feminism in particular occupies a political position and an activist stance that it claims can be enacted through the appropriation of objecthood as a universal position.
43 Behar, "Introduction to OOF," 8.
44 Ibid., 9.
45 Ibid.
46 Ibid., 8.
47 Ibid.
48 Ibid.
49 Ibid., 14.
50 Ibid., 16.
51 Ibid.
52 Ibid., 18.
53 Ibid.
54 Ibid., 23.
55 Timothy Morton, "All Objects Are Deviant: Feminism and Ecological Intimacy," in *Object Oriented Feminism*, ed. Katherine Behar (Minneapolis: University of Minnesota Press, 2016), 65.
56 Ibid.
57 Ibid.
58 Ibid.
59 Ibid., 72.
60 Ibid., 68.
61 Ibid., 69.
62 Ibid., 72.
63 Ibid., 73.

64 Ibid., 78.
65 Sontag, "In Plato's Cave," 24.
66 Frenchy Lunning, "Allure and Abjection: The Possible Potential of Severed Qualities," in *Object Oriented Feminism*, ed. Katherine Behar (Minneapolis: University of Minnesota Press, 2016), 83.
67 Ibid., 84.
68 Graham Harman, *Guerilla Metaphysics: Phenomenology and the Carpentry of Things* (Chicago: Open Court, 2005), 150.
69 Lunning, "Allure and Abjection," 84.
70 Ibid., 86.
71 Graham Harman, *Object-Oriented Ontology: A New Theory of Everything* (London: Pelican Books, 2018).
72 Lunning, "Allure and Abjection," 86.
73 Ibid., 87.
74 Ibid., 102.
75 Ibid.
76 Julia Kristeva and Philippe Sollers, *Marriage as a Fine Art*, trans. Lorna Scott Fox (New York: Columbia University Press, 2016), 34.
77 Ibid.
78 Kristeva, *Intimate Revolt*, 62.

Chapter 6

1 Behar, "Introduction to OOF," 19.
2 Althusser, *Reproduction of Capitalism*, 269.
3 Ibid., 247.
4 Kelly Oliver, "What Is Response Ethics?" *Response Ethics*, ed. Alison Suen (Lanham: Rowman & Littlefield International, 2018), 43.
5 Behar, "Introduction to OOF," 5.
6 Ibid.
7 Ibid., 24.
8 Susan Silas, "Thoughts on the Life and Art of Barbara DeGenevieve," *Hyperallergic*, August 14, 2014, hyperallergic.com/143339/thoughts-on-the-life-and-art-of-barbara-degenevieve.
9 Behar, "Introduction to OOF," 24.
10 Saidiya V. Hartman, *Scenes of Subjection: Terror, Slavery, and Self-Making in Nineteenth-Century America* (New York: Oxford University Press, 2010), 22.
11 Michael Weinstein, "Beyond the Binaries: Crossing the Boundaries of Identity Politics," in *Objectifying the Abject: Exploitation, Political (In)Correctness, and

Ethical Dilemmas, ed. Barbara DeGenevieve (Chicago: University of Illinois at Chicago, Gallery 400), 2006.
12 Ibid.
13 *The Panhandler Project. The Panhandler Project from Barbara DeGenevieve on Vimeo* (2011), https://player.vimeo.com/video/29540736.
14 Hartman, *Scenes of Subjection*, 29.
15 School of the Art Institute of Chicago, "Documenting: The Panhandler Project by Barbara Degenevieve." *Vimeo*, June 8, 2021, https://vimeo.com/52015733.
16 Behar, "Introduction to OOF," 24.
17 Ibid.
18 Ibid., 5.
19 "Exhibitions." Daniel Cooney | Fine Art, https://www.danielcooneyfineart.com/exhibitions (accessed July 27, 2022).
20 "Art—Photo: Dream Factory," JOSEPH MAIDA, http://josephmaida.net/gallery-category/photo/#dream-factory-2 (accessed July 15, 2019).
21 Elizabeth Avedon, "JOSEPH MAIDA: New Natives at Daniel Cooney," *Elizabeth Avedon Journal*, September 15, 2013, elizabethavedon.blogspot.com/2013/09/joseph-maida-new-natives.html.
22 Joseph Maida, "Reciprocal Fantasy: Joseph Maida's New Natives," interview by Matthew Leifheit, *Art F City*, October 9, 2013, artfcity.com/2013/10/09/reciprocal-fantasy-joseph-maidas-new-natives/.
23 Priscilla Frank, "8 Scantily Clad Reasons to Rethink Masculinity," *HuffPost*, December 7, 2017, https://www.huffpost.com/entry/joseph-maida_n_3797229.
24 Maida, "Reciprocal Fantasy."
25 Ibid.
26 "About," JOSEPH MAIDA, http://josephmaida.net/about-2/ (accessed July 15, 2019). BA from Columbia University, MFA from the prestigious Yale Photography Department, and current chairmanship of the School of Visual Arts BFA Photography and Video Department.
27 Geraldine Pratt and Victoria Rosner, "Introduction: The Global and the Intimate," in *The Global and the Intimate: Feminism in Our Time*, ed. Geraldine Pratt and Victoria Rosner (New York: Columbia University Press, 2012), 20.
28 "Art—Photo: Isaac," JOSEPH MAIDA, http://josephmaida.net/gallery-category/photo/#isaac-2 (accessed July 15, 2019).
29 "Art—Photo: Things 'R' Queer," JOSEPH MAIDA, http://josephmaida.net/gallery-category/photo/#things-r-queer (accessed July 15, 2019).
30 "Art—Video: Hula Kahiko Kane," JOSEPH MAIDA, http://josephmaida.net/gallery-category/video/ (accessed July 15, 2019).
31 Tina Chanter and Ewa Płonowska Ziarek, "Introduction," in *Revolt, Affect, Collectivity: The Unstable Boundaries of Kristeva's Polis*, ed. Tina Chanter and Ewa Płonowska Ziarek (Albany: State University of New York Press, 2005), 6.

32. "Art—Video: Hula Kahiko Kane," JOSEPH MAIDA.
33. Christopher Pinney, "Introduction: 'How the Other Half . . . ,'" in *Photography's Other Histories*, ed. Chrisopher Pinney and Nicolas Peterson (Durham: Duke University Press, 2003), 4.
34. Kristeva, *Sense and Non-Sense*, 144.
35. Kristeva, *Powers of Horror*, 73.
36. Behar, "Introduction to OOF," 7.
37. Ibid.
38. José Esteban Muñoz, *Cruising Utopia: The Then and There of Queer Futurity* (New York: New York University Press, 2009), 1.
39. Maida, "Reciprocal Fantasy."
40. Ibid.
41. Jacques Lacan, *Anxiety: The Seminar of Jacques Lacan, Book X*, ed. Jacques-Alain Miller, trans. A. R. Price (Cambridge: Polity Press, 2016), 101.
42. "Art—Video: Hula Kahiko Kane," JOSEPH MAIDA.
43. Kristeva, *Sense and Non-Sense*, 28.
44. Sara Beardsworth, "From Revolution to Revolt Culture," in *Revolt, Affect, Collectivity: The Unstable Boundaries of Kristeva's Polis*, ed. Tina Chanter and Ewa Płonowska Ziarek (Albany: State University of New York Press, 2005), 39.
45. Kristeva, *Sense and Non-Sense*, 18.
46. Sara Beardsworth, *Julia Kristeva: Psychoanalysis and Modernity* (Albany: State University of New York Press, 2004), 50.
47. Ibid.
48. Alex Greenberger, "'The Painting Must Go': Hannah Black Pens Open Letter to the Whitney About Controversial Biennial Work," *ARTnews*, Mar 21, 2017, www.artnews.com/2017/03/21/the-painting-must-go-hannah-black-pens-open-letter-to-the-whitney-about-controversial-biennial-work. Hannah Black castigated Dana Schutz for attempting to express "white shame" in the painting *Open Casket*. Randy Kennedy, "White Artist's Painting of Emmett Till at Whitney Biennial Draws Protests," *The New York Times*, 21 March 2017, www.nytimes.com/2017/03/21/arts/design/painting-of-emmett-till-at-whitney-biennial-draws-protests.html. Schutz expressed empathy with Till's mother and a desire for connection as motivating factors in producing the piece.

Chapter 7

1. Lorraine O'Grady, "Performance Statement #1: Thoughts About Myself, When Seen as a Political Performance Artist (1981)," in *Writing in Space, 1973-2019*, ed. Aruna D'Souza (Durham: Duke University Press, 2020), 38.

2. Lorraine O'Grady, "Olympia's Maid: Reclaiming Black Female Subjectivity (1992/1994)," in *Writing in Space, 1973-2019*, ed. Aruna D'Souza (Durham: Duke University Press, 2020), 98.
3. Ibid., 97.
4. Sheldon George, *Trauma and Race: A Lacanian Study of African American Racial Identity* (Waco: Baylor University Press, 2021), 72–3.
5. Lorraine O'Grady, "Interview with Jarrett Earnest (2016)," in *Writing in Space, 1973-2019*, ed. Aruna D'Souza (Durham: Duke University Press, 2020), 245.
6. Fred Moten, *In the Break: The Aesthetics of the Black Radical Tradition* (Minneapolis: University of Minnesota Press, 2003), 1.
7. Ibid., 8.
8. Behar, "Facing Necrophilia," 123.
9. Ibid.
10. Ibid.
11. O'Grady, "Olympia's Maid," 99.
12. Carla Williams and Deborah Willis, *The Black Female Body: A Photographic History* (Philadelphia: Temple University Press, 2002), 89.
13. "Body Is the Ground of My Experience," Lorraine O'Grady, May 31, 2022, https://lorraineogrady.com/art/body-is-the-ground-of-my-experience/.
14. Williams and Willis, *The Black Female Body*, 89.
15. O'Grady, "Body Is the Ground of My Experience."
16. O'Grady, "Olympia's Maid," 100.
17. O'Grady qtd. Williams and Willis, *The Black Female Body*, 89.
18. Williams and Willis, *The Black Female Body*, 89.
19. O'Grady, "Olympia's Maid," 100.
20. O'Grady, "Body Is the Ground of My Experience."
21. O'Grady, "Olympia's Maid," 95.
22. Williams and Willis, *The Black Female Body*, 89.
23. O'Grady, "Body Is the Ground of My Experience."
24. Behar, "Introduction to OOF," 11.
25. O'Grady, "Body Is the Ground of My Experience."
26. Ibid.
27. Ibid.
28. George, *Trauma and Race*, 73.
29. O'Grady, "Body Is the Ground of My Experience."
30. O'Grady qtd. Williams and Willis, *The Black Female Body*, 89.
31. O'Grady, "Body Is the Ground of My Experience."
32. George, *Trauma and Race*, 64.
33. O'Grady, "Olympia's Maid," 99.
34. Ibid., 101.

35 Ibid., 104.
36 Ibid., 98.
37 Kristeva, *Powers of Horror*, 30.
38 O'Grady, "Olympia's Maid," 105.
39 Ibid.
40 Ibid.
41 Ibid., 105–6.
42 Ibid., 106.
43 Ibid.
44 Ibid.
45 Ibid., 105.
46 Ibid.
47 Kristeva, *Intimate Revolt*, 8.
48 Lorraine O'Grady, "Interview with Laura Cottingham (1995)," in *Writing in Space, 1973-2019*, ed. Aruna D'Souza (Durham: Duke University Press, 2020), 230.
49 Kristeva, *Powers of Horror*, 37.
50 Ibid.
51 Ibid., 37–8.
52 Ibid., 38.
53 Ibid.
54 Ibid.
55 Ibid., 39.
56 Ibid.
57 O'Grady, "Interview with Laura Cottingham," 230.
58 Kristeva, *Powers of Horror*, 40.
59 Ibid., 41.
60 O'Grady, "Olympia's Maid," 97.
61 Ibid.
62 Ibid.
63 Ibid., 102.
64 Ibid., 107.
65 Ibid., 108.
66 "About," Katherine Behar (2019), http://katherinebehar.com/info/index.html.
67 "Buffering (From 'Modeling Big Data')," Katherine Behar (2019), http://katherinebehar.com/art/modeling-big-data/buffering/index.html.
68 "Knock Knock," Katherine Behar (2019), http://www.katherinebehar.com/art/knock-knock/index.html
69 "Katherine Behar," CUNY Graduate Center, last modified 2022, https://www.gc.cuny.edu/people/katherine-behar. Behar is Associate Professor, Data Analysis

and Visualization/New Media Arts, and Deputy Chair of Art in the Fine and Performing Arts Department at Baruch College, CUNY Graduate Center.
70 Behar, "Facing Necrophilia," 139n1.
71 Behar, "Introduction to OOF," 4.
72 Ibid., 13.
73 Ibid., 7.
74 Ibid.
75 Kristeva, *Revolt, She Said*, 101–2.
76 Behar, "Introduction to OOF," 13.
77 Behar, "Facing Necrophilia," 129.
78 Behar, "Introduction to OOF," 16.
79 Ibid.
80 Ibid., 17.
81 Ibid., 9.
82 Ibid.
83 Ibid., 3–4.
84 Kristeva, *Revolt, She Said*, 99.
85 Ibid., 85.
86 Ibid.
87 Ibid., 87.
88 Ibid., 100.
89 Ibid.
90 Behar, "Introduction to OOF," 10.
91 Ibid., 18.
92 Ibid.
93 Greenberger, "The Painting Must Go."
94 Coco Fusco, "Censorship, Not the Painting, Must Go: On Dana Schutz's Image of Emmett Till," *Hyperallergic*, March 29, 2017, hyperallergic.com/368290/censorship-not-the-painting-must-go-on-dana-schutzs-image-of-emmett-till/.

Coda

1 Kristeva, "Psychic Life," 88.
2 Kristeva, *Intimate Revolt*, 10.
3 Julia Kristeva, *In the Beginning Was Love: Psychoanalysis and Faith*, trans. Arthur Goldhammer (New York: Columbia University Press, 1987), 9.
4 Baudrillard, "Radical Thought," 61.
5 Kristeva, *Intimate Revolt*, 10.
6 Ibid.

7 Althusser, *Reproduction of Capitalism*, 259.
8 Jacques Lacan, "On Freud's 'Trieb' and the Psychoanalyst's Desire," in *Écrits: The First Complete Edition in English*, trans. Bruce Fink (New York: W. W. Norton & Company, 2006), 722.
9 Žižek, *Sublime Object*, 191
10 Kristeva, *Sense and Non-sense*, 55.
11 Behar, "Introduction to OOF," 8.
12 Morton, "All Objects Are Deviant," 78.
13 Andrea Fraser, "From the Critique of Institutions to an Institutional Critique," *Artforum* 44 (September 2005): 281.
14 Elizabeth A. Harris and Robin Pogrebin, "Warren Kanders Quits Whitney Board After Tear Gas Protests," *New York Times*, July 25, 2019, www.nytimes.com/2019/07/25/arts/whitney-warren-kanders-resigns.html. Board member Warren Kanders was forced to resign in July 2019, after numerous artists threatened to pull their works mid-show in protest of his ownership of a company that sells tear gas that has been used against protesters and at the border, as well as at other contested sites.
15 Greenberger, "The Painting Must Go."
16 Linda Yablonsky, "Everything Is Good at the Whitney Biennial but Nothing Makes a Difference," *The Art Newspaper*, May 14, 2019, www.theartnewspaper.com/review/whitney-biennial-2019.
17 Paddy Johnson, "Critique of Inequality Is Aimed in All Directions at the 2019 Whitney Biennial," *Observer*, May 15, 2019, observer.com/2019/05/whitney-museum-biennial-2019-review-art-critiquing-injustice.
18 Yablonsky, "Everything Is Good"; subsequent to Yablonksy's review, multiple artists withdrew from the exhibition in protest of Warren Kanders's position on the board, compelling him to resign.
19 Deborah Solomon, "Review: The Whitney Biennial Cops Out." *WNYC News*, May 17, 2019, www.wnyc.org/story/review-whitney-biennial-cops-out.
20 Ibid.
21 Seph Rodney, "Probing the Proper Grounds for Criticism in the Wake of the 2019 Whitney Biennial," *Hyperallergic*, June 7, 2019, hyperallergic.com/503513/probing-the-proper-grounds-for-criticism-in-the-wake-of-the-2019-whitney-biennial.
22 Ibid.
23 Yablonsky, "Everything Is Good."
24 Fraser, "Critique of Institutions," 282.
25 Kristeva, *Intimate Revolt*, 50.
26 Timothy Morton, *The Ecological Thought* (Cambridge, MA: Harvard University Press, 2010), 10.

Bibliography

Aletti, Vince. "Galleries—Downtown: Ellen Jong." *The New Yorker*, July 9, 2012.

Althusser, Louis. *On the Reproduction of Capitalism: Ideology and Ideological State Apparatuses*. Translated by G. M. Goshgarian and Ben Brewster. London: Verso, 2014.

Andronis, Dionysos and Aldo Lee, directors. *The Pandrogeny Manifesto*. Greece, 2006.

Avedon, Elizabeth. "JOSEPH MAIDA: New Natives at Daniel Cooney." *Elizabeth Avedon Journal*, September 15, 2013. elizabethavedon.blogspot.com/2013/09/joseph-maida-new-natives.html.

Aydemir, Murat. *Images of Bliss: Ejaculation, Masculinity, Meaning*. Minneapolis: University of Minnesota Press, 2007.

Barthes, Roland. *Camera Lucida*. Translated by Richard Howard. New York: Hill and Wang, 1980.

Baudrillard, Jean. *Forget Foucault*. Translated by Nicole Dufresne. Los Angeles: Semiotext(e), 2007.

Baudrillard, Jean. "Radical Thought." *Parallax: Cultural Studies and Philosophy* 1, no. 1 (1995): 53–62. http://doi:10.1080/13534649509361992.

Baudrillard, Jean. *Seduction*. Translated by Brian Singer. New York: St. Martin's Press, 1990.

Beardsworth, Sara. "From Revolution to Revolt Culture." In *Revolt, Affect, Collectivity: The Unstable Boundaries of Kristeva's Polis*, edited by Tina Chanter and Ewa Płonowska Ziarek, 37–56. Albany: State University of New York Press, 2005.

Beardsworth, Sara. *Julia Kristeva: Psychoanalysis and Modernity*. Albany: State University of New York Press, 2004.

Behar, Katherine, "An Introduction to OOF." In *Object Oriented Feminism*, edited by Katherine Behar, 1–38. Minneapolis: University of Minnesota Press, 2016.

Behar, Katherine, "Facing Necrophelia, or 'Botox Ethics.'" In *Object Oriented Feminism*, edited by Katherine Behar, 123–44. Minneapolis: University of Minnesota Press, 2016.

Behar, Katherine (website). http://www.katherinebehar.com (accessed 2019).

Bengala. "The Intuitive Lure of Flesh: Genesis P-Orridge's Erotic Mailart." In *Painful But Fabulous: The Lives & Art of Genesis P-Orridge*, edited by Genesis P-Orridge, 111–20. New York City: Soft Skull Press, 2003.

Blake, Matt. "Is This Really Art? Artist Photographs His MOTHER Having Sex with Young Men as Part of Controversial Exhibition." *Daily Mail*, October 11, 2013. http://www.dailymail.co.uk/news/article-2454175/Is-really-art-Artist-photographs-MOTHER-having-sex-young-men-controversial-exhibition.html.

"Body Is the Ground of My Experience." LORRAINE O'GRADY: concept-based art, updated May 31, 2022. https://lorraineogrady.com/art/body-is-the-ground-of-my-experience/.

Breyer P-Orridge, Genesis. "Acknowledgemeants." In *Thee Psychick Bible*. Port Townsend: Feral House, 2006.

Breyer P-Orridge, Genesis (website). "Genesis BREYER P-ORRIDGE Art." *Genesis BREYER P-ORRIDGE Art*, no longer available (accessed November 23, 2015).

Brother Words. "Even Further: The Metaphysics of Sigils." In *Thee Psychick Bible*, edited by Genesis Breyer P-Orridge, 391–402. Port Townsend: Feral House, 2006.

Butler, Judith. *Gender Trouble*. New York: Routledge, 2007.

Cecil, Paul, ""Even Further: The Metaphysics of Sigils." In." In *Painful But Fabulous: The Lives & Art of Genesis P-Orridge*, edited by Genesis P-Orridge, 121–130. New York City: Soft Skull Press, 2003.

Chanter, Tina and Ewa Płonowska Ziarek, "Introduction." In *Revolt, Affect, Collectivity: The Unstable Boundaries of Kristeva's Polis*, edited by Tina Chanter and Ewa Płonowska Ziarek, 1–18. Albany: State University of New York Press, 2005.

Connolly, Holly. "Genesis P-Orridge on Activating a Dead Twin's Spirit." *Dazed*, October 20, 2017. http://www.dazeddigital.com/film-tv/article/37819/1/uncovering-a-dead-twin-obsessed-cult-with-genesis-p-orridge.

DeGenevieve, Barbara. *The Panhandler Project from Barbara DeGenevieve on Vimeo* (2011), https://player.vimeo.com/video/29540736.

"Exhibitions." Daniel Cooney | Fine Art, https://www.danielcooneyfineart.com/exhibitions (accessed July 27, 2022).

Fallis, Greg. "Leigh Ledare," Sunday Salon, UTATA, March 16, 2012, http://www.utata.org/sundaysalon/leigh-ledare (accessed 2019).

Ford, Simon. *Wreckers of Civilisation: The Story of COUM Transmissions & Throbbing Gristle*. London: Black Dog, 1999.

Foster, Hal. "Obscene, Abject, Traumatic." October 78 (1996): 106–24. https://doi.org/10.2307/778908.

Frank, Priscilla. "8 Scantily Clad Reasons to Rethink Masculinity." *HuffPost*, December 7, 2017. https://www.huffpost.com/entry/joseph-maida_n_3797229.

Fraser, Andrea. "From the Critique of Institutions to an Institutional Critique." *Artforum* 44 (September 2005): 278–83.

Freud, Sigmund and Peter Gay. "Civilization and Its Discontents." In *The Freud Reader*, edited by Peter Gay, 722–72. New York: W. W. Norton & Company, 1989.

Fusco, Coco. "Censorship, Not the Painting, Must Go: On Dana Schutz's Image of Emmett Till." *Hyperallergic*, March 29, 2017. http://hyperallergic.com/368290/censorship-not-the-painting-must-go-on-dana-schutzs-image-of-emmett-till.

George, Sheldon. *Trauma and Race: A Lacanian Study of African American Racial Identity*. Waco: Baylor University Press, 2021.

Greenberger, Alex. "'The Painting Must Go': Hannah Black Pens Open Letter to the Whitney About Controversial Biennial Work." *ARTnews*, March 21, 2017. http://

www.artnews.com/2017/03/21/the-painting-must-go-hannah-black-pens-open-letter-to-the-whitney-about-controversial-biennial-work.

Guagnini, Nicolás. "Pretend You're Actually Dead." In *Leigh Ledare, et al.*, edited by Elena Filipovic, 57–82. Bruxelles: Mousse/Wiels, 2012. https://leighledare.com/Press-and-Texts.

Haraway, Donna. *Simians, Cyborgs, and Women: The Reinvention of Nature*. New York: Routledge, 1991.

Harman, Graham. *Guerilla Metaphysics: Phenomenology and the Carpentry of Things*. Chicago: Open Court, 2005.

Harman, Graham. *Object-Oriented Ontology: A New Theory of Everything*. London: Pelican Books, 2018.

Harris, Elizabeth A. and Robin Pogrebin. "Warren Kanders Quits Whitney Board After Tear Gas Protests." *New York Times*, July 25, 2019. http://www.nytimes.com/2019/07/25/arts/whitney-warren-kanders-resigns.html.

Hartman, Saidiya V. *Scenes of Subjection: Terror, Slavery, and Self-Making in Nineteenth-Century America*. New York: Oxford University Press, 2010.

Hoby, Hermoine. "The Reinventions of Genesis Breyer P-Orridge." *The New Yorker*, June 29, 2016. http://www.newyorker.com/culture/culture-desk/the-reinventions-of-genesis-breyer-p-orridge.

Hossenally, Rooksana. "Anish Kapoor on His Controversial New Exhibition at the Chateau De Versailles." *Forbes*, June 10, 2015. http://www.forbes.com/sites/rooksanahossenally/2015/06/10/interview-anish-kapoor-talks-about-his-new-controversial-show-at-the-chateau-de-versailles-france/#2a4ea204151a.

Irigaray, Luce. "Of Relations and Rights—Interview with Luce Irigaray." *YouTube*, GBTIMES, March 12, 2013. http://www.youtube.com/watch?v=ODD8-wayDhM.

Irigaray, Luce. *This Sex Which Is Not One*. Translated by Catherine Porter and Carolyn Burke. Ithaca: Cornell University Press, 1985.

Irigaray, Luce. "When Our Lips Speak Together." Translated by Carolyn Burke. *Signs: Journal of Women in Culture and Society* 6, no. 1 (Autumn 1980): 69–79.

Johnson, Paddy. "Critique of Inequality Is Aimed in All Directions at the 2019 Whitney Biennial." *Observer*, May 15, 2019. http://observer.com/2019/05/whitney-museum-biennial-2019-review-art-critiquing-injustice.

Jong, Ellen. "@peenessenvy_af." Artist (@peenessenvy_af) Instagram Photos and Videos. https://www.instagram.com/peenessenvy_af/ (accessed August 15, 2022).

Jong, Ellen. "Contemporary Artist Mixed Media—Ellen Jong." (2020). https://ellenjong.com/.

Jong, Ellen. *Getting to Know My Husband's Cock*, 2nd ed. Ellen Jong, 2011.

Jong, Ellen and Annie Sprinkle. *Pees on Earth*. New York: PowerHouse Books, 2006.

Kapoor, Anish and Julia Kristeva. "Blood and Light." In *Anish Kapoor: Versailles*. Paris: RMN-Grand Palais, 2015. http://www.kristeva.fr/.

"Katherine Behar." CUNY Graduate Center (2022). https://www.gc.cuny.edu/people/katherine-behar.

Kennedy, Randy. "White Artist's Painting of Emmett Till at Whitney Biennial Draws Protests." *New York Times*, March 21, 2017. http://www.nytimes.com/2017/03/21/arts/design/painting-of-emmett-till-at-whitney-biennial-draws-protests.html.

Kinsella, Tim, Genesis P-Orridge, and Robert Ryan. "Undifferentiated Light: A Conversation with Genesis P-Orridge." In *The Inborn Absolute: The Artwork of Robert Ryan*. Chicago: Featherproof Books and Mandible Projects, 2016.

Kotz, Liz. "Aesthetics of 'Intimacy.'" In *The Passionate Camera: Photography and Bodies of Desire*, edited by Deborah Bright, 204–15. London: Routledge, 1998.

Kristeva, Julia. *In the Beginning Was Love: Psychoanalysis and Faith*. Translated by Arthur Goldhammer. New York: Columbia University Press, 1987.

Kristeva, Julia. *Intimate Revolt: The Powers and Limits of Psychoanalysis*. New York: Columbia University Press, 2002.

Kristeva, Julia. *Melanie Klein*. Translated by Ross Guberman. New York: Columbia University Press, 2010.

Kristeva, Julia. *Powers of Horror: An Essay on Abjection*. Translated by Leon S. Roudiez. New York: Columbia University Press, 1982.

Kristeva, Julia. "The Psychic Life: A Life in Time, Psychoanalysis and Culture." *Journal of French and Francophone Philosophy* 26, no. 2 (2018): 81–90. https://doi.org/10.5195/jffp.2018.860.

Kristeva, Julia. *Revolt, She Said: An Interview by Philippe Petit*. Los Angeles: Semiotext(e), 2002.

Kristeva, Julia. *The Sense and Non-Sense of Revolt: The Powers and Limits of Psychoanalysis*. Translated by Jeanine Herman. New York: Columbia University Press, 2000.

Kristeva, Julia and Philippe Sollers. *Marriage as a Fine Art*. Translated by Lorna Scott Fox. New York: Columbia University Press: 2016.

Lacan, Jacques. *Anxiety: The Seminar of Jacques Lacan, Book X*. Edited by Jacques-Alain Miller. Translated by A. R. Price. Cambridge: Polity Press, 2016.

Lacan, Jacques. *Encore: The Seminar of Jacques Lacan, Book XX, On Feminine Sexuality: The Limits of Love and Knowledge, 1972–1973*. Edited by Jacques-Alain Miller. Translated by Bruce Fink. New York: W. W. Norton & Company, 1999.

Lacan, Jacques. *The Four Fundamental Concepts of Psychoanalysis: The Seminar of Jacques Lacan Book XI*. Edited by Jacques-Alain Miller. Translated by Alan Sheridan. New York: W. W Norton & Company, 1998.

Lacan, Jacques. "God and the *Jouissance* of The Woman. A Love Letter." In *Feminine Sexuality: Jacques Lacan and the école freudienne*, edited by Juliet Mitchell and Jacqueline Rose, translated by Jacqueline Rose, 137–48. New York: W. W. Norton & Company, 1985.

Lacan, Jacques. "On Freud's 'Trieb' and the Psychoanalyst's Desire." In *Écrits: The First Complete Edition in English*, translated by Bruce Fink, 722–5. New York: W. W. Norton & Company, 2006.

Lacan, Jacques. *The Seminar of Jacques Lacan: Book I: Freud's Papers on Technique, 1953–1964*. New York: W. W. Norton & Company, Inc., 1991.

Lacan, Jacques. *The Seminar of Jacques Lacan: Book VII: The Ethics of Psychoanalysis, 1959–1960*. Edited by Jacques-Alain Miller. Translated by Dennis Porter. New York: W. W. Norton & Company, Inc., 1997.

Lange, Christy. "Leigh Ledare." *Frieze*, May 5, 2009. https://www.frieze.com/article/leigh-ledare.

Lauer, Christopher. *Intimacy: A Dialectical Study*. London: Bloomsbury, 2016.

Ledare, Leigh. Interviewed by David Joselit, "An Interview." In *Leigh Ledare, et. al.*, 99. Milan: Mousse Publishing, 2012.

Ledare, Leigh. "Pretend You're Actually Alive (Leigh Ledare)." Interview by Chris Kraus in *Social Practices* by Chris Kraus (Semiotext(e), 2018): 246–64. Originally printed in *BOMB* 132 (2015).

Ledare, Leigh. *Pretend You're Actually Alive*. New York: PPP Editions, 2008.

Ledare, Leigh. "In the Studio: Leigh Ledare." By Steel Stillman. *ARTnews*, December 1, 2017. https://www.artnews.com/art-in-america/features/leigh-ledare-63320.

Ledare, Leigh (website), https://leighledare.com/ (accessed July 26, 2022).

Ledare, Leigh and Steel Stillman. *Leigh Ledare and Steel Stillman.* Presentation at the SVA Theatre by BFA Photography and Video and *Dear Dave*, magazine, October 5, 2017.

Losier, Marie, Steve Holmgren, Martin Marquet, Genesis P-Orridge, and Lady Jaye Breyer P-Orridge. *The Ballad of Genesis and Lady Jaye*. Paris: Epicentre Films, 2011.

Lukacher. Ned. *Primal Scenes: Literature, Philosophy, Psychoanalysis*. Ithaca: Cornell University Press, 1986.

Lunning, Frenchy. "Allure and Abjection: The Possible Potential of Severed Qualities." In *Object Oriented Feminism*, edited by Katherine Behar, 83–106. Minneapolis: University of Minnesota Press, 2016.

Maida, Joseph. "Reciprocal Fantasy: Joseph Maida's New Natives." Interview with Matthew Leifheit. *Art F City*, October 9, 2013. http://artfcity.com/2013/10/09/reciprocal-fantasy-joseph-maidas-new-natives/.

Maida, Joseph (website). http://josephmaida.net/ (accessed 2019).

Massumi, Brian. *Semblance and Event: Activist Philosophy and the Occurrent Arts*. Cambridge, MA: The MIT Press, 2013.

Mathieson, Frankie. "Does Photographing Your Mother Having Sex Really Qualify As Art?" *Refinery29*, October 11, 2013. http://www.refinery29.com/2013/10/55129/leigh-ledare-mother-having-sex-photo.

Meredith, Charlotte. "Oedipal Art? Man Takes Photos Of His Own Mother Having Sex." *HuffPost UK*, October 10, 2013. http://www.huffingtonpost.co.uk/2013/10/10/oedipal-art-man-mum-sex-pictures_n_4075627.html.

Micchelli, Thomas. "Leigh Ledare: You Are Nothing to Me. You Are Like Air." *The Brooklyn Rail*, October 5, 2008. https://brooklynrail.org/2008/10/artseen/leigh-ledare-you-are-nothing-to-me-you-are-like-air.

Miller, Jacques-Alain. "Another Lacan." Translated by Ralph Chipman, *The Symptom* 10, *Lacanian Ink* (Spring 2009). https://www.lacan.com/symptom10a/another-lacan.html.

Miller, Jacques-Alain. "Extimity." Edited by Elisabeth Doisneau. Translated by Françoise Massardier-Kenney, *The Symptom 9, Lacanian Ink* (Fall 2008). http://www.lacan.com/symptom/extimity.html.

Miller, Jacques-Alain. "The Wolfman I." Translated by Asunción Lopez. *Lacanian Ink* 35 (Spring 2010): 6–83.

Mitchell, Juliet. "Introduction I." In *Feminine Sexuality: Jacques Lacan and the école freudienne*, edited by Juliet Mitchell and Jacqueline Rose, translated by Jacqueline Rose, 1–26. New York: W. W. Norton & Company, 1985.

Morton, Timothy. "All Objects Are Deviant: Feminism and Ecological Intimacy." In *Object Oriented Feminism*, edited by Katherine Behar, 65–82. Minneapolis: University of Minnesota Press, 2016.

Morton, Timothy. *The Ecological Thought*. Cambridge, MA: Harvard University Press, 2010.

Moten, Fred. *In the Break: The Aesthetics of the Black Radical Tradition*. Minneapolis: University of Minnesota Press, 2003.

Mulholland, Neil. "Dynamic Perversity." In *The Cultural Devolution: Art in Britain in the Late Twentieth Century*, 55–78. Aldershot and Hants: Ashgate, 2003.

Muñoz, José Esteban. *Cruising Utopia: The Then and There of Queer Futurity*. New York: New York University Press, 2009.

O'Grady, Lorraine. "Interview with Jarrett Earnest (2016)." In *Writing in Space, 1973–2019*, edited by Aruna D'Souza, 239–49. Durham: Duke University Press, 2020.

O'Grady, Lorraine. "Interview with Laura Cottingham (1995)." In *Writing in Space, 1973–2019*, edited by Aruna D'Souza, 219–38. Durham: Duke University Press, 2020.

O'Grady, Lorraine. "Olympia's Maid: Reclaiming Black Female Subjectivity (1992/1994)." In *Writing in Space, 1973–2019*, edited by Aruna D'Souza, 94–109. Durham: Duke University Press, 2020.

O'Hagan, Sean. "Oedipal Exposure: Leigh Ledare's Photographs of His Mother Having Sex." *The Guardian*, October 9, 2013. http://www.theguardian.com/artanddesign/2013/oct/09/leigh-ledare-photographs-mother-having-sex.

Oliver, Kelly. "What Is Response Ethics?" In *Response Ethics*, edited by Alison Suen, 32–50. Lanham: Rowman & Littlefield International, 2018.

Osto, Douglas. *Altered States: Buddhism and Psychedelic Spirituality in America*. New York: Columbia University Press, 2019.

Pangburn, DJ. "Worship at Genesis Breyer P-Orridge's Cut-Up Altar." *Vice*, April 15, 2016. http://www.vice.com/en_us/article/4xqm4d/worship-at-genesis-breyer-p-orridges-cut-up-altar.

Pinney, Christopher. "Introduction: 'How the Other Half…'" In *Photography's Other Histories*, edited by Christopher Pinney and Nicolas Peterson, 1–16. Durham: Duke University Press, 2003.

P-Orridge, Genesis. *Nonbinary*. New York: Abrams Press, 2021.

P-Orridge, Genesis and Richard Metzger. "Annihilating Reality: An Interview with Genesis P-Orridge." In *Painful But Fabulous: The Lives & Art of Genesis P-Orridge*, 41–50. New York: Soft Skull Press, 2003.

Pratt, Geraldine and Victoria Rosner. "Introduction: The Global and the Intimate." In *The Global and the Intimate: Feminism in Our Time*, edited by Geraldine Pratt and Victoria Rosner, 1–28. New York: Columbia University Press, 2012.

Regan, Sheila. "After Protests from Native American Community, Walker Art Center Will Remove Public Sculpture." *Hyperallergic*, May 29, 2017. http://hyperallergic.com/382141/after-protests-from-native-american-community-walker-art-center-will-remove-public-sculpture/.

Rodney, Seph. "Probing the Proper Grounds for Criticism in the Wake of the 2019 Whitney Biennial." *Hyperallergic*, June 7, 2019. http://hyperallergic.com/503513/probing-the-proper-grounds-for-criticism-in-the-wake-of-the-2019-whitney-biennial.

Rose, Jacqueline. "Introduction II." In *Feminine Sexuality: Jacques Lacan and the école freudienne*, edited by Juliet Mitchell and Jacqueline Rose, translated by Jacqueline Rose, 27–58. New York: W. W. Norton & Company, 1985.

Rose, Jacqueline. *Sexuality in the Field of Vision*. London: Verso, 2005.

Sayej, Nadja. "We Skyped with Genesis P-Orridge About Their First Retrospective." *Vice*, June 17, 2014. http://www.vice.com/en_us/article/8gdm33/we-skyped-with-genesis-p-orridge-about-their-first-retrospective.

School of the Art Institute of Chicago. "Documenting: The Panhandler Project by Barbara Degenevieve." *Vimeo*, June 8, 2021. https://vimeo.com/52015733.

Schürmann, Reiner. *Broken Hegemonies*. Translated by Reginald Lilly. Bloomington: Indiana University Press, 2003.

Silas, Susan. "Thoughts on the Life and Art of Barbara DeGenevieve." *Hyperallergic*, August 14, 2014. http://hyperallergic.com/143339/thoughts-on-the-life-and-art-of-barbara-degenevieve.

"The Social Sex Revolution." *MakeLoveNotPorn*, 2019. www.makelovenotporn.com/.

Solomon, Deborah. "Review: The Whitney Biennial Cops Out." *WNYC News*, May 17, 2019. http://www.wnyc.org/story/review-whitney-biennial-cops-out.

Sontag, Susan. "In Plato's Cave." In *On Photography*, 3–26. New York: Picador, 2001.

Sontag, Susan. *Regarding the Pain of Others*. New York: Farrar, Straus and Giroux, 2017.

Sophocles. *Oedipus the King*. Translated by David Grene. Chicago: University of Chicago Press, 2010.

Tutti, Cosey Fanni. *Art Sex Music*. London: Faber & Faber, 2017.

Velasco, David. "Leigh Ledare: ROTH." *Artforum International* 44 (September 2008): 463. Gale Academic OneFile, https://link.gale.com/apps/doc/A185040867/AONE?u=nysl_me_sova&sid=AONE&xid=c4c840c5.

Weinstein, Michael. "Beyond the Binaries: Crossing the Boundaries of Identity Politics." In *Objectifying the Abject: Exploitation, Political (In)Correctness, and Ethical*

Dilemmas. Exhibition pamphlet by Barbara DeGenevieve. Chicago: University of Illinois at Chicago, Gallery 400, 2006.

Williams, Carla and Deborah Willis. *The Black Female Body: A Photographic History*. Philadelphia: Temple University Press, 2002.

Wilson, Siona. "Prostitution and the Problem of Feminist Art: The Emergent Queer Aesthetic of COUM Transmissions." In *Art Labor, Sex Politics: Feminist Effects in 1970s British Art and Performance*, 93–138. Minneapolis: University of Minnesota Press, 2015.

Yablonsky, Linda. "Everything Is Good at the Whitney Biennial but Nothing Makes a Difference." *The Art Newspaper*, May 14, 2019. http://www.theartnewspaper.com/review/whitney-biennial-2019.

Zappe, Florian. "'When Order Is Lost, Time Spits': The Abject Unpopular Art of Genesis (Breyer) P-Orridge." In *Unpopular Culture*, edited by Martin Lüthe and Sascha Pöhlmann, 129–46. Amsterdam: Amsterdam University Press, 2016.

Žižek, Slavoj. "Introduction: The Spectre of Ideology." In *Mapping Ideology*, edited by Slavoj Žižek, 1–33. London: Verso, 1994.

Žižek, Slavoj. *The Sublime Object of Ideology*. London: Verso, 2008.

Index

Note: Page numbers followed by 'n' refer to notes

abjection/abject
  abject   49, 53, 60–1
  analytic *après-coup*—retroactive
    signification   76–7
  borderlander   72–3
  the corpse   71–2
  cultural taboos   52–3
  cycle of life and death   57–8
  death drive   49
  effect of   66–7
  extimacy of speech   75
  intersubjectivity   65
  and intimacy (*see* intimacy)
  Lacan's extimacy   74
  libidinal desire   74
  mother to child's body, primordial
    relationship of   70
  notion of "self"   49–50
  Oedipus   53
  par-don   75–7
  paternal law   70
  performance theory   64
  performative gestures   72
  phantasmatic mother   67–74
  poetic pathways   77
  poetic play with language and
    images   48
  from pre-Oedipal *paranoid-schizoid*
    position   69–70
  Pretend You're Actually Alive
    48–63
  psychoanalysis   64
  purgation process of unwanted
    material   73
  radicalizing intimacy   63–4
  regulatory laws   67–8
  satisfaction   65–6
  taboos, role of   66, 68
  transference/countertransference
    74–8
  transgressive positioning   51

  women in contemporary
    capitalism   57
Abrahamsson   92
"Aesthetics of Intimacy"(Kotz)   39
"All Objects Are Deviant: Feminism
  and Ecological Intimacy"
  (Morton)   147
Althusser, Louis   3, 13–15, 17, 25, 28–9,
  31–3, 36–7, 40–1, 44–5, 49, 157,
  177, 184, 204
Andrew Roth Gallery   50
art, object, and beauty   202–4
Art Institute of Chicago   64, 160
authentic femininity, notion of   43
Avedon, Elizabeth   168
Aydemir, Murat   134–5

Baldessari, John   81
The Ballad of Genesis and Lady Jaye
  (Losier)   84, 104, 216 n.32
The Ballad of Sexual Dependency
  (Goldin)   39
Barthes, Roland   51, 100–1, 152
Baudrillard, Jean   15–18, 47, 114, 118,
  179, 202
Behar, Katherine   4, 8, 45–6, 118, 121,
  126, 133, 145–8, 158–9, 166–7,
  172, 176–9, 181, 191, 193–9
Black, Hannah   199, 204
Body Is the Ground of My Experience   176
Breyer, Jacqueline, *see* P-Orridge, Lady
  Jaye Breyer
Burden, Chris   81
Burroughs, William   95, 104
Butler, Judith   3, 7–8, 42–7, 64

capitalism   32, 40, 57, 87, 91, 145, 194
Cease to Exist 1-5   85–6
Cease to Exist no. 4   81
Cease to Exist performances (1967-81)
  19, 109

Châteaux de Versailles,
    2015 exhibition   12
Childhood heroes and *Girls I wanted to
    do*   52
Christopherson   85-6
*The Clearing: or, Cortés and La
    Malinche, Thomas Jefferson
    and Sally Hemings, N. and Me*
    (O'Grady)   179-80
colonialism   185, 188, 194
the corpse
    and abjection   71-2
    and death   142
    incest taboo and the horrific apparition
        of   60
    and maternal   19
    phantasmatic mother   71-2
    site of abjection   71-2
    taboos of intimate contact with   72
Cosmic Organicism of the Universal
        Molecular (COUM),
        transmissions   19, 81-9,
        215 n.25, 216 n.29
    Cease to Exist performances   19, 81,
        84-90
    focus on the phallus   89
    nonconformity to gender and sex   85
    notion of "self"   87
    performances involving bodily fluids,
        stress, and nudity   86
    practice of intimate collaboration   88
    queer form of activist aesthetic   87
    self-realisation   88
    sexual power structures   86
    Throbbing Gristle (TG)   85, 88-9
Creon   35
cultural taboos   52-3, 82
cyborg   146, 219 n.105

Dadaists   84
Daniel Cooney Gallery   167
David Zwirner Gallery   181
death drive   9, 49, 120, 124, 203
DeGenevieve, Barbara   3, 20, 158-66,
    172, 175, 192, 196, 198-9, *see
    also The Panhandler Project*
    (DeGenevieve)
disruptive gesture, in Ledare's work   25
Double Bind   210 n.26
Drang (thrust)   5

Dream Factory (Maida)   168
the drive
    as a constant force   5-6
    death drive   9, 11-12, 120, 124, 189,
        203
    and enjoyment   49
    Freudian   6, 203
    and jouissance   40, 47, 60
    language and   6, 30
    primordial   2, 40
    race and associated   192
    semiotics of   66
    sex drive   186
    unconscious   184

*Encore: On Feminine Sexuality: The
    Limits of Love and Knowledge*
    (Lacan)   114
enjoyment and fantasy, role of   48,
    see also fantasy
erotic photographs   27-8
essentialism   7, 10, 43, 149
exorcisms   86
exoticism   168
extimacy   13, 32, 74-5, 107, 126, 147, 179

Fallis, Greg   50
fantasy   37, 40-8, 54-5, 59, 61, 63, 104,
    116-17, 119, 144, 173-4, 189-90
    and desire   100
    of incest   68
    reality and   30
    and repetition   41
    seductive visual   170
feminist object   4-10
    concept of satisfaction   5-6
    drive and language   9
    essentialism   7
    language and drive   5-6
    objectivity   44-5
    object-oriented feminism (OOF)   8
    psychoanalytic models of gender
        difference   7
Ford, Simon   81, 84, 86, 88, 127
Foster, Hal   66, 143, 158, 195
Fraser, Andrea   204-5
Freud, Sigmund   1, 3-6, 8-9, 11-13,
    26-7, 30-4, 39, 42, 68-70, 77-8,
    104-5, 116, 118, 121-3, 127,
    132, 133, 140, 186, 188-90, 203

discovery of unconscious   1, 4, 33
duality of *eros* and *thanatos*   190
model of subjectivity   11, 42
Oedipal model   34, 42, 186, 190
paternal law   70
primal scene   27, 30, 68
psychoanalysis   6, 105
semiology   132–3
sexual difference   127
Trieb (drive)   5–6, 203
Frieze, Christy Lange of   51
Fusco, Coco   199

Gallery 400   161
Gallop, Cindy   119
gender
  difference   7, 128
  essentialism   10
  and performativity/sexuality   42
  qualities of   104
gender-nonconforming people   116, 128
George, Sheldon   20, 177
Getting to Know My Husband's Cock (Jong)   20, 113–14, 118, 122, 133
Goldin, Nan   27, 38–9, 50, 62
Gosine, Andil   183
Grosz, Elizabeth   196
Guagnini, Nicolás   53, 55, 58
Gysin, Bryon   95, 104

Haraway, Donna   8, 44–6, 148
Harman, Graham   149–51
Hartman, Saidiya   161–2
Home Truths: Photography, Motherhood and Identity (Ledare)   50
Hula Kahiko Kane (Maida)   20, 158, 167, 169–70, 173–5

IDEA Gallery   86
Ideological State Apparatus (ISA)   15, 40, 157, 199
ideology
  definition   13–14
  and intimacy, co-presence of   122
  into intimacy   198–200
  intimacy of   14–15
  of objectivity   145
  subjectivity   15

and theories on interpellation of subjectivity   3
imagining intimacy
  destitute subject   46–7
  disruptive gesture   25
  erotic photographs   27–8
  image-making   29
  interpellation   29
  intimacies and feminist ethics   38–46
  misrecognition   47
  mutual recognition   28
  notion of subject-formation   47
  power relations   26
  primal scene   30–3
  process of subjectification   29
  sacrifice in the Oedipal cycle   34–8
  subjective destitution   47
  subject's relationship to reality   29
incest
  and apparition of corpse   60
  claustrophobia   59
  copresence of abjection and beauty in   54
  incestuous desire for the mother   43
  incestuous jouissance   50, 54, 58, 72, 74
  and murder taboo   34–5
  poetic enjoyment-of incest taboo   73
  prohibition with the death   55
  rituals of   34
  and symbolic order   68
  taboo   26–7, 46, 60
  tragedy of   53
interpellation   3, 14, 29, 31–3, 40–1, 44–5, 69, 75, 122, 177–8, 184
intimacy, *see also* imagining intimacy; postcolonial intimacy
  extimacy   13
  and feminist ethics   38–46
    act of subjective interpellation   41
    authentic femininity   43
    fantasy and repetition   41–2
    feminist objectivity   44
    gender and performativity   42
    ideology   40
    intimate curse of Oedipus   46
    jouissance and the drive   40
    masochism   45
    patriarchy   39–40, 43
    poetic language   43–4

power structures   45
ritual of subjectivity   39
scientific objectivism   44–5
surplus-jouissance   41
and instability   63–7
desire as a dialogical process   65
effect of abject   66–7
intersubjectivity   65
performance theory   64
psychoanalysis   64
radicalizing intimacy through the abject   63–4
satisfaction   65–6
taboos, role of   66
jouissance   11 (*see also* jouissance)
of psychoanalysis   10
as radical activism   2–4
revolt through arts   12
of sexual differentiation and desire   2, 10
and thought   1–2
Intimate Revolt (Kristeva)   10
Invisible Exports Gallery   84
Irigaray, Luce   3, 8, 115, 118, 120, 126–33, 135, 137, 139, 145, 148–9, 151, 153, 167, *see also* materialism, Irigaray's

Jackie and Genesis   105
Jacosta   35–6, 67
Johnson, Paddy   204
Jong, Ellen, *see* object-oriented intimacy, Jong's monograph; radical objectification, Jong; sex and the symbolic
jouissance   11, 140–1
and the drive   40, 203
feminine   114–15
infinite   110
Lacanian   11
masculine and feminine   126
mutual   118, 126, 152
phallic   117, 126
semiotics of poetic speech   65
surplus-   41, 68, 73, 77, 117, 203

Kapoor, Anish   12, 208 n.26
Klein, Melanie   64, 69
Kotz, Liz   39

Kraus, Chris   26
Kristeva, Julia   1, *see also The Sense and Non-Sense of Revolt* (Kristeva)
gender essentialism   10
Intimate Revolt   139
language and drive   6
on practice of psychoanalysis   10
psychoanalysis   6–7
relationship to feminism   7
revolt, definition   1
theories on abjection and revolt   6, 137–8

Lacan, Jacques   5–6, 13, 30–2, 36–7, 46–7, 69, 74–5, 100, 104, 114, 116–18, 121, 126–9, 131–2, 151, 167, 173, 203
big Other   35
emphasis on paternal law   70
feminine position   117
imago   31
jouissance   11
misrecognition   177
photo-graphs   36
psychoanalysis   105
semiotics   190
sexual differentiation   121
symbolic order   7–8, 30, 40
theory and her performative writing   8
transference-in Lacanian theory   190
Lange, Christy   51, 62
'the last taboo'   181
Leber, Laure A.   105
Ledare, Leigh   3, 7, 19, 25, 28, 48, 53, 62, *see also* abjection/abject; imagining intimacy
Leifheit, Matthew   168–9
libido   32–3, 122, 203
life art sex magick   81–5, 217 nn.48, 49
automation, simulation, and violence in contemporary society   82–3
Cease to Exist no. 4   81
exploration of abjection in sexual intimacy   82
performative practices, P-Orridge's   83
Powers of Horror (1982)   81, 82
psychoanalytic discourse on abjection   83

research in sexuality, P-Orridge's 217 n.41
  ritual purification 81
loquela, St. Augustine's 140
Los Angeles Institute of Contemporary Arts (LAICA) 81, 86, 216 n.29
Losier, Marie 84, 216 n.32
Love, Guilt and Reparation (Klein) 64
Lunning, Frenchy 4, 118, 133, 149–51

Maida, Joseph 3, 20, 158, 226 n.26, *see also New Natives* (Maida)
makelovenotporn.com 119
Marxist model 40
masochism 45, 58
Massumi, Brian 12, 19, 83, 97–102
materialism, Irigaray's 126–31
  discourse on the 'feminine' 128
  Lacan's Freudian approach to sexual difference 127–28
  masculine and feminine jouissance 126–8
  phallic language 127, 129–30
  phallogocentrism 130
maternal
  body 1, 43, 59, 69, 74
  boundaries 67
  care 43, 70
  and the corpse 19
  femininity 64
  function 7, 70, 74
  pre-monotheistic maternal cults 68
  sexuality 56
  as a site of nondifferentiation 107
  and speech 36
  into the subjectivity and desire 67
  taboo of maternal sexuality 71–2
Mathieson, Frankie 50
Metzger, Richard 86
Micchelli, Thomas 51, 64
Miller, Jacques-Alain 12, 13, 76, 107, 116, 122, 127
mimesis, Platonic notion of 99
Mitchell, Juliet 115, 118, 121
modernity 3, 40, 109
  hegemony of 21
  recoding 78
Morton, Timothy 4, 118, 133, 147–9, 203, 206

Moten, Fred 178
mutual jouissance 118, 126, 152
mutual recognition 33–4, 46, 49
  gestures of 28
  interpellation 29
  of subjecthood 14

Naked Beach Day 125–6
narcissism 58, 138, 149, 174, 203
New Natives (Maida)
  beauty and eroticism 168–9, 171
  ethnic heritage 167–8
  forgiveness for the shame 175
  Hula Kahiko Kane 167
  human beings as objects of sexual desire 167
  identity 172–3
  identity, cultural and ethnic heritage as signifiers 174
  intimacy, role of 170–1
  object-oriented model of inquiry 166
  photography in the hegemonic field 166–75
  "primal" or primordial nature, concept of 171
  "queerness" 172
  relativity of exoticism 168
  revolt 171–2

Obama, Barack 168
objectification, *see* radical objectification, Jong
Objectifying the Abject: Exploitation, Political (In)Correctness and Ethical Dilemmas. (exhibition) 161
object-oriented feminism (OOF) 4, 6, 8, 18, 20, 115, 150–1, 191, 224 n.42, *see also* OOF as politics of intimate revolt
  Behar's explanation 194
  discourse on sexual intimacy 145
  intervention 178
  intimacy and ideology 194
  and Jong's "experimental and process driven art practice" 115
  nuanced vocabulary of intimacy 167
  political challenge to subjectivity 158
  and the power 176

power and agency   176, 178
practice-based artistic activism   159
proposal for radical objecthood   121
and revolt   194
role of radical intimacy   194
tenets of   192-3
object-oriented intimacy, Jong's monograph, *see also* objects, intimacy of
object revolts   152-3
sex in the sensorium (*see* sex in the sensorium)
object-oriented ontology (OOO)   145, 148-9, 193-4
object revolts   152-3
objects, intimacy of   144-52, 224 n.42
allure, notion of   149-51
capitalism   145
correlationism   145
ecological awareness   148
generative thinking and doing   147
hegemonic thinking   146
ideology of objectivity   145
language of kinesthesis   148
"A New Theory of Everything"   150-1
object of desire in sexual relation   149
objects in relation with other objects   146
OOF (*see* object-oriented feminism (OOF))
OOO (*see* object-oriented ontology (OOO))
patriarchy   145
political activism   146
politics   145
radical immanence, philosophy of   148
resistance to patriarchy   151
weird essentialism   149
withdrawal, notion of   147-9
objet petit a   117, 121
Oedipal/Oedipus   7, 19, 26, 28, 33, 35, 42, 52, 58, 65-6, 68-71, 77, 115, 135, 184-7, 190, *see also* sacrifice in Oedipal cycle
complex   37, 185
cycle   19, 34-8
intimate curse of   46
myth   39

O'Grady, Lorraine   3, 8, 20, 176-7, 179-87, 189-92, 199
"Olympia's Maid: Reclaiming Black Female Subjectivity" (essay, O'Grady)   158, 177
OOF as politics of intimate revolt   192-8
conflict between subject and object   197-8
contemporary studio practices   193-4
intimate revolt   197
objecthood as a political tool   194-5
objectification and exploitation   196
ontologically 'correct' master theory   196
performativity   195
pleasure and failures, role of   197-8
political engagement through art practice   193
power, desire, and oppression in postcolonial relationships   192
race and intimate relationship   192
revolt   197
tenets of OOF   192-3
Open Casket, Dana Schutz's painting   204
orgasm   83, 88-96, 98, 103, 124-5, 135, 140, 144, 183
orgasmic sigil   85, 91-6, 98, 101-2, 108, 109

pandrogeny   103-8
aesthetico-political practice   103
description   104
desire for Lady Jaye   107
extimacy   107
maternal as a site of nondifferentiation   107
performative works towards autonomous self   108
plastic surgeries and physical transformations   103
ultra-genetic terrorists   105
The Pandrogeny Manifesto (Breyer P-Orridge)   107
The Panhandler Project (DeGenevieve)   20
categorization, ambiguity of   162
enactment of sexual objectification and exploitation   164-5

exchanges of power and need   160, 163
exploitation of vulnerable populations   162–3
notion of cool exploitation   160–1
objectification and self-possession   166
photographic series   159–66
sexual reciprocity   164
slavery-themed melodrama   161
white violence upon a Black body   165–6
patriarchal masculinity   134
patriarchy   19, 32, 40, 42–3, 59, 70–1, 86–7, 91, 121, 151, 154, 184–5
Pees on Earth (Jong's photographic series)   136
performance art   84, 179
performative writing   8
Personal Commissions (exhibition)   50
Peterson, Tina   26, 48, 58
Petit, Philippe   7
phallic jouissance   117, 126
phallogocentrism   20, 44, 130
phantasmatic mother   67–74, *see also* abjection/abject
    biblical injunctions against taboos   68
    borderlander   72–3
    continual recycling of ideologies in performative gestures   72
    the corpse   71–2
    extimacy   74
    fantasy of incest   68
    flat encephalograph, example of   72
    intimacy and abjection   70–1
    libidinal desire   74
    Mom Fucking in Mirror   68–9
    paternal law   70
    pre-Oedipal *paranoid-schizoid* position   69–70
    primordial relationship of mother to the child's body   70
    regulatory laws   67–8
pharmakos   36
photo-graphs   36
photography
    creating alternate reality   149
    in the hegemonic field (*see New Natives* (Maida))

indexical representational system of   114
intimacy in   38
intimate   27, 113
sex and   120
use for access to a semblance of power   136
Photography's Other Histories (Pinney)   171
Pierson, Jack   39
Pinney, Christopher   171
pornography   114, 119, 134–5
P-Orridge, Genesis   3, 12, 81, 84, 86, *see also* Thee Temple ov Psychick Youth (TOPY)
    performances with body fluids   109–10
    performative practices   83
    sigils   96
    visual and object-based artworks   96
P-Orridge, Lady Jaye Breyer   19, 81–2, 85, 101–3
postcolonial intimacy
    Althusser's ideological model   157–8
    exposing the object   157–9
    intimacy   159
    material reality and economic power   161
    object-oriented feminism   158
    OOF's object-oriented discourse   158
    photography in the hegemonic field (*see New Natives* (Maida))
    power and possession (*see The Panhandler Project* (DeGenevieve))
    radical intimacy in artistic practice   159
    radical thought   160
    society's laws and cultural institutions   157
post-1968 resistance movements   5, 7, 21
power relations   26, 45, 135, 182, 184, 194
Powers of Horror (1982)   82, 138
Pratt, Geraldine   169
Pretend You're Actually Alive (Ledare)   19, 26, 32, 48–63
    abjection   49, 53, 60–1

archive of autobiographical
       material   55
Childhood heroes and *Girls I wanted to
       do*   52
cultural taboos   52–3
cycle of life and death   57–8
death drive   49
economic relationships   56
family members   52
family's breakdowns   56
Hot Licks   54
image series after Grama's death   60–1
intimacy on the other side   48–63
Me and Mom in Photobooth   62
memoir page   57
Mom as Baby Jane   52
Mom in New Home   61–2
Mom Spread with Red Heels   53
Mom with Hand on Bed   52
nonconformity with societal roles   58
notion of self   49–50
Oedipus (*see* Oedipal/Oedipus)
performance and photographic
       practices   53–4
performative structure as
       mechanism   62
Peterson's role as abject and abjected
       mother   60
poetic play with the language and
       images   48
power of literature as   49
scenes of Ledare and his
       girlfriend   58–9
sexuality and relationships, social and
       economic constructs   50
social rites   55–6
transgressive positioning   51
voice of narration   52
women in contemporary
       capitalism   57
primal scene   30–3
    complicity of viewer   32
    extimacy   32
    Freudian   30
    interpellation   33
    libido   32–3
    memories from infancy   30
    patriarchal, capitalist ideologies   32
    psychic destabilization   30

rituals   33
role of sexual intimacy in subject-
       formation   33
symbol of distortion and
       dissolution   30–1
Prince, Richard   39
protests in France, 1968   5–6, 25
psychic bisexuality   7
psychic destabilization   30
psychoanalysis   10–13, 20, 26, 64–5, 75,
       82, 115, 118, 139, 185–7, 202
    discourse of intimate materialist art
       practice   5
    Freudian-Lacanian school of   105
    Freudian structure of   6
    impact of   47
    intimacy of   10–13
    intimate revolt of   140
    investigation of intimacy   132–3
    Klein's school of   69
    Kristeva, on practice of   10
    narcissism   174
    patriarchal categories of   6
    radicality of   139
    structuralism of   8
    Žižek, on   45

race/racism   8, 18, 20, 147, 159, 182, 185,
       187, 199
    component of ideology   8
    dynamics   161
    hegemonic structures of   192
    identifying attributes   18, 147, 177
    mixed-race children   180
    threats to   206
radical intimacy   4, 177–8, 201–2
    abjection or the abject   201
    in aesthetic and political fields   205–6
    in artistic practice   159
    discourse of   118
    lack of intimacy in contemporary
       communications   201
    role of   194
    viability of art practice as a culture of
       revolt   202
radicality   3, 15–18
    in contemporary art   204–6
       definition   204
       ideology and intimacy   206

intimacy's radicality 206
  politics 204
  radical intimacy in aesthetic and political fields 205–6
materialist feminist approach 18
mechanism of instant commutation 17
object-oriented feminism 18
principle of modern subjectivity 16
radical thought, Baudrillard's 16
radical objectification, Jong 118–26
  abjection and revolt 121
  attributes of contemporary Western marriage 119
  camera as an apparatus of power 125
  complicity and participation 121
  co-presence of intimacy and ideology 122
  exploration of abjection 123
  feminine enjoyment 131
  Getting to Know My Husband's Cock 113, 118
  humor and absurdity, use of 125
  images, description 120, 123–4
  intersectional feminist intervention 113
  love, definition of 130
  object of desire 121
  Pees on Earth, photographic series 121–2
  phallic jouissance 126
  phallic power, symbol of 129
  poetics, use of 120
  radical objecthood 121
  representation of rapport and collaboration 125
#realworldsex 119
reclaiming subjectivity
  black-and-white diptych photo-montage 180
  Black female subjectivity 176
  Cartesian/Kantian thinking subject 178
  discourse of intimacy 179
  hegemonic ideologies 184–5
  ideological interpellation, Althusserian notion of 177
  interconnectedness, model of 178
  interracial relationships 182–3
  O'Grady 176–85
  OOF intervention 178
  power, social discourse of 183
  radical intimacy 177–8
  radical work employing sexuality as tool 181–2
  seeing and naming, notion of 177
  sexual difference 185
  slavery 176
  subjectivity and objecthood in creative practice 179
  victimization and agency for the black female 180–1
Refinery 29 (Mathieson) 50
the *Reiz* (excitation) 5–6
revolt
  intimacy (*see also* intimacy)
    concept of satisfaction 5–6
    in contemporary art practice 1
    drive and language 9
    essentialism 7
    function of drive 5
    gender difference, psychoanalytic models 7
    ideology 13–15
    language and drive 6
    OOF (*see* OOF as politics of intimate revolt)
    radicality 3, 15–18 (*see also* radicality)
  and ritual
    COUM (*see* Cosmic Organicism of the Universal Molecular (COUM), transmissions)
    jouissance, infinite 110
    life art sex magick 81–5
    loss of intimate 108
    media, effects 109
    pandrogeny (*see* pandrogeny)
    P-Orridge's performances with body fluids 109–10
    sacred in intimate revolt and in love 109
    TOPY (*see* Thee Temple ov Psychick Youth (TOPY))
  subjectivity 15
  subject to feminist object 4–10
ritual purification 81
Rivington Arms Gallery 50, 64

Rodney, Seph   205
Rodriguez, V.   165
Rose, Jacqueline   104, 115, 118
Rosner, Victoria   169
Rubin Museum of Art   84

sacrifice in Oedipal cycle   34–8
　artistic practice   37
　awareness of own subjectivity   38
　Ledare as subject of symbolic order   35–6
　Oedipal complex   37
　photo-graphs   36
　power and authority   35
　relationship between tragedy and ideology   34
Sartre   152
School of the Art Institute of Chicago   160
Schürmann, Reiner   34–5
Schutz, Dana   199, 204
scientific objectivism   44–5
Semblance and Event (Massumi)   83, 98
semiotic   73, 75
　activity in borderlands   63
　aspect of Ledare's practice   65
　of body   130
　conceptions of   7–9
　COUM transgress boundaries   87
　of drives   66
　of intimacy   198
　Lacanian semiotics   190
　O'Grady's semiotics and politics   189
　of poetic speech via jouissance   65
　P-Orridge's sigils operate as   96
　semiotic, "a primal mapping of the body by Kristeva"   64
　semiotic *chora*   174
　Symbolic and   101–2, 130, 170, 172, 174, 197
The Sense and Non-Sense of Revolt (Kristeva)   10, 82–3, 89
　interiority and transformation   90
　Italian baroque sculptures, analysis of   89–90
　language and symbol   90
　relationship to ritual and interiority   90
sensorial cave   140–1, 150

difference from the Real   141
　intimacy in   144
　of Jong's consciousness   144
　mutual jouissance and   152
　word-presentations and thing-presentations in Kristeva's   150
sex and the symbolic   116–18
　discourse of radical intimacy   118
　feminine jouissance   114–15
　intimate photography   113
　materialism (*see* materialism, Irigaray's)
　mutual jouissance   118
　object-oriented feminism   115
　phallic jouissance   117
　poetics of objecthood   113–15
　pornography   114
　radical objectification (*see* radical objectification, Jong)
　sexual act, description   116
　sexual intimacy   116
sex in the sensorium   132–44
　abjection and revolt   132–3
　Cartesian philosophy   140
　concept of style   141
　Freudian semiology   132–3
　gender ambivalence in Jong's monograph   142
　intimate revolt of psychoanalysis   140
　Jong's image   135–6, 139
　jouissance   140–1
　Kristeva's *Intimate Revolt*   139
　Kristeva's theories on abjection   137–8
　mummifying transference   138
　mutual pleasure   144
　patriarchal masculinity   134
　photography and semblance of power   136
　pronouncement of ambivalence   143
　psychoanalysis   132
　role of imaginary in relation to mind-soul dichotomy   140
　speech-language and communications of the body   139
　symbolic function of body fluids   136
　word-presentations in Jong's monograph   141–2
sexual economics   59

sexual intimacy   116
   exploration of abjection in   82
   OOF discourse on   145
   revolutionary potentiality of   15
   role in subject-formation   33
   sex and the symbolic   116
   in subject-formation   33
   taboos   189, 191
sociopath   52
Sollers, Philippe   152
Solomon, Deborah   205
Sontag, Susan   120, 125, 135–6, 149
Sophocles   34
soul (*psukhê*)   3
Spare, Austin Osman   95
Stewart, Michael   164
subjectification   15, 19, 27, 29–31, 34, 46–7, 167
subjective destitution   46–7
subjective interpellation   41, 75
subjectivity, *see also* reclaiming subjectivity
   acts of auto-expression   185
   anti-racist consciousness   199–200
   architecture of Black sexuality   186
   Behar's *being-with*   199
   black-and-white diptych photomontage   180
   Black female subjectivity   186, 191
   The Clearing, description   188
   complicated   185–91
   cultural differences and power   187
   desire, aggression and prohibition   189–90
   emphasis on Oedipal   186
   ideology and desire, co-presence of   198–9
   interpreting emotional state of the woman   188–9
   knowledge of abjection   186
   OOF as a politics of intimate revolt   192–8
   phobia
      description   188–9
      phobic hallucination   190
   psychoanalysis   187
   radicality and intimacy   199
   ritual of   39
   subject-object divide   191

surplus-jouissance   41, 68, 73, 77, 117, 203
taboos
   aesthetic resistance to social and political orders   101
   age   53
   biblical injunctions against   68
   cultural   52–3, 82
   incest   34–5, 46, 60, 73
   intimacy outside of sanctioned spaces and relationships   89
   of intimate contact with the corpse   72
   of maternal sexuality   71–2
   physical and psychical   87
   prohibition of   70
   role in symbolic order and paternal law   66
   and sacrifice   44
   sexual intimacy   189, 191
   transgression of taboo incestuous desire   27
   willingness to confront   26
Thee Grey Book (P-Orridge)   93
Thee Psychick Bible: Thee Apocryphal Scriptures Ov Genesis Breyer P-Orridge (Breyer P-Orridge)   85, 91–3, 104
Thee Temple ov Psychick Youth (TOPY)   19, 81, 85, 90–1
   activating mind through experiences and sensations of body   94
   aesthetico-political artwork   98
   Barthes's '*punctum*'   100
   constructive deconstruction, process of   94–5
   Coyote 37   94
   discourse on abjection and body fluids, Kristeva's   101–2
   evental art practice   101
   intimacy   100–1
   occurrent art   99–100
   orgasm
      as a "magickal" practice   92
      as occurrent art   90–103
      as a resistant mechanism   93
   orgasmic sigil   91–3
   poetics of resistance   96–7

P-Orridge's work with TOPY   91–2
process philosophy, influence of   98
ritual, definition   98–9
ritualized living gender re-evolutionary exploration   91
ritual space, creation of   102
self-actualization, strategies for   97
visual and object-based artworks, P-Orridge's   96
Things "R" Queer   170
Throbbing Gristle (TG)   84–5, 88–90
transference   10, 26, 74–8
   analytic *après-coup*—retroactive signification   76–7
   countertransference   74–8
   extimacy of speech   75
   identification in the transference-relation   174
   intersubjective relationship   75
   mechanism of language and recollection   75–6
   mummifying transference   138
   par-don   75–7
   poetic pathways   77
   poetic rifts in discourse   74–8
   surplus-jouissance through speech   77
Trieb (drive)   5
Tutti, Cosey Fanni   19, 81–2, 84–6, 88, 90, 103, 115

unconscious   4
   and eroticism of psychoanalytic discourse   3
   fantasies and defenses   2
   Freudian   4, 33
   of Genesis   107
   imaginary manifestations of   188–90
   impact of analytic speech   1
   intersubjective forces   26
   libidinal desire   74
   memory and desire   174, 183
   movement of   78
   as radical exteriority   74
   relationship to the ego   13
   role of language in   5
   stirrings of such revolt   197

Velasco, David   63
voyeurism   26–7, 39, 44, 55, 143

Warhol, Andy   62
Waters, John   181
Weinstein, Michael   161–2
weird essentialism   149
Western religions, oppression and limitations   91
When Our Lips Speak Together (Irigaray)   128
white patriarchy   184–5
Whitney Biennial of American Art, 2017   199, 204
Williams, Carla   180–1
Willis, Deborah   180–1
withdrawal
   boredom   189
   in Kristeva's writings   149–50
   Morton's notion of   147–9
   of objects   147
   poetic language of   149
   power of   192–3
"Wolfman" case study, Freud and primal scene   30
Wooten, Gordon K.   160–3, 165–6
Wreckers of Civilisation: The Story of COUM Transmissions and Throbbing Gristle (Ford)   84

Yablonsky, Linda   204–5
You Are Nothing to Me, You Are Like Air (exhibition, Ledare)   50

Žižek, Slavoj   31, 33, 37, 40–2, 46–7, 49, 59, 203